D0359957

FORTUNE

SCANDAL!

AMAZING TALES of SCANDALS that SHOCKED THE WORLD and SHAPED MODERN BUSINESS

Copyright 2009 Time Inc. Home Entertainment

Published by Fortune Books

Time Inc.
1271 Avenue of the Americas
New York, NY 10020

ISBN 10: 1-60320-009-6
ISBN 13: 978-1-60320-009-7
Library of Congress Number: 2008902356

All of the articles in this book were previously published in substantially the same form in FORTUNE magazine between 1933 and 2009; all have been edited for length and updated with forewords and/or afterwords.

FORTUNE

★★★★   ★★★★

SCANDAL!

AMAZING TALES of SCANDALS that SHOCKED THE WORLD and SHAPED MODERN BUSINESS

TABLE OF CONTENTS

I. LOOTING

chapter 1
◆

How an Italian thug looted MGM, brought Credit Lyonnais to its knees, and made the Pope cry.

chapter 2
◆

Roman-style excess comes to New Hampshire.

chapter 3
◆

In the 1920s, Ivar Kreuger was known as the savior of Europe. A month after his death in 1932, he was known as its greatest swindler.

chapter 4
◆

Once the country's sixth-largest cable company, Adelphia was the pride of Coudersport, Pennsylvania. Then it wasn't.

chapter 5
◆

For decades, Robert Vesco was an international man of mystery. Here is how it all started.

II. BAD DEALS

III. SCAMS

IV. DOWNFALLS

INTRODUCTION

by CAIT MURPHY

Think of it: $50 billion. That's the estimate of the amount of money Bernie Madoff allegedly vaporized, though the exact figure may never be known. How much is that? Well, a company with $50 billion in revenues would place 46th on the 2008 FORTUNE 500, just behind Microsoft and Sears. You could buy every Major League Baseball team, and have enough left over to buy most of pro football. It's almost twice the worldwide revenues of the movie business. In short, when Madoff confessed his deeds to his family in late 2008, he was admitting to the most money ever taken by an individual swindler. "Madoff" looks likely to become a verb (meaning: to be ripped off by someone you trust), in the same way Ponzi has become an adjective. If it does, there is grammatical justice here, because Madoff's scheme was classic in its simplicity: By his own account, he used new money to pay returns to existing clients (see Chapter 20). That is exactly what Charles Ponzi did back in 1920, when his own scam fell apart.

Madoff is unique in terms of scale; but in terms of what he did, he is only the latest in a long line of scoundrels. Like Ivar Kreuger, the Swedish match king (Chapter 3), Madoff's end began with a falling market that exposed his hedge fund's weaknesses. Like the Carlows, father and son (Chapter 12) or Dennis Helliwell (Chapter 14), Madoff's alleged actions betrayed a cosmic indifference to their consequences, in the process devastating charities, friends and even family members. And finally, like many another scandal, Madoff's financial tsunami will almost certainly result in new rules, as regulators swear, "Never again"—once again.

Since its founding in 1930, FORTUNE has covered the Madoffs of the world. But when it comes to business, sin and scandal go back much further than that. In fact, the American republic was a toddler when it suffered its first major financial scandal. In January 1792, less than two years after George Washington took the oath of office at a site just around the corner from Wall Street, one William Duer indulged his compulsion for gambling in the nascent market for government securities. Duer's big bet: an attempt to corner the market on 6% bonds, which Treasury Secretary Alexander Hamilton had created to pay off Revolutionary War debt.

Duer's "6% club" failed, following the usual course. The price rose fast at first, then fell faster. Duer kept borrowing, betting prices would recover. They didn't. By March 1792, he owed more than $230,000 to the government alone. A few weeks later, Duer was sitting in a debtor's prison, alone and distraught, as a mob screamed and threatened him from without.

The debacle emboldened Hamilton's critics. A brilliant and irascible visionary, Hamilton believed the U.S. needed a capital market and a credit system to thrive—indeed, to survive. The scandal struck close to home because Hamilton himself had been accused of speculating in Revolutionary War debt. A scoundrel named James Reynolds told some of the Treasury Secretary's many political enemies that Hamilton had paid Reynolds to trade on insider information.

It wasn't true, and Hamilton was able to prove it. His defense: He was sleeping with Reynolds's wife, and paying blackmail to the husband. Adultery, yes; corruption, no.

Money and sex and scandal: These realities are as certain in life as death and taxes. What is sometimes not appreciated, though, is how critical scandal has been in the shaping of the U.S. economy.

Take the unfortunate Duer. He was stewing in prison when 24 brokers and merchants, determined to bring order to the unruly business, met under a tree near what is now 68 Wall Street. Under the historic Buttonwood Agreement of May 1792, they agreed to trade securities among themselves, charging a standard commission—and shutting out the auctioneers, whom they believed, correctly, were trying to rig prices. That was the beginning of the New York Stock Exchange.

In the following century, the market struggled to maturity. The vicious brawl in the 1850s and '60s over control of the Erie railroad, which became known as the "Scarlet Woman of Wall Street," for the richness of the skullduggery surrounding it, forced the exchange to clean house. Among other things, it ordered new rules to tighten practices on the registration of securities and forbade insiders from shorting their own stock. As a result of these and other reforms—many of them prompted by scandals of less spectacular scale—by the turn of the century, New York was a sophisticated and powerful financial market. It's worth noting that these changes were made by the exchange itself; there were few criminal convictions, even after the disastrous attempt to corner the gold market on "Black Friday" in 1869. Scandal can be criminal but it doesn't have to be. No laws were broken because there were few laws to break. The Stock Exchange was a self-regulating, privately–run entity—and no one saw fit to challenge that.

The willingness—and eventually eagerness—of government to police business developed with the rise of very big business in the late 19th century. The Sherman Antitrust Act of 1890 was the first attempt to limit the scope of the cartels that dominated the economy—particularly John D. Rockefeller's Standard Oil. But enforcement was minimal. Only when prompted by Ida Tarbell's famous series of magazine articles that ran in *McClure's* from 1902-04, which took aim at what she called Rockefeller's "commercial Machiavellism," did the Sherman Act become more than a government-issued paper with which to wrap fish.

Stung into action by the muckrakers and a truly irritated public, in the early 1900s, the federal government broke up hundreds of trusts, including that of Standard Oil, to enormous popular acclaim. Washington also began to be more assertive in terms of protecting consumers. In 1906, Congress passed the first federal laws to protect the food supply and to rid the worst quack remedies from the nation's medicine cabinets. These successes emboldened public agencies to take a more active interest in the management of business, even on fairly dubious grounds.

There was, for example, the famous ball of 1905, given by 28-year-old James Hazen Hyde, the Francophile scion of the Equitable Life Assurance Society, then the world's third-largest life insurance company. Guests were told to dress in the costume of the court of Versailles. In an era of fabulous parties, Hyde's was opulent but hardly out of the ordinary. And yet, something about this one struck a disgusted chord. It was just too much: Roses piled to the ceiling; women so encrusted with jewels they could not walk; an ice sculpture of Michelangelo's "David," through which vodka issued (a touch repeated by Dennis Kozlowski; see Chapter 2). And Hyde, by virtue of his position, had enemies, both inside and outside the company. Goaded by the newspapers, who accused Hyde of paying for the bacchanalia with company money (not true), what began as a tabloid frenzy of familiar mien became a challenge to Hyde's management of the Equitable—and eventually provoked an investigation of the entire insurance industry.

Though the pretext could not have been flimsier, the Armstrong Committee did solid work, uncovering various abuses and incidents of sharp-dealing in the industry. The result was a host of measures that changed forever the relationship between Wall Street and the insurance companies and that went far to protect consumers. More than a dozen other states followed New York's lead.

The 1907 panic marked another milestone on the road to widespread regulation. In mid-October, a couple of rogue speculators attempted to corner United Copper. They failed. The stock, like a canary in a poisoned mine, fluttered, then crashed. In a matter of hours, there was a full-blown rush for the exits, as stocks sunk to levels last seen in 1893.

In fact, the financial system, looked at rationally, was not in that bad shape. But fear is not always rational, and when it comes to money, neither are people. They wanted their cash, and they wanted it now, camping out outside their banks.

Financier J.P. Morgan came to the rescue. Because the U.S. did not have a central bank, the federal government lacked the means to pump money into the system. To his office at 23 Wall—George Washington could have thrown a dollar to the site of the Buttonwood Agreement down the street—Morgan summoned New York's most important money men. On the crucial day, October 24, with dozens of brokerage firms on the verge of collapse from margin calls, Morgan got them to pledge $25 million to keep the Stock Exchange open and to reduce the interest rate on margin loans. The floor of the exchange gave a standing O on the news. Still, the crisis was far from over.

Finally, in early November came one of the most dramatic moments in American financial history. Morgan again gathered the city's bankers, this time to his magnificent Manhattan library and locked the door. His unmistakable message: *No one was getting out until they fixed the mess.* And they did, agreeing to a complex rescue plan around dawn on Sunday. President Theodore Roosevelt, a rich man who didn't think much of Wall Street, approved the deal. When the market opened on Monday, it rallied. The worst was over.

The panic of 1907 was sharp, but blessedly short. The larger problem was that the U.S. had had such scares about once a decade; some deteriorated into full-blown depressions. And while there was nothing illegal about many of the actions that triggered the panics, business as usual was clearly not good enough. By the early 20th century, even the most ardent Jacksonian—it was Andrew Jackson who in 1832 killed the national bank that Hamilton had created—began to concede that the lack of a central bank contributed to the creation of financial crises, and then hindered the government's ability to stop them. In 1908, Congress began to investigate how to stabilize the financial system. The result: the creation of the Federal Reserve, in 1913.

"The 1907 panic would be the last time that bankers loomed so much larger than regulators in a crisis," concludes Ron Chernow in *The House of Morgan*. "Afterward, the pendulum would swing decidedly toward government financial management... Everybody saw that thrilling rescues by corpulent old tycoons were a tenuous prop for the banking system." There is no clearer example of how a scandal forced actions that fundamentally shaped the U.S. economy.

Even so, it was not until the Depression that such intervention became frequent, and eventually routine. The shock of the 1929 stock market crash, combined with spectacular frauds like those of Ivar Kreuger (see Chapter 3), "made it easy for Congress, especially with a new president, to pass very major pieces of legislation," says Marc Hodak, an adjunct professor in the market, ethics and law program at New York University's Stern School of Business. Today, Hodak points out, expectations are different; people believe they should be protected from wrong-doers, and sometimes even from risk.

FORTUNE, which published its first issue in 1930, has been able to chronicle this evolution from a front-row seat. These 20 stories, drawn from the magazine and adapted for this volume, offer a modern history of scandal. In fact, we could have filled another 500 pages with wonderful stories like the $600 million cigarette scam, Operation Boris, the downfall of Milberg & Weiss, and the great Florida oil swindle. But *Scandal!* hits the high points, with stories ranging from 1933 through 2009.

There was so much to choose from because FORTUNE has made it its business to track both the business world's more dubious achievements—and the legal and regulatory response to them. So, for example, when a small-time con artist named Philip Musica managed to rip off millions from a century-old drug business in the late 1930s (see Chapter 11), he didn't just compromise a family firm; he helped to drag accounting standards into something like the modern age.

Closer to our own times, the savings-and-loan scandals led to a total overhaul of the industry in 1989, while the many Wall Street scandals of the same decade led to such legislation as the Insider Trading Sanctions Act of 1984. This, in turn, set the stage for more and more legislation as more and more unseemly stories emerged (Chapters 13 and 14). The dense network of scandals—Adelphia (Chapter 4), HealthSouth (Chapter 17), Enron (Chapter 16), *ad nauseum*—that made the early 2000s such interesting times for FORTUNE journalists, gave the world Sarbanes-Oxley. Many business people regard SarbOx with unconcealed distaste. Necessary evil or no, SarbOx did not come out of nowhere; it was a considered reaction to a set of serious crimes.

Finally, there is the mortgage crisis. With Fannie Mae providing financing of last resort, and Congress cheering it on (see Chapter 18), far too many people leveraged themselves into taking loans they could ill afford. For millions, the American dream of owning a home turned into a financial nightmare. Fannie Mae committed no crime, nor did most private-sector lenders or borrowers. The scandal here was avarice, abetted by carelessness. And the result was economic crisis. "Scandals of any size provoke a desire to regulate," concludes Hodak. "Now it is basically an expectation." In a sense, business has only itself to blame for such officiousness.

Not all the chapters in *Scandal!* fit this framework. Check-kiting has always been illegal, for example. But it can still happen—and break a city's heart in the process (Chapter 12). Ditto for the numerous price-fixing cartels that were all over the electrical industry in the 1950s (Chapter 6). And when Billie Sol Estes moved ammonia tanks around the plains of West Texas with the facility of a three-card Monte dealer, (Chapter 15) he had to know he was doing wrong. But it was just too damn tempting to rip off the smart-asses from the city.

FORTUNE loves business, and is happy to write about the good guys, too—the innovators, managers, and laborers who work hard and well. But the nature of modern business is that it is not self-contained—for good or ill. Ideas blast across cyberspace in microseconds; geniuses in Haifa tap capital in California overnight. But on the downside, teachers in Ontario can and do lose a chunk of their pensions to the crooks at Enron, and investors from Minneapolis to Sao Paolo and Tel Aviv lost their shirts after investing with Bernie Madoff. The result is that business scandals tend to hit the headlines and then stay for a while. There is no reason to believe that the percentage of venal or rotten people is greater in business than in any other field; nor does business have a monopoly on scandalous misjudgments. There is also no doubt that it doesn't always seem that way.

For the best, most highly regarded businesses, ethics matter and internal checks prevent small mistakes from ballooning into big ones. The list of great-performing companies with poor values and whimsical management is a short (and short-lived) one. Honesty really is the best policy; and wisdom really is the better part of performance.

But scams and spies and stupidity—that makes the best reading.

February 2009

LOOTING

1

THE PREDATOR

*How an Italian thug looted MGM, brought Credit
Lyonnais to its knees and made the Pope cry.*

---

by DAVID McCLINTICK

July 8, 1996

I t was a "harem," as Florio Fiorini recalls it, and the young women
were kept on the company payroll. There was Carla from Milan,
fair, quiet, tall, so tall that she was never seen walking alongside her
sugar daddy, a squat little man; and Marina from Venice, red hair,
green eyes, a Shakespeare scholar; and Cinzia from Rome, black hair,
smoldering, indolent, a chain smoker.

They were all women kept by Giancarlo Parretti, an Italian tycoon of
stunning vulgarity and shrewd charm, the man who had just acquired
MGM studios for $1.3 billion. It was early 1991, and Parretti had come
a long way in a very short time from his days as a petty crook in Sicily.
A $9 million mansion in Beverly Hills, a brown $200,000 Rolls-Royce,
a private jet, a rich social life, and a major presence in Hollywood
were all his. And it had all been so easy: a matter of a few well-placed
bribes to senior officials of a vast global bank, which had subsequently
sprung—and sprung and sprung—for more than $2 billion.

But already cracks had begun to appear in the gaudy edifice. On January

10, 1991, a six-figure check to Dustin Hoffman bounced. Lack of funds forced MGM to postpone the opening of *Thelma & Louise*. The studio withheld a letter of credit due Sean Connery until the actor threatened to boycott the premiere of *The Russia House*. A month into Parretti's ownership, the studio missed a payment of bond interest. The company was running a cash-flow deficit of, by one estimate, $1 million a day.

Even a gala event meant to legitimize Parretti instead sent an ominous signal. On the evening of Thursday, February 28—four months after acquiring MGM—Parretti beamed from the head table in the Beverly Hilton Hotel's International Ballroom; he was being honored with a "distinguished achievement award" at a glittering black-tie ball given by the National Council on the Aging, to which he had just promised $500,000. At Parretti's table were Alan Ladd Jr., Robin Leach, and Carlo Ponti. But the genuine Hollywood elite—actors, studio heads, leading agents—were conspicuously absent, like birds that vanish before an earthquake. They missed the slick color program, which gushed that Parretti was "worthy of any Hollywood film script."

And, in his own way, he was: In less than a year, Parretti's Hollywood edifice would blow apart with epic force, and a shaky global empire constructed from the oldest building material known to man—the bribe—would topple. Parretti's fabled studio would be snatched away. The corrupt bank that had lent him over $2 billion, the august Credit Lyonnais of Paris, would shrivel and watch its grand dreams of global influence go up in flames.

Today the Parretti affair occupies a U.S. grand jury, two federal prosecutors and a group of FBI and IRS agents in Los Angeles, who are weighing evidence of racketeering, criminal securities fraud, tax fraud, and money laundering by Parretti and others. It is also the focus of criminal proceedings in France, Italy, Switzerland, and the state of Delaware.

In the annals of pilgrims with or without money who have come to Hollywood seeking sex, grandeur, riches, and triumph, the little man who began as a hotel waiter in Italy would wreak more havoc in less time than anyone before. In the resulting debacle, the biggest banking swindle ever would fuse with the biggest Hollywood swindle ever, in a story of elegant skullduggery, bald greed and breathtaking opportunism.

From the private screening room of the Vatican, where he talked Pope John Paul II into sitting through the screening of a movie (the Pontiff was deeply moved), to the grand ballroom of the Beverly Wilshire Hotel, where he offered the helm of MGM to former President Ronald Reagan (he declined), to the Parretti mansion in Beverly Hills, where he tried to lure Meryl Streep into his bed (she laughed him out of the room), Parretti never feared rejection or even jail in pursuit of the big score.

YOUNG MAN IN A HURRY

Raised on an olive farm 50 miles north of Rome near Orvieto, a small city famous for its striking cathedral, Parretti went to sea as a young man, working as a waiter aboard the *Queen Elizabeth.* An eager employee, he befriended a passenger named Graziano Verzotto, a powerful tycoon and political boss from Sicily. Verzotto hired him to work as a waiter and maitre d' at one of his hotels, the Villa Politi in the Sicilian city of Siracusa.

It wasn't long before Parretti had become the protege and confidant of Verzotto. Giancarlo Parretti had met his first angel. In 1975 an Italian government investigation revealed that Verzotto had taken bribes to run money for Michele Sindona, the Mafia's notorious banker. Verzotto was shot in the arm and hospitalized. It was alleged that he had arranged a fake assassination attempt to delay prosecution. Giancarlo Parretti spent time at his bedside.

Once Verzotto recovered, he fled Italy, and his wife named Parretti to manage his business interests, which included the Siracusa soccer team. Parretti paid the team every week from a bag full of cash. No one knew where the money came from. The team eventually went bankrupt; years later the ensuing investigation would produce an indictment for fraud.

Parretti was doing more than just bankrupting a soccer team; he was building a rap sheet—for violating public securities laws, conspiring to commit bodily harm, issuing bad checks—though he never served significant time. In 1976 he formed a chain of newspapers called Il Diario in several Italian cities. Eventually the newspapers, too, would go bankrupt, resulting in a fraud conviction, but not before Parretti, as publisher, formed a close relationship with two brothers who were prominent Socialist Party activists, Gianni and Cesare DeMichelis.

The fraud indictments kept coming. In 1984, Parretti was indicted for fraud in the bankruptcy of the hotel company in Sicily. That same year he was prosecuted in Sicily for forging a savings bond. In 1986 he gained control of a Socialist newspaper in Paris, *Le Matin*, which went bankrupt a year later.

PARIS GOES TO HOLLYWOOD

Credit Lyonnais by the mid-1980s was on its way to becoming the world's leading lender to Hollywood studios. Its point man in that effort was Frans Afman, who loved to hang out in Hollywood. Afman treated his clients lavishly. On occasion he would advance millions without the required documentation or collateral. To keep the funds flowing, some clients paid Afman money on the side. Carolco Pictures paid Afman a "consulting fee" of $225,000 a year. Afman became a director of several client companies, giving him access to confidential information and deliberations within companies that were competing with each other.

Founded in 1863 and nationalized after World War II, Credit Lyonnais had been among the world's largest banks for decades. Its opulent headquarters, on the Boulevard des Italiens near the opera, loomed for years as the largest nongovernment building in Paris. But it sought more than size; it sought worldwide prestige and power.

Frans Afman was ready to help. Between 1981 and 1988, Afman's lending to Hollywood increased sixfold, to around $775 million. His clients included Dino De Laurentiis; Alexander Salkind, who had made *Superman*; Hemdale Films, which had made the Academy Award-winning *Platoon* and the megahit *The Terminator*; Carolco Pictures, which had made some of the Rambo movies; and Gladden

Entertainment, which made *The Fabulous Baker Boys.* (On Oscar night, 1987, the producer of *Platoon*, accepting the Academy Award for best picture, thanked Afman by name for "having the money in the Philippine jungle when I really needed it.")

Afman actually reported to the Dutch branch of Credit Lyonnais, called Credit Lyonnais Bank Nederland (CLBN), which had a checkered past, including allegations of laundering money for drug kingpins. In 1981, Credit Lyonnais appointed Georges Vigon, a rising star in its senior echelons, to straighten out the Dutch. One of Vigon's first moves was to create a new division of the bank exclusively for the movie loans. He named Frans Afman to run it.

While Credit Lyonnais was building its presence in Hollywood, Giancarlo Parretti was building his fortune in Europe. In the mid-1980s he gained control of a big Italian insurance company, then a Spanish hotel and travel company called Melia International, and finally a real estate firm called Renta Immobiliaria. Along the way he made a crucial alliance—with Florio Fiorini, a chubby, good-humored Tuscan businessman.

"Parretti was wearing a tie the way the charcoal merchants wear them," Florio Fiorini said years later of their first meeting, describing an unfashionably wide black necktie that Parretti wore tucked into his pants. If Parretti was a deceptively comic figure, an "Italian Ralph Kramden," as someone in Hollywood later called him, Fiorini was his foil—an urbane kibitzer and occasional restraining influence who by the mid-1980s had secretly become one of the biggest, if not the biggest, political briber and money launderer in Europe. He had learned those skills from the master criminals Roberto Calvi and Michele Sindona, the notorious Vatican-connected bankers whose violent deaths in the wake of banking scandals in the late 1970s and 1980s remain unsolved.

The two hustlers—Parretti and Fiorini—set about creating a vast nebula of shell holding companies that would obscure the ownership of all their acquisitions to come. Fiorini's principal vehicle, Sasea, eventually had more than 300 subsidiaries all over the world, many of them entwined with Parretti's holding companies, which were ultimately controlled by a shadowy entity called Comfinance Panama.

The two partners got their first taste of the movie business in 1986, a very long way from Hollywood. A Roman Catholic organization Parretti had worked with in Rome asked him to oversee the production of *Bernadette*, a motion picture based on the life of a peasant girl who saw visions of the Virgin Mary in the French town of Lourdes in the 1850s and was sanctified. Parretti loved it, but Fiorini insisted that Parretti get rid of it. Instead, Parretti decided he wanted to buy the distributor, the Cannon Group, which was run by two former Israeli paratroopers, Menahem Golan and Yoram Globus. Cannon, based in Los Angeles and traded on the New York Stock Exchange, was the largest movie theater operator in Europe and made ninja and vengeance films with actors like Charles Bronson and Chuck Norris. "Parretti, may God strike you dead!" Fiorini exclaimed in early 1987. "I send you to sell a movie and you come back wanting to buy a whole studio with a billion dollars in debt!"

The Cannon Group's debt was actually a little under a billion, but still the company was in considerable financial and regulatory trouble. Golan and Globus were amenable to a takeover; they saw it as a way to save Cannon.

Parretti convinced Fiorini that they could sell some of Cannon's assets and get control of its more valuable properties. But they would need the approval of Cannon's principal bank. The bank was the Dutch branch of Credit Lyonnais.

As it happened, the Cannes Film Festival was about to open. Golan and Globus invited Parretti to meet their banker, Frans Afman. As soon as the elegantly dressed banker walked through the door of the lavish suite, according to sources who witnessed the scene, Parretti pointed his finger at him and shouted across the room: "You, Afman!"

"Yes," replied Afman, taken aback.

"How much money you make at that bank?" Parretti shouted in heavily accented English.

Afman hesitated. There were other people in the suite.

"I double it!" Parretti shouted.

Afman looked at Globus. Was this a joke?

"Not enough?" Parretti continued. "I triple it! I triple your salary—if you come into my company."

"Wait a moment, Mr. Parretti," Afman retorted quietly, settling with his assistant Ria Jankie on a sofa across from Parretti. "I'm not here to discuss my salary with the bank. I'm here to discuss your possible investment in Cannon." But Parretti wouldn't relent. Finally Afman said, "I'd have to give up my job at the Credit Lyonnais." Parretti beamed and replied: "That wouldn't be necessary—on the contrary."

Only then did Afman grasp what Parretti was offering—a bribe of triple the banker's salary if he went to work secretly for Parretti while still running entertainment lending at CLBN. Frans Afman didn't know when he had been so repelled by another human being. It wasn't the bribe proposal; Afman had been bought before. It was Parretti's manner—shouting a bribe offer across a crowded room—that offended him. If Parretti's brazenness was repulsive, his vulgarity was worse. As they talked, Parretti began gazing at Ria Jankie, an attractive and thoroughly professional business woman, in an overtly lascivious way while gesturing at his genitals. Jankie was disgusted, as was Afman. Nor was Afman impressed by Parretti's proposal for refinancing Cannon. "This is not a bankable proposition," Afman told him. "There is nothing I can do."

Offended, Parretti rose to his feet. "I'm going to take my private plane and fly to Rotterdam to meet your chairman. You may lose your job."

"You won't need to go to Rotterdam," Afman replied, with false confidence. "Georges Vigon is here." The next day, Vigon met with Parretti, Fiorini and Globus; Afman was nowhere to be seen. Parretti's words proved prophetic—it was the beginning of the end for Afman's career at the bank.

Vigon was, Fiorini recalls, "smoking like a Turk" as they talked. A short, barrel-chested, ex-Foreign Legion paratrooper, he had once killed an Algerian rebel with the rebel's own bayonet after the Algerian's gun jammed. His hands moved constantly—not nervously but with the swift grace of a prestidigitator. Vigon extracted the soft center of a piece of French bread, compressed pieces of it into cubes, took out a pen, marked them like dice, and played with them as he listened to Parretti's proposals for the Cannon Group. Movie people from all over the world stopped at the table to pay their respects. Parretti flirted with starlets. Globus departed. By the end of the afternoon, Parretti, Fiorini, and Vigon had struck the outlines of a deal.

After a single meeting, the president of the Dutch subsidiary of one of the world's largest banks had agreed, against the advice of his principal loan officer, to turn over control of the Cannon Group to two men he had never before met, and whose movie experience was limited to the financing of a minor film about a minor saint. Then, things got weird.

Back in Rotterdam after the Cannes meeting, Georges Vigon ordered a background investigation. The report, delivered on July 22, 1987, detailed the true extent of Parretti's criminal rap sheet; a separate report detailed Fiorini's involvement in bank scandals and political bribery. Undeterred, Vigon and his colleagues okayed Parretti and Fiorini's takeover of the Cannon Group. The bank lent them $250 million. Parretti was required to use some of the money to pay down Cannon's old debt, but Parretti and Fiorini still had plenty of money to work with.

To show his appreciation, Parretti began giving Vigon and other CLBN bankers works of art—color drawings purportedly by Picasso and Miró. And he flew Georges Vigon and his family aboard a private jet for a South Pacific vacation.

The Dutch central bank knew nothing of the conflicts of interest at CLBN, nothing of Parretti's attempted bribe of Frans Afman at the Cannes Film Festival, nothing of Parretti's and Fiorini's reputations, and nothing of Parretti's "gifts" to Georges Vigon. The central bank, however, had by early 1988 noticed the sharp rise in CLBN's loans to Hollywood and to Parretti and Fiorini, and expressed its concern about the concentration of loans with a few borrowers in a single industry and about an apparent imbalance of debt over equity among the borrowers.

Georges Vigon sprang into action—not by demanding that delinquent clients pay off overdue loans but by funneling new funds their way, often through shell corporations set up to cloud the money trail. Even as he papered over bad loans, Vigon continued to shovel money to new Hollywood clients. According to papers filed in California Superior Court, he put $30 million of Credit Lyonnais's money into a small movie company called Film Accord, with offices in Los Angeles and Montreal. Some $13.5 million of the money was spent to make the film *Honor Bound*, starring Tom Skerritt, which proved unreleasable. Another $550,000 was spent on a yacht, kept in the Caribbean, called *The Iliad and The Odyssey*. None of the financing was covered by loan documents until much later. According to Film Accord's former senior vice president for finance, Anthony Friscia, Film Accord funneled $1.8 million in kickbacks to Vigon and other CLBN officers through a Canadian bank account.

Partly as a result of his impolitic clash with Parretti, Frans Afman, who had built the entertainment loan business, had been forced to resign. He became a consultant to the bank, dealing only with a few of his old clients. The Dutch central bank, which had learned Afman was on the payroll of the Cannon Group, endorsed the termination of "this double function which, in our opinion, is undesirable."

With his problem loans hidden and CLBN seemingly prospering, Vigon was promoted to Paris to head all European lending (including CLBN, and by extension the Hollywood lending). From Credit Lyonnais's magisterial headquarters, the man who had sanctioned Afman's conflicts of interest and who was himself now taking artwork and South Seas vacations from Giancarlo Parretti, suddenly had vastly broader responsibilities. The cancer had spread from a limb to the torso of one of the world's largest financial institutions.

But at Credit Lyonnais, the supply of executives willing to be corrupted proved ample. Credit Lyonnais named Jean-Jacques Brutschi, another rising star, to replace Vigon at CLBN. Replacing Afman was one Jacques Griffault, who had headed Credit Lyonnais's branch in Milan, where he had known Florio Fiorini. Brutschi and Griffault quickly became intimates of Parretti, who kept the expensive gifts coming.

Loans weren't the only service CLBN provided to Parretti. Ten months after it learned of his criminal background, a CLBN officer wrote an effusive "To Whom It May Concern" letter of recommendation. "Since the commencement of our relationship with him...we have come to know Mr. Parretti as a capable and astute businessman...."

By the late 1980s, Credit Lyonnais had become the largest lender in Hollywood—but its film portfolio had become a massive Ponzi-like scheme, with lavish new loans to disreputable borrowers paying off uncollectible old loans as a means of keeping at bay Dutch and French banking regulators, and perpetuating a gravy train of bribes to bank officers.

Flush with Credit Lyonnais cash, Giancarlo Parretti in late 1988 moved his base of operations to Los Angeles, where he indulged himself like the proverbial Roman emperor. Parretti took over Dino De Laurentiis's Wilshire Boulevard office, lavish even by Beverly Hills standards, and bought a Rolls-Royce. His home was an opulently landscaped two-acre property that included a seven-bedroom house, Olympic-sized swimming pool, and a tennis court that ran north and south to minimize sun in players' eyes.

Parretti installed his wife, Maria Cecconi, and his children, Valentina, Evelyn, and Mauro, in the mansion, along with a lot of expensive-looking art. At Cannon, meanwhile, the man whose lewd behavior had so offended people in Cannes the previous year put three young Italian women under contract as "actresses" to service him sexually. In addition to payroll checks to Carla, Marina, and Cinzia (who had once been second runner-up in the Miss Universe pageant), Parretti apparently gave the women jewelry worth up to $1 million. He promised them acting lessons.

He launched a $150 million bid to acquire Pathé Cinema, the venerable

French motion picture company, and went so far as to change the name of the Cannon Group to Pathé Communications Corp. in anticipation. And he hired Alan Ladd Jr., an experienced studio executive and son of the late movie star, to make pictures for Pathé Communications. Ladd also joined the board of directors.

In Hollywood, all this gave Parretti instant cachet. He invited *le tout* Hollywood to his mansion and they came. The entertaining culminated just before Christmas 1988 with a festive party for 200. Among the guests were Georges Vigon and Jacques Griffault, flown in with their families from Europe to California by Parretti.

During the party, Parretti took Vigon and Griffault, together with Florio Fiorini, Menahem Golan and a few others, into the seclusion of his library. There he presented each banker with a certificate for 200,000 shares of stock in a small, publicly traded motion picture company that Parretti controlled, called 21st Century Distribution Corp. He also gave them certificates for 200,000 of 21st Century's Class A warrants and 200,000 of its Class B warrants, convertible under certain conditions into common stock, for a potential total of 600,000 common shares. Twenty-First Century, which had recently emerged from bankruptcy, is "going to become a big company in the motion picture business," Parretti told the bankers, according to Golan's declaration. Its stock "might soon be selling at $30 or $40 a share." Based on those numbers, the inescapable inference was that each gift had a potential value of between $18 million and $24 million. Even if that possibility were discounted, the shares of 21st Century were then being quoted over the counter at 50 cents bid, $1 asked, giving the stock, excluding the warrants, an indicated value of between $100,000 and $200,000.

The gifts made Vigon and Griffault among the largest individual shareholders of 21st Century Distribution. Two months later Pathé acquired 21st Century and made plans to guarantee $50 million in credit for the small company. That meant that 21st Century became a client of Credit Lyonnais. Messrs. Vigon and Griffault, by lending money to Pathé, were in a position to line their own pockets.

Parretti sent the same "gift" to CLBN President Jean-Jacques Brutschi, who had been unable to travel to California for the party. The morning after bribing the bankers, Parretti flew Vigon to Bora Bora again.

Before year-end, Pathé's credit line was extended. CLBN's loans to Pathé, Parretti, Fiorini, and related corporate entities doubled in the following year, from $600 million to over $1 billion.

Whether in Beverly Hills or New York, Paris, or Rome, Giancarlo Parretti was rarely out of the entertainment headlines in the early months of 1989. "Parretti is very appealing. He's going to be a very big player in our industry," Alan Ladd Jr. told *The Wall Street Journal.* Parretti announced that Pathé Communications had earned a profit for 1988 against a loss the previous year. He announced plans to bail Dino De Laurentiis out of bankruptcy. He announced he would buy New World Entertainment, a company that produced TV shows and B movies. He announced he would take over Kings Road Entertainment, which was known for *The Big Easy.* And most spectacular of all, he elaborated on plans to purchase control of Pathé Cinema, the legendary French movie company.

No one, not even the Pope, was too exalted to meet with Parretti or take his call as he jetted between Europe and the U.S. aboard his Credit Lyonnais-financed private jet. In Rome, Parretti showed *Bernadette,* the movie he had produced in 1986 about the girl who became a saint, to Pope John Paul II in the Pontiff's private screening room in the Vatican. The Pope sat in the first row. Parretti sat in the second row with Menahem Golan and Yoram Globus. When the movie ended, the Pope, tears running down his face, didn't move for several minutes.

And then, like a spent Roman candle, Parretti began to sputter. He was outbid for New World entertainment and Kings Road Entertainment. The De Laurentiis deal fell through. Pathé Communications posted a loss for the second quarter of 1989. Parretti's bid for Pathé Cinema was tentatively blocked by the French government, which didn't want a French shrine to be owned by an Italian of dubious background. *The*

Wall Street Journal caught Parretti lying about his criminal background in Italy, and the SEC forced him to put a longer disclosure statement in Pathé's filings. Even the new statement fell short of candor; it failed to mention that Parretti had been charged with "falsifying balance sheets" in the collapse of his *Il Diario* newspapers.

Concerned about the burgeoning loans, the Dutch central bank in the spring of 1989 imposed a lending limit on CLBN of $200 million per client or related group of clients. The bank's exposure to the Parretti-Fiorini group already exceeded $900 million, but instead of reducing that exposure, the bank schemed with Fiorini and Parretti to expand the exposure while making it appear it was shrinking.

In one such ruse, the bank and the borrowers set out to make it appear that Pathé Communications had reduced its indebtedness to the bank by $184 million. A company called Cinema V, purportedly controlled by Italian media mogul Silvio Berlusconi and newly incorporated in the Netherlands, purchased a group of Pathé's movie theaters in England and Holland for $184 million. Pathé used the money to pay down the combined Parretti-Fiorini debt at CLBN. What the central bank wasn't told was that Cinema V was a shell created by Fiorini, with the knowledge not only of Jacques Griffault and Jean-Jacques Brutschi of CLBN but also of Georges Vigon of Credit Lyonnais in Paris, for the sole purpose of deceiving the Dutch central bank. The $184 million wasn't from Silvio Berlusconi at all—in fact, he may not have known his name was used in the transaction. It had been put up by CLBN. The central bank wasn't told that Parretti and Credit Lyonnais controlled both ends of the transaction, or that the Parretti-Fiorini loan portfolio was still expanding.

Frans Afman no longer headed entertainment lending, but as a consultant still serviced several of his old clients. He tried to tune out new information about Parretti and Fiorini. He felt their relationship with the bank was out of control and sure to attract attention sooner or later from U.S. law enforcement. Whenever he was in the U.S., he felt queasy; he expected FBI agents or SEC investigators with subpoenas to knock at his door.

At a screening one evening at the Writers Guild on Wilshire Boulevard, Afman was approached by CLBN's manager in charge of the Parretti account, a nervous young man named Dirk van Swaay.

"I need to talk to you very urgently," van Swaay whispered. "I need your advice. It's about Parretti."

"Sorry, I don't want to talk about him."

"But I need to tell you something."

"No, I don't want to hear it," Afman said, trying to walk away.

"We're now in over a billion dollars!" van Swaay shouted, dashing after Afman.

The 28-page fax from the European private detective to the head of an independent Hollywood film company, in August 1989, was headed STRICTLY PERSONAL AND CONFIDENTIAL. Two years after Credit Lyonnais had received its background report on Giancarlo Parretti, and then proceeded to lend him hundreds of millions of dollars, a few Hollywood people whose business Parretti was soliciting were ordering their own briefings. In addition to detailing Parretti's and Fiorini's checkered backgrounds, the new report speculated about the origins of Parretti's funds—maybe the Italian Socialists, maybe the Mafia.

By early 1990, Parretti had been eyeing MGM for more than a year. He had found the perfect centerpiece for the global empire he aspired to build. Founded in the Twenties, symbol of Hollywood's Golden Age, once home to "more stars than there are in Heaven," MGM had produced *Gone With the Wind, The Wizard of Oz,* and *Singin' in the Rain.* But MGM's owner since the late Sixties, Kirk Kerkorian, had never made the studio pay the way he wanted it to. So in 1986, Kerkorian sold the rights to the MGM library, and the fabled 44-acre Culver City lot to Ted Turner. By the end of the decade, Kerkorian was looking to sell the rest. And Giancarlo Parretti was looking to buy.

On March 6, Parretti's Pathé Communications offered Kerkorian $1.25 billion for MGM. Kerkorian accepted and gave Parretti and Fiorini, four months to come up with the money. They would have to pay Kerkorian nonrefundable deposits of $50 million a month until the deal was closed.

At MGM, people were thrilled by the prospect of new ownership after years of upheaval. "I think the world of Parretti," said Jeffrey Barbakow, the studio's chairman. "He's extremely bright, and he's a global thinker."

But where would the global thinker raise $1.25 billion? Parretti and Fiorini had already gone through much of the $1 billion-plus that Credit Lyonnais had loaned them. Steve Ross, chairman of the newly formed Time Warner, decided to advance Parretti $650 million—a bit more than half the purchase price for MGM—in exchange for the rights to distribute the studio's television and video offerings and the movies not owned by Turner. But Ross conditioned his offer on Parretti's raising the rest of the money in the form of equity rather than debt. Both Hollywood and Wall Street were skeptical; while Credit Lyonnais could supply endless loans, it couldn't create investors.

The ultimate responsibility for the bank's role lay with its Paris-based chairman and chief executive officer, Jean-Yves Haberer, an appointee of President Francois Mitterrand. Mitterrand had given Haberer a blank check to transform the state-owned Credit Lyonnais into the French equivalent of Germany's all-powerful Deutsche Bank, competing at the highest levels of global finance—a cultural force, more than just a bank.

Jean-Yves Haberer was more than just a banker. He was also a published fiction writer, an art connoisseur, an Alpine hiker. He had headed Paribas, another large French bank, and had run the French Treasury. Upon taking command at Credit Lyonnais, Haberer installed a unique "floating floor" containing his office, a luxurious dining room, a sitting room, and a full bathroom, insulated from the vibrations of the street, the Metro, and the real world.

As chief executive, Jean-Yves Haberer had been actively involved in his Dutch subsidiary's financing of Giancarlo Parretti and Florio Fiorini. Haberer was on the CLBN supervisory board. In fact, one of his first important decisions after he took the helm of Credit Lyonnais had been to approve CLBN's financing of Parretti's attempted acquisition of France's Pathé Cinema. And when the Dutch central bank expressed alarm that CLBN was lending too much money to Parretti and Fiorini and their myriad corporations, Haberer tried to paint Parretti and Fiorini as separate borrowers, independent of each other, individuals who should be analyzed separately. The central bank rejected that reasoning. To resolve the dispute, Haberer had the parent Credit Lyonnais issue a guarantee of Parretti and Fiorini's CLBN obligations and at the same time promised to reduce those obligations.

The Dutch central bank had broader concerns. In another letter to Haberer, headed STRICTLY CONFIDENTIAL, the central bank implored him to heed rumors that Parretti and Fiorini's major corporate entities were being used to launder "dirty money." Haberer did not reply, and the Dutch central bank informed the French central bank and its enforcement branch, the Commission Bancaire.

Then, in March 1990, a court in Naples convicted Giancarlo Parretti of fraud in connection with the bankruptcy of his *Il Diario* newspapers. He was sentenced in absentia to three-and-a-half years in prison and appealed. Back in the U.S., where Parretti had yet to actually put the MGM deal together, the ridicule began. "MGM is being bought by an Italian who has promised only one small change," Billy Crystal quipped from the stage of the Oscars. "From now on the lion is not going to roar—it will be taking the Fifth."

If such quips, plus the Italian news reports, plus the private background investigation of Parretti that Credit Lyonnais had received in 1987, weren't enough—and they weren't—Jean-Yves Haberer got a personal warning. Over lunch, a film producer friend warned him to avoid doing business with Giancarlo Parretti.

Back in Hollywood, Steve Ross began to have his doubts. He was troubled by reports of Parretti's criminal problems in Italy. And then one day he made a sobering discovery.

Parretti had given Ross what appeared to be a Picasso drawing worth millions. Ross had turned the piece over to Time Warner, which had called in an appraiser in order to insure it. The appraiser declared the drawing a fake. (It was later learned that much of Parretti's art collection was not genuine.)

Then, Parretti failed to produce equity investors. For Ross, that was too much. He withdrew his commitment of $650 million.

With the centerpiece of their financing suddenly gone, Parretti and Fiorini faced a crisis. They had already paid Kirk Kerkorian $200 million that was nonrefundable. He granted them an extension until October, but raised the price of MGM to $1.34 billion. Plus, Kerkorian was due $50 million more each month. Credit Lyonnais had surreptitiously financed more than two-thirds of the monthly deposits so far, but would it spring for a billion more, a doubling of its commitment?

The first $1 billion, greased by bribes, had come easy. The second $1 billion, a different order of magnitude, might require another kind of inducement. As they had in the past, Giancarlo Parretti and Florio Fiorini turned to friends in high Italian places for what Fiorini would later call, in a written statement, "help from above." Parretti consulted his longtime associate Gianni DeMichelis, the Italian Foreign Minister, who, according to Fiorini, suggested that Parretti and Fiorini see Bettino Craxi, the former Prime Minister. DeMichelis denies Fiorini's account.

In his written statement, Fiorini says Craxi received Parretti and Fiorini in Rome, in the Socialist Party's headquarters on the Via del Corso. In his pocket, Fiorini carried two "bearer certificates," drawn on July 10 from the Milan branch of the Banca Novara Suisse, one for 600 million lire (then about $485,000), the other for 200 million lire—certificates any "bearer" could cash without reference to their origin.

Parretti and Fiorini said that they needed "high-level intervention" at Credit Lyonnais. According to Fiorini's written statement, the inventive Craxi suggested that they link the MGM deal to a major commercial negotiation then under way between the governments of France and Italy. The French government was trying to persuade the Italian government to purchase a new high-speed rail network from manufacturers in France instead of Germany. Craxi recommended to Parretti that he pay another call on his friend Foreign Minister

DeMichelis. Perhaps DeMichelis could prevail upon the chairman of the Italian state rail company, Lorenzo Necci, to condition any agreement by Italy to purchase high-speed trains from France upon the good treatment of Giancarlo Parretti by Credit Lyonnais.

After the meeting, according to Fiorini's statement, he delivered the 600 million lire bearer certificate to the Socialist Party treasurer, Vincenzo Balsamo, and asked him to remind Craxi of their conversation.

Parretti dined with DeMichelis at the nearby Plaza Hotel and asked him to "intervene" to achieve a quid pro quo between the rail deal and the MGM deal. He gave the 200 million lire bearer certificate to Gianni DeMichelis's secretary.

"I am sure," Fiorini wrote in his statement, "that Mr. DeMichelis called the chairman of the Italian rail company to instruct him to mention the interest of Italy in Italians' taking control of MGM and that any help of Credit Lyonnais will be duly appreciated by the authorities that had to decide the approval of the high-speed train deal."

Shortly thereafter, the government of Italy picked Credit Lyonnais and Haberer to lead the financing of the train consortium.

Parretti and Fiorini then traveled to Nice and briefed Georges Vigon at his weekend home. Vigon suggested that they also should see Alexis Wolkenstein, Vigon's boss, the general manager in charge of Credit Lyonnais's international affairs, who reported directly to Haberer and who aspired to succeed him. Wolkenstein would presumably welcome an opportunity to ingratiate himself with the government, which would one day be choosing a successor to Haberer. Parretti and Fiorini arranged for Italian Foreign Minister DeMichelis to meet with Wolkenstein.

By October 1990, Parretti and Fiorini had paid Kirk Kerkorian a total of $353 million. With a month before Kerkorian's deadline was to expire, they still had to come up with more than $900 million and had few legitimate sources. Time Warner, having withdrawn its commitment of $650 million, decided to chip in a more modest $125 million for home-video distribution rights to MGM films. Turner Broadcasting put up $200 million for television rights to the 1,000 MGM movies it didn't already own. That left Parretti and Fiorini over $600 million short.

At Dino De Laurentiis's suggestion, Parretti solicited the aid of Marvin Davis, the oil billionaire who had sold 20th Century Fox to Rupert Murdoch but who remained a Hollywood player. After an inconclusive meeting at Davis's Palm Springs weekend home, Davis's driver returned Parretti and two associates to the airport. "This guy is stupid," Parretti said of Davis, in Italian, in the back of the limo. "He's a big, fat, rich, dumb Jew. You know Jews. They always want something for nothing. Well, this time he won't get it. He'll be an easy touch."

The following Monday, Parretti arrived at Davis's Century City office in Los Angeles. "I'm going to teach you something," the oil man said. "Remember the driver who took you to the airport? He speaks Italian. He understood everything you said." Davis, a large man, gestured to the plate-glass window facing the ocean from his majestic 28th-floor office. "Now," he said, "you have a choice. You can get out of this office in the next 30 seconds. Or I'm going to throw you through this window." Parretti fled.

Florio Fiorini had laid a foundation that summer for more borrowing by seeming to spruce up the creditworthiness of Sasea, the vast Swiss holding company and money laundry that he controlled and that partially underpinned the Parretti-Fiorini empire. He had raised 340 million francs through an offering of Sasea debentures on the Geneva stock exchange. It appeared that public investors had purchased the bonds, endorsing Sasea's financial health, even as Fiorini and Parretti were bidding for MGM. In fact, Sasea was deep in debt, using fake balance sheets, and had secretly bought 88% of the bonds itself through a Dutch subsidiary in a way meant to resemble public support.

Now, with just days to go, Parretti and Fiorini, backed by the "health" of Sasea, embarked upon a dizzying sequence of deceptions to prompt the bribe-primed Credit Lyonnais to lend them the rest of the money. The details of the deceptions emerge from an examination of sealed depositions. Parretti told CLBN that Fininvest, the Italian media empire of Silvio Berlusconi, would invest $50 million in the MGM deal. (In fact, it isn't known whether Berlusconi had any intention of investing, or whether he was merely allowing Parretti to use the "commitment" as a means to instill confidence in others.) Pointing to Sasea and Fininvest, Parretti then elicited a commitment of $168 million from Reteitalia, another media company in Italy, for television and pay-per-view rights to distribute MGM material in Italy and Spain. What he didn't disclose was a secret side deal under which Pathé Communications would have to refund most of the money, if Reteitalia demanded it, for up to a year after the agreement.

Most important, Parretti indicated that the corporate parent and grandparent of Pathé Communications—Melia and Comfinance, both shells he controlled—would make equity investments in Pathé totaling $350 million. He didn't reveal that neither Comfinance nor Melia had nearly enough cash or credit to make such investments.

To conceal from the Dutch central bank the deepening role of Credit Lyonnais, which knew how weak Melia and Comfinance were, Florio Fiorini recruited the help of the second-largest shareholder of Sasea, Jean-Rene Bickart, a member of the Seneclauze family, one of the oldest clients of Credit Lyonnais. There then ensued an especially complicated example of the kind of fraudulent transaction at which Fiorini had grown so adept: making yet another bank loan appear to be an equity investment. That seemingly brought in another $150 million.

With that, plus several contingent or phony commitments such as those from Fininvest and Reteitalia, and bolstered by Fiorini's misrepresented summer debenture offering, Parretti asked CLBN and Credit Lyonnais in Paris to lend him enough money to close the MGM deal on November 1. He promised to repay this "bridge" loan later when he received funds from Fininvest, Reteitalia, and his other investors.

The staff of CLBN's Entertainment Business Division opposed further loans to Parretti. But Parretti didn't need the support of EBD. He had not bribed the staff of EBD. He had bribed Georges Vigon, Jacques Griffault, and Jean-Jacques Brutschi. Parretti was in constant contact with them by late October. The circular Bickart charade was part of about $550 million in last-minute loans the three bankers approved—Vigon in Paris gave the final okay—so that Parretti and Fiorini could close their purchase of MGM. In all, the two Italians had borrowed at least 76% of the $1.3 billion purchase price from Credit Lyonnais, much of it in secret to get around restrictions by Dutch and French banking regulators.

Giancarlo Parretti and Florio Fiorini's takeover of Metro-Goldwyn-Mayer closed on November 1, 1990, in Los Angeles. MGM executives broke out champagne and paraded a 400-pound live lion through the studio in celebration. "Non me mangia!" Parretti yelled in fright, "Don't eat me!" Parretti issued a press release declaring a "goal of being the most powerful Euro-American communications group of the Nineties."

Once MGM was his, almost without pause, Parretti began looting the studio in earnest, firing most of the financial staff and naming his 21-year-old daughter, Valentina, to an important financial post. Various of Parretti's many women were seen entering his office suite each afternoon. Sounds of sex could be heard from behind closed doors.

CLBN's largesse continued. The bank lent the studio another $97 million early in 1991.

But the party didn't last long. Looted and hopelessly in debt, the MGM studio was already little more than a tottering shell. The entire structure was so precarious that it was all but undone by one man, a canny Los Angeles lawyer named Stephen Chrystie. The great tangled Ponzi-esque skein of debt began to unravel.

Chrystie had made a good living over the years forcing corporations into bankruptcy when they didn't pay their creditors. In March several clients had complained to Chrystie that MGM owed them money—a total of about $18 million—and wasn't paying. Chrystie became the latest in a lengthening line of lawyers and executives to obtain Parretti's Italian rap sheet. He promptly filed a formal complaint against MGM in the U.S. Bankruptcy Court, invoking Chapter 7 of the federal bankruptcy code, the chapter governing involuntary bankruptcy. It was barely five months since Parretti had acquired MGM. If upheld by a judge, the complaint would cause $300 million to $400 million of MGM bonds to come due in 60 days. It might also transfer control of MGM from Giancarlo Parretti, Florio Fiorini, and the Credit Lyonnais bank to an independent bankruptcy examiner.

When news of Chrystie's complaint broke, the two Haberer deputies had just returned to Paris from Los Angeles, where they had been laying plans to reduce MGM's debt. Haberer, the bank's CEO, didn't give them time to unpack. François Gille, the Credit Lyonnais general manager in charge of finance, and Wolkenstein immediately flew back to Los Angeles to deal with the crisis.

Of the two, Wolkenstein was more familiar with MGM. He was Georges Vigon's boss and had supervised the bank's loans to Parretti and Fiorini leading up to the acquisition the previous year. Wolkenstein also had met at least twice with Foreign Minister DeMichelis in connection with Parretti's purchase of MGM.

Since his fateful lunch with Georges Vigon at the Cannes Film Festival in 1987, Giancarlo Parretti had become one of CLBN's biggest customers. It didn't matter. In the eyes of Gille and Wolkenstein, Parretti was history.

Everything Gille and Wolkenstein learned in the days to come only strengthened their conviction. First, in his conference room in Century City, lawyer Steve Chrystie put Giancarlo Parretti's rap sheet in front of the French bankers. "How could you loan money to a man like this?" Chrystie demanded. Visibly nervous, they averted their eyes from the legal documents freshly faxed from Naples. "He's a fine gentleman," one of them said of Parretti.

In meetings with MGM's and Pathé's auditors, Wolkenstein and Gille grew even more alarmed. It appeared he had lied about the companies' debt-to-equity ratios in the wake of the hidden Credit Lyonnais loans. Parretti also had lied in official reports to the SEC about the Cinema V transaction in 1989, in which $184 million of debt had been disguised, and about the merger financing that had been made to look like an equity investment made by him and Fiorini. The auditors told Gille and Wolkenstein that Pathé's SEC reports on the MGM acquisition would have to be revised forthwith.

Alan Ladd Jr., too, had lost confidence in Parretti. He was telling Credit Lyonnais that Parretti was a disaster, and offered to take command of the company—for a $1 million bonus, atop his $3.3 million salary.

Gille and Wolkenstein told Parretti that the bank would be willing to loan MGM still more millions to keep it out of bankruptcy and away from an independent examiner—but only if he relinquished control. Parretti agreed to leave as chief executive of MGM, but insisted on remaining a director. After initial reluctance, he also ceded his job as head of Pathé Communications to his old acquaintance Cesare DeMichelis, brother of Gianni. The bankers crafted a "corporate governance agreement" that purported to insulate Ladd from control by Parretti.

Credit Lyonnais would loan MGM an additional $145 million to stanch its $1-million-a-day cash-flow deficit. Chrystie's clients would be made whole, and he would drop his complaint. As security for the loan, the bank would take voting control of Pathé's MGM stock.

The agreement was signed on April 15, 1991. As a gesture of good will, Parretti treated everyone to champagne and dinner.

But the day after the new agreement took effect, he sent Ladd a memorandum demanding that Ladd inform him, as MGM's majority owner, of all important decisions and meet with him weekly. Ladd dispatched his own memorandum saying he was boss. Parretti countered with another memo, and the company was soon mired in a debilitating civil war of memos that left it without effective governance.

By late May, the bank was seeking alternatives to the standoff between Parretti and Ladd. It recruited Charles Meeker, the White & Case lawyer who had been in charge of getting Steve Chrystie's bankruptcy complaint dismissed, to join MGM as president. As it turned out, Meeker did little more than courier memos between Ladd and Parretti, adding his own memos to the mix and angering Parretti. In Paris, on Thursday, June 6, Parretti told Meeker (whom he called "Meekers"): "I want you to understand, Meekers, that I am really crazy.... I want you to understand that I am really dangerous. I am very dangerous. Do you understand, Meekers? I'm very dangerous." The bankers took the rumors of violence, and Parretti's alleged connection to the mob, seriously; they began holding their meetings under armed guard.

On June 14, Parretti called a meeting of the MGM board in Los Angeles. Ladd and Meeker boycotted the meeting. The directors who attended—all Parretti allies—passed several "resolutions" that, in effect, purported to revoke the "corporate governance agreement" that the bank had imposed in April and that Parretti was now claiming he had signed "with a gun to my head."

Parretti flew to Paris that night and had a tense meeting Saturday with Gille and Wolkenstein. It was the last straw. On Monday, June 17, invoking its rights under the April agreement, the bank seized control of MGM, removed Giancarlo Parretti from the company, and began a lawsuit against him in the Chancery Court of Delaware, where MGM is incorporated.

Charles Meeker, meanwhile, called the FBI and the SEC, both of which began investigations of Parretti and his stewardship of MGM. Meeker also hired the retiring special agent in charge of the FBI's Los Angeles office to probe the company.

Credit Lyonnais's sudden emergence as the de facto owner of the world's most famous movie studio, after years of shadowy dealings with two disreputable Italian tycoons, broke like an intense summer storm in the French press. The bank came under increasing pressure from the French Ministry of Finance and various deputies in the National Assembly to provide details of its links to Parretti and Fiorini. The aloof Jean-Yves Haberer found himself in the rare position of issuing a written press statement defending the bank's conduct. He tried to have it both ways. On the one hand, he blamed Georges Vigon for loans to Parretti in the face of contrary instructions. On the other hand, he complained that the bank was the victim of a disinformation campaign. Citing widespread rumors about Parretti's background, Haberer said he had no proof from any government that Parretti was undesirable. Haberer did not mention bribery or high-speed trains.

Credit Lyonnais announced that Georges Vigon had taken early retirement and that Jean-Jacques Brutschi had been reassigned to Southeast Asia. The bank did not mention Jacques Griffault, but he too was soon sidelined.

With Credit Lyonnais trying to fathom its losses, the business relationship between the bank and its Hollywood clients shifted rapidly from one of self-dealing, deception and bribery to one of intense legal combat. The bank and Parretti sued each other in both Delaware and California over whether the bank had improperly seized MGM. The bank and Kirk Kerkorian sued each other, in both federal and state courts in Los Angeles, over whether the bank had defrauded Kerkorian and whether he bore any responsibility for MGM's financial condition at the time he sold it. The bank and several of its smaller Hollywood clients, such as Hemdale, Epic, and a former officer of Film Accord, fought over who was to blame for those companies' difficulties.

The Delaware Chancery Court found that the bank had been justified in seizing MGM. The judge accused Parretti of lying on the witness stand; Parretti accused the bank of suborning perjury by Fiorini.

Parretti's suit against Credit Lyonnais in California would take longer to resolve, as would the bank's battles with Kerkorian and Epic Pictures.

In one of the many sealed depositions taken by Kerkorian's lawyers and obtained by FORTUNE, the attorneys try various approaches, including sarcasm, to penetrate the hubris of Credit Lyonnais bankers. An exchange between the lawyers and François Gille:

"Mr. Gille, are you aware that there is a lawsuit filed in California today wherein it is alleged that Mr. Vigon received $2 million as a bribe that was set up in a Canadian bank account in connection with a loan extended by CLBN to a company called Film Accord?... Have you been able to do any investigation with respect to whether that is an accurate rendition of the facts?"

"No."

"Do you intend to?"

"I have formed no decision."

"You've got to be a little curious, though, right?"

"Thank you for your recommendation."

The lawyers also asked Gille how much debt was carried on the books of Credit Lyonnais in connection with MGM:

"The debt should reach an approximate amount of $1.1 billion," he replied.

"And how much of the $1.1 billion has been reserved?"

"For the moment, nothing."

Where did the money go—the $2 billion-plus that Credit Lyonnais lent Parretti and Fiorni? According to the investigation by the former FBI official, Lawrence Lawler, Parretti misappropriated roughly $100 million, directly or indirectly, from MGM and Pathé Communications. More than $1 billion went to Kirk Kerkorian, who then paid a small percentage back to CLBN to settle litigation between them. Much of the rest of the money was spent operating Pathé from 1987 to 1991 and covering MGM's operating losses for the eight months Parretti owned it. Even now, not every dollar is accounted for. Nor is it known whether the bank's officers ever benefited from the bribes they took. Jacques Griffault testified that he kept the 21st Century Distribution Corp. stock certificates in a drawer at his home. Jean-Jacques Brutschi testified that he "eliminated" the stock certificates when he changed offices. Just as well: 21st Century currently is back in bankruptcy. The value of the artworks the bankers took is also in doubt. One of the many lawyers looking into the Parretti-Credit Lyonnais affair compares it to *Chinatown*, the Roman Polanski movie in which ambiguity clouds verifiable facts to the end.

On May 5, 1997, the opulent Paris headquarters of Credit Lyonnais, a hulking French Empire pile, was gutted by fire.

◆

AFTERMATH

MGM lost nearly $1.7 billion between 1992 and 1996, when Credit Lyonnais finally sold the beleaguered studio. The buyer? Kirk Kerkorian, who paid $1.3 billion to become MGM's owner for the third time. In 2004, a Sony-led a group of investors (including cable giant Comcast) bought MGM for $5 billion.

The MGM defaults were just one in a series of bad loans that nearly forced Credit Lyonnais into bankruptcy. The French government bailed it out and it was privatized in 1999. In 2003, it was acquired by France's Credit Agricole. Florio Fiorini's holding company, Sasea, filed for bankruptcy in 1992. It was the largest bankruptcy in the history of Swtizerland; Credit Lyonnais was one of its largest creditors. Fiorini stands convicted of bankruptcy and fraud in Switzerland. In 1997, Credit Lyonnais's Jacques Griffault pleaded guilty in the Italian part of the Sasea bankruptcy.

Even after losing control of MGM, Giancarlo Parretti continued to live his life as if it was a Hollywood caper. In late 1996, he was convicted of perjury and tampering with evidence in the 1991 Delaware Chancery Court trial that gave Credit Lyonnais control of the studio. He fled the country before sentencing.

Parretti's absence did not stop the law from taking its course. In 1997, a California Superior Court judge entered a judgment of $1.5 billion against Parretti in a civil suit brought by Credit Lyonnais. No one expected him to pay, but the verdict carried a certain psychic satisfaction. Ditto for his conviction on corruption charges two years later in France; he was sentenced him in absentia to four years in prison and a $165,000 fine.

In 1999 Parretti and Florio Fiorini were taken into custody near Orvieto on an extradition request by the U.S., which had indicted them on 55 counts, including conspiracy and fraud. Credit Lyonnais, named as an unindicted co-conspirator, paid a $4 million fine to the U.S. government. Fiorini agreed to be extradited from Italy and pleaded guilty to conspiracy, securities fraud, and filing false reports with the SEC in 2001. He received a sentence of 41 months in prison, a $100,000 fine, and banishment from the U.S. for ten years. As part of the plea agreement, Fiorini returned to Italy to face criminal cases there before beginning to serve his sentence. He has yet to return.

Parretti, too, remains in Italy, where he faces numerous legal proceedings. When those are exhausted, he could be extradited to the U.S.

2

THE BIG KOZLOWSKI

---

by NICHOLAS VARCHAVER

November 18, 2002

In the 1990s, industrial products maker Tyco grabbed Wall Street's attention with a series of acquisitions that CEO Dennis Kozlowski appeared to manage with canny skill. But in 1999, questions about accounting practices surfaced, and Tyco's stock suffered. Then in 2002, Kozlowski resigned while under criminal investigation for evading New York sales tax on the purchase of artwork. A broader probe soon uncovered lavish spending on the company's dime. Within months, Kozlowski and his CFO, Mark Swartz, were indicted for taking Tyco for hundreds of millions.

Midas had his gold. Elvis had his Cadillacs. Dennis Kozlowski had his, um, shower curtain.

Yes, this is what it all comes down to. Forget Enron and WorldCom. When Americans think back on the corporate scandals of the early 21st century 25 years from now, they aren't likely to summon more than a blurry memory.

What they will remember is the bald guy with the $6,000 shower curtain. And, say, the $15,000 dog umbrella stand. Ditto for the now infamous $2.1 million birthday bash that Kozlowski, the former CEO of Tyco, threw in Sardinia for his wife's 40th birthday. It featured a giant cake with exploding breasts and an ice sculpture of Michelangelo's "David" dispensing Stoli through an appendage that in more modest times would've been covered by a fig leaf.

By comparison Jeff Skilling and Ken Lay seem like pallid figures. For all their vilification, they didn't have to endure, as Kozlowski did, their photos on the front page of the *New York Post* under the giant headline, "Oink, oink."

You could call it his big fat Greek tragedy. Kozlowski's tale resonates because it appears to have been based on the classic human quality of greed (with a little gluttony thrown in). Many of the crimes he's accused of—for example, his machinations to avoid paying sales tax on art—are based on acts that would not be unknown to many Americans. To an average person, of course, that might mean crossing state lines to save a few bucks on a carton of cigarettes, not shipping empty crates to New Hampshire in an apparent effort to shirk $1 million in taxes on art by the likes of Monet and Renoir. But why quibble?

It's precisely the scale of Kozlowski's conduct—whatever the ultimate result of the legal proceedings against him—that takes the breath away. It's why a person who not long ago was seen as a latter-day Jack Welch (back when that was an unadulterated compliment) is now seen as the demon love-child of Gordon Gekko and Caligula. It's proof that in the end, nothing exceeds like excess.

The truth of the matter is that the $6,000 shower curtain is a side issue. One person close to Kozlowski goes so far as to assert that the "valance trimmed" burgundy-and-gold tasseled curtain in question wasn't even a shower curtain—it was a "wall covering" that allowed the Kozlowskis to avoid spending $50,000 in renovations. (Who knew? It was all a push to save money.) Ah, then better give him equal credit for the $2,200 gilded wastebasket and $2,900 in coat hangers that Kozlowski put on Tyco's tab as well.

One suspects that there's more than one CEO mansion in the glitzy precincts of Squam Road on Nantucket—where Kozlowski owns a $5 million home—that's got a coat hanger priced in four figures. The point isn't the *objet* itself; it's how those moguls came by the money to pay for them. Kozlowski, who declined to be interviewed for this article, isn't charged with tasteless spending—if that were a crime, he'd really be in trouble—he's charged with conspiring with CFO Mark Swartz to loot $170 million from Tyco (or $600 million, if you include his allegedly tainted stock sales).

Kozlowski's friends profess total shock and amazement that he would be accused of misappropriating money. Then again, it'd be rather more surprising if they proclaimed that they'd always known he had a multimillion-dollar fraud in him. To a person, they're quick to cite myriad examples of how generous Kozlowski was with various charities and causes.

That may not be the best example of Kozlowski's good character, given that Tyco has charged him with loosening the strings on the company's corporate giving program and dispersing $106 million of shareholders' money to charity. This would make Kozlowski a new kind of Robin Hood. Taking from the rich to give to the poor has an undeniable appeal to it—but maybe not so much when the people you're filching from are your own shareholders. And maybe not so much when you're using some of those shillings to throw blowout parties in Sherwood Forest.

Kozlowski shared his company's bounty with conspicuous alacrity. Robert Monks, who served on Tyco's board from 1985 to 1994, recalls driving down to meet Kozlowski at Tyco's New Hampshire offices in the summer of 2000 to solicit money for a corporate governance group. It turned out to be a brief meeting. "I thought it a little odd that Dennis didn't invite me to have lunch," Monks recalls. "But I thought, what the hell, he's a busy man. Dennis said, 'Well, what do you need?' And I said, 'Four million dollars.' And he said, 'We can do that. I'll give $2 million, and the company will match it.' I never raised $4 million dollars from anyone before, to say nothing of as quickly as that."

How's that for supporting corporate governance! But observe the ease with which the erstwhile CEO opened Tyco's coffers. Armchair psychologists might say it suggests that the Big Kozlowski saw himself as a divine monarch of sorts, free to bestow his company's largesse on any worthy supplicant. Certainly, we would never engage in such speculation. And yet ... Kozlowski seemed to consider Tyco little more than an extension of himself. It was the corporate equivalent of Louis XIV's famous phrase, *L'état, c'est moi.*

FROM FRUGAL TO OUTLANDISH

Before Kozlowski was indicted, he had gained a reputation as the outlandishly compensated CEO of a relatively unknown company with a soaring stock price. But what few recall is that only a few years before, Kozlowski was the frugally paid CEO of a relatively unknown company with a soaring stock price.

Indeed, as late as 1997, Kozlowski seemed a paragon of parsimony. Articles were replete with references not only to Tyco's "lean" staffing and spartan headquarters but also to Kozlowski's modest pay. In April 1997 *The Wall Street Journal* noted approvingly that "Mr. Kozlowski's $1 million salary has remained unchanged for four years. Directors limit his annual bonus to no more than $1 million... Tyco doesn't offer him any stock options [though] he can receive performance-linked restricted shares... In addition, Mr. Kozlowski lacks the usual executive perquisites such as club memberships, financial planning and post-retirement medical insurance. He sometimes pilots his own plane for business trips—without charging Tyco. 'I like to avoid costs wherever I can in the company,' says Mr. Kozlowski."

That, it turns out, was the year Tyco merged with ADT and adopted ADT's practice of issuing stock options. Tyco's endless acquisitions had transformed it into a giant conglomerate. Its stock was flying; it rose 13-fold between July 1992, when Kozlowski took over as CEO, and December 2001, when it peaked. But Kozlowski's compensation—that is, his legal, duly approved compensation—grew more than four times as much as the stock price during those glory years.

The oddest aspect of Kozlowski's conduct, for those of us naïve enough to think that people take money because they somehow need it, is that he began availing himself of what became hundreds of millions of dollars in company loans (most of which, to be fair, he paid back) precisely at the moment that his pay was exploding. For example, according to the indictment and Tyco's SEC filings, Kozlowski began regularly taking loans in 1996 and 1997—just as his board-approved compensation leaped from $8.8 million in 1996 to $52.8 million in '97. It wasn't until '98 and '99, though, that he really went hog-wild on the borrowing. Apparently his approved compensation of $136.1 million in 1999 left him in a bit of a cash squeeze.

He was in a frenzy of making and spending, shuttling among properties in New Hampshire, Florida, New York, Connecticut, Massachusetts, and Colorado. His Florida home, in Boca Raton on the Intracoastal Waterway, cost $29.8 million—including the money Kozlowski spent to buy an adjacent property so that he could reposition his tennis court. (The sun had reportedly been getting in the players' eyes.) The New York City apartment, which belonged to Tyco, cost $30.8 million, including his infamous shower curtain, er, wall covering. There were his three Harley-Davidsons and the company planes and helicopters that he piloted (Kozlowski was not the type to relax with a book). There was his 130-foot 1934 America's Cup sailboat, *Endeavour,* which reportedly ran him $20 million. The yacht's maintenance—just for upkeep and crew—was $700,000 a year. Pretty soon, as the old saying goes, you're talking about real money.

Kozlowski displayed a curious mix of ostentation and lack of pretension. He pledged $4.5 million of Tyco's money and got himself a seat on the board of the Whitney Museum in New York. That said, he seems to have eschewed the stuffy enclaves of old money in New York and Palm Beach.

In fact, when it came to his friends, Kozlowski was strikingly down to earth, preferring the company of ordinary folks to CEOs. Many of the Nantucket friends who attended his wife's birthday fete in Sardinia owned or ran small businesses; one ran an outfit called Spanky's Raw

Bar. "Some of the events that Dennis and Karen hosted were in fact lavish," says a Kozlowski friend, "but they were always very inclusive also. They would invite their contractors, the people who took them on fishing expeditions, their gardeners, their lawn-care people, right down the line."

If it seems at odds that a man would prefer to have his fishing buddies with him on his historic 130-foot sailboat, well, that was Kozlowski. After all, he'd risen from humble origins in Newark, the self-made son of a school crossing guard and a cop.

But then, it is precisely Kozlowski's incredible rise that makes his descent so dramatic. Or maybe the Greek drama is this: For all of his legitimate accomplishments—Tyco's revenues grew tenfold during his tenure—Kozlowski will find it near impossible to shake the type of notoriety that attaches to the fall of American emperors. Especially those with a $6,000 shower curtain.

◆

AFTERMATH

Kozlowski's first trial began in September 2003 and ended in mistrial six months later, after a juror who appeared to gesture favorably to the defense received threatening letters. At the 2005 retrial, Kozlowski took the stand in his own defense but failed to sway the jury. Both he and Swartz were found guilty on multiple counts of grand larceny, securities fraud and false filings with the SEC. Kozlowski was sentenced to eight to 25 years in prison and ordered to repay $97 million to Tyco, in addition to paying $70 million in fines. He began serving time in a medium-security state prison in Marcy, New York, in 2005 and sold his homes and yacht to pay the court-ordered restitution. In November 2007, the state Supreme Court's Appellate Division upheld Kozlowskis and Swartz's convictions. In September 2008, Kozlowski and Swartz appealed again, this time to the New York State Court of Appeals. They lost again.

As for the company, in 2006, Tyco paid $50 million to the SEC to settle charges stemming from accounting fraud allegations. The following year, Tyco paid nearly $3 billion to settle a class-action lawsuit brought by shareholders after Kozlowski's conviction. (Tyco's auditor, PricewaterhouseCoopers, also paid $225 million to settle with investors.) In June 2007, the conglomerate split into three public companies, separating its former electronics and health-care units from the security and fire-protection divisions.

3

THE SWEDISH MATCH KING

by ARCHIBALD MACLEISH

May, June, July 1933

In the 1920s, Ivar Kreuger was known as the savior of Europe. A month after his death in 1932, he was known as its greatest swindler. What follows is a condensation of a three-part FORTUNE series on the man who would be the world's match king—but whose hubris left his reputation in ashes.

Land reform in Estonia; the migration of Greeks and Turks; the building of railways in Peru; Mussolini in full spout: All these events are linked by the suicide of a man in a Paris apartment in March 1932. And that man, Ivar Kreuger, was the heart and brain of what may be the greatest business scandal of the 20th century. At the peak of his fame in the late 1920s, he was easily the most respected business man in the world, and the shares in his company, Swedish Match, were the most widely traded. He invented the "B" share. He was referred to as the "savior of Europe" for providing loans to cash-strapped countries in the aftermath of the Great War.

The Kreuger empire was built on the humblest of things—the match. And in fact, Swedish Match really did make matches, but it was also a complicated pyramid that sent money from tens of thousands of American investors to Europe, where it disappeared forever.

How could this happen? His U.S. bankers, the white-shoe Boston firm of Lee, Higginson, later confessed they had simply taken Kreuger at his word. His U.S. accountants relied on the bona fides of the Swedish accountants, and vice versa. The books of the foreign subsidiaries—and there were literally hundreds of these—were never seen, or asked for. And Kreuger himself made sure that no one else saw anything but the shadow of an occasional corner of his far-flung operations

In a three-part series that ran in May, June, and July 1933—the same year he won the Pulizer Prize for poetry—FORTUNE writer Archibald MacLeish laid out the entire history of Ivar Kreuger. What follows is an edited version of Part II, with a few elements from Parts I and III included for clarity.

On March 22, 1932, ten days after his suicide in Paris, Ivar Kreuger's funeral was held in the North Cemetery of Stockholm.

Ivar Kreuger, heavy between the eight uniformed chauffeurs on the 22nd of March, was a victim of the Depression, a martyr of the economic wars. No one doubted that—not *Pravda*, not *The Economist*, not the chief banker, Donald Durant of Lee, Higginson & Co.

It was not easy to sit there staring at the coffin while a Swedish soprano choked on a phrase of Handel. And it was not easy, Ivar being dead, to estimate the future of his house, which held upward of $8 million of the dead man's stocks and bonds. None of it was easy. But doubting Ivar was another thing. Doubting Ivar meant forgetting all the profits and the brilliance and the companionship of the first nine years and thinking only of the last week in February and the first two weeks in March of 1932. And it was precisely those three weeks of which Donald Durant was most unwilling to think.

And it was precisely those three weeks of which Mr. Donald Durant was most unwilling to think. There had been the 4 million loan falling due on February 27, which Ivar had been unable to pay. But that was because the money hadn't come in from Country Y (Spain) and he was going to send a man down to see about it...

Then there was the 50 million of German bonds belonging to

International Match which were supposed to be deposited in a bank in Germany but weren't there. So Durant made Ivar promise to put them back and he showed the accountants, Ernst & Ernst, a cable saying the bonds had been returned, but when Ernst & Ernst sent their agents to the bank in Berlin to see, the bonds weren't there...

Then, on the crossing to Europe, Ivar had been very nervous and ill. And then in Paris he had shot himself. It was all very complicated. Or perhaps it wasn't complicated at all.

On March 25, three days after Durant watched his friend's light-wood coffin, burdened by flowers, slip into the furnaces, the Investigating Commission made its preliminary report—a mild but disquieting document. "The preliminary results of the inquiry seem to indicate that the position of the company is not strong... To what extent other circumstances may have contributed cannot be ascertained until later." Other circumstances? Bondholders in America reread the passage. Patriotic Swedes sweat under their high, stiff collars. And Lee, Higginson issued to investors a nervous leaflet in which it was announced with perfect if somewhat unconvincing truth that "the conclusion reached ... is strongly at variance with the company's published reports." But even so the world was troubled.

But the talk of the 25th and the 26th and the 27th of March was merely rumor, merely guesswork. It was not until the report of Price, Waterhouse and Company, accountants, was read in the Swedish Parliament, just before midnight on the 5th of April that suspicion changed to certainty. Price, Waterhouse's phrases were colorless and dry: the December 31, 1930, balance sheets of Kreuger and Toll "grossly misrepresent the true financial position of the company," the fraudulent entries were made "under the personal direction of the late Mr. Kreuger"; Continental Investment, the vital organ of Kreuger's U.S. International Match Corporation, was in the same condition; profit-and-loss accounts had been cooked for years. Even Lee, Higginson gave in. The accountants' statement, they told investors, must be accepted "as evidence that gross frauds have been perpetrated by Mr. Kreuger."

Suspicion, with the 6th of April, changed to belief. And belief became action. Stockholm was, at one stroke, the financial capital of the world. Auditors and experts, protective committee agents, rival protective committee agents, New York lawyers, German treasury officials, diplomats, newspapermen, novelists climbed aboard the Nord Express at Victoria Station, or rattled up from Berlin to find themselves in a town of 500,000 souls and another world—a kind of bourgeois paradise with clean and quiet streets and few automobiles and a conventional palace and long arms of the Baltic reaching in along neat quays and well-dressed sober people who waited in line for taxis and crossed the streets at their proper intersections and drank good beer and German hock and sometimes sweet sauterne (when the pocketbook permitted)—a city of much food and dinner anywhere from 5 to 8 with a liqueur glass of schnapps and a great quantity of raw fish, dried fish, sausages, and pickled beets for hors d'oeuvres and the three wines served at once and no retreat from the ladies afterward and tea at 10 p.m.—a world of fine modern buildings and sunset at 2:58 on December 21 and no sunset at all in June but a kind of twilight and half day through the night and snow until April and skiing country out of a man's back door—a society in which theatres began at 8 and American movies ran in English with flashes of explanatory Swedish and Greta Garbo was not loved and the great winter sport was watching the king play tennis—an exceedingly law-abiding and honest and unmoral country with the highest illegitimacy rate in the West and the laxest auditing laws on earth and the greatest mutual confidence conceivable.

And while the creditors and the accountants and the lawyers were filling the Grand Hotel, the police were rummaging in his apartment and finding documents so compromising they could never be published, and the Investigating Commission was showing Benito Mussolini a package of 47 bonds issued with a guaranty by the Italian government, and Il Duce was explaining, with some heat, that the signatures on the bonds were forgeries and that the Italian words were even misspelled.

And eventually on April 15, it was announced to an already hysterical world that the great financier, the creditor of governments, was not only suicidal and not only bankrupt but common and a very clumsy forger of bad bonds. Hell, in the expressive phrase, broke with that news. Within two hours of the announcement Bjorn Prytz of the Investigating Commission had three callers—the German Minister asking that the German transactions of Kreuger be verified as his government suspected the dead man of traffic with the Nazis, the Polish Minister demanding that the Polish conversations be examined as his government suspected Kreuger of bribing the dead finance minister Glowacki, and the Spanish Minister protesting that the Spanish dealings must be aired since his government suspected Kreuger of improper dealings with the dead dictator Primo de Rivera. Within a week the suicides were coming in—a municipal clerk who had bought Kreuger and Toll when the big boys were unloading and who was found with his wrists cut; another clerk, his savings wiped out; a leading baker Sievertz, his money lost; a lumberman of Bavaria. And with the suicides came the arrests, culminating in that of brother Torsten himself.

And the whole structure of the state was shaken. Prime Minister Ekman was forced to resign because of his denial of the receipt by his party of gifts from Kreuger shortly before Kreuger was granted an important credit by the Swedish central bank. The foreign exchange reserves of the bank were weakened and the powerful financiers, the Wallenbergs, were forced to intervene. Municipal tax collections fell by 10% and membership in the Communist Party doubled. Many of the richest men of the country were bankrupt. The king's brother Carl, father of the Crown Princesses of Norway and Belgium, moved into humble quarters. The racing season collapsed. Kreuger's furniture and pictures and towels were sold at auctions in Stockholm, London, Paris, Amsterdam, Berlin—the Stockholm auction turning into a society levee with rich women and grocers wrangling over skillets and with steel scissors engraved "Ivar Kreuger" going at $12. In Manhattan the Irving Trust was appointed receiver for International Match on the 13th of

April and International Match filed a voluntary petition in bankruptcy on the 19th.

BUT these events were merely consequences, repercussions. They explained nothing. The real question was still in the summer of 1932, as it had been on the March 12, the day he died: What was it precisely that had happened? Was Ivar Kreuger really a common crook? If he was a crook, how long had he been a crook? Why had he killed himself at the precise moment when he did kill himself?

As rumor fed rumor, only the employees of Price, Waterhouse and Company were in a position to apply the hard edge of fact.

All through the summer and fall of 1932, 30 men and a dozen calculating machines and hundreds of ledgers and great stacks of correspondence were collaborating in the writing of 57 fact-finding reports. What the accountants discovered was that Kreuger's career in the years from 1911 to 1923 had been approximately what the world believed it to be.

The central story, the official account, was clear enough. Born in 1880 of a bourgeois family in the little Swedish wooden town of Kalmar, Kreuger had worked through grammar school and technical college, emigrated to America at the age of 20, tried real estate and wire stringing, worked on a bridge in Vera Cruz and on the Flatiron Building, Macy's, the Metropolitan Life Building, the St. Regis, and the Plaza in New York, tried his luck with a construction company in London in 1903, started a Johannesburg restaurant, served a hitch in the British Militia at the Cape, toured the Far East, passed three months in Paris at the age of 24, swung back to Canada and the States, worked on the Syracuse Stadium, and ended up in Sweden in 1907 with no money, a sound knowledge of reinforced concrete, and an ambition to rebuild the city of Stockholm after the American heart's desire.

At 30, Kreuger had joined forces with a young Swedish engineer named Toll, run away with the building business in Stockholm (where the firm must be credited with a large part of the excellent modern construction which the city now boasts), extended his interests into Finland, Russia, and Germany, run his capital from 1 million kronor up to 6 million kronor, turned to the family match business in 1913, formed Swedish Match in 1917 in the face of enormous and worldwide difficulties, and by shrewd management and consolidation restored to Sweden her predominance in match production lost during the War.

Kreuger the builder and Kreuger the Match King were not frauds. Both existed. Both made large and apparently justifiable profits. From 1917 to 1924, the Swedish Match Company paid dividends of 12% or better and Kreuger and Toll paid dividends of 20% or more. In 1923, Kreuger was a great industrialist and his companies were approximately what they represented themselves to be. From about 1923 until his suicide in Paris, the colors changed. What the world knew, or thought it knew, was that Kreuger extended the Match Trust's operations into every European country except Spain, Russia, and France and to 16 non-European countries, bought or built 250 match factories, set up fabulous subsidiaries in America, acquired absolute monopolies in 15 countries, de facto monopolies in nine, and market dominance in ten more, associated with himself the great banking names, with very few exceptions, of Europe and America, lent almost $400 million to 15 countries including France and Germany at a time when Europe was desperately short of credits and American credits were no longer to be had, made possible by his loans the monetary stabilization of Rumania, the purchase of seed grain in Latvia, the construction of railroads in Estonia, and the repatriation of refugees in Greece, paid large and steady dividends to his stockholders, and received the public thanks of France for his part in the Curtius-Tardieu negotiations at The Hague.

His interests touched the world at every point. His telephone company, Ericsson, had factories in 12 countries and concessions in five. His Swedish Pulp Company was the largest European producer of sulphite and sulphate pulp. His newspapers included the *Svenska Dagbladet,* one of the best in Scandinavia. Through Kreuger and Toll he had also minority interests in major Swedish banks while his own banks were set up in Paris and Amsterdam and Berlin and Warsaw. The Swedish Film Industry Company was one of his companies.

It is this latter narrative, alas, that does not bear scrutiny.

Though some of the assets were real, the entire foundation was a financial fantasy. Until 1923, Kreuger was a moderately honest man and an industrialist by profession; after, he became an immoderately dishonest man and a stock promoter by trade. In that year, Kreuger, with his passion for power, discovered the New York glut of gold and the inexhaustible New York appetite for stocks. In doing so, he discovered the superiority of the stock market to the match factory as a means of conquest. If that discovery implies a weakening of the mind then there were many other Wall Street idiots in the 1920's. There is only one conclusion: In 1923 and 1924 Kreuger and Toll changed from a productive entity to a Stock Exchange show window.

PRICE, WATERHOUSE began its investigations of that period with the three central beams of the Kreuger house—Kreuger and Toll, Swedish Match, and International Match. These companies were as open and clean as the columns of a Greek porch. Kreuger and Toll was a super-holding company owning Swedish Match. Swedish Match was a holding company that owned factories and also International Match of New York. And International Match, founded in 1923, was a holding company that owned other match factories. All that seemed clear enough.

But the accountants had not gone very far before they began to find that the seeming cleanness and openness were a pure illusion. From a distance the beams stood clear. But up close they were caught, like the timbers of a dusty barn, in a mesh and tangle of spider-web subsidiaries. Some of these subsidiaries were real, some were a set of books, some were a name; but name, books, or reality the entries spun back and forth, the debit and credit items tangled from roof to wall. One, the great net of the N. V. Financieele Maatschappij Kreuger and Toll (Dutch Kreuger and Toll), was everywhere. Another, Continental

Investment A. G., hung between International Match and the rest of the structure. Still others filled in the corners and sent long threads out to twist and turn and disappear. Some, particularly Dutch Kreuger and Toll, were known to the investing public by name but not by function. Others, like Continental, were known vaguely to the directors of the principal concerns which owned them. But the great majority, International Finance Syndicate, Finanzgesellschaft fur die Industrie, Mercator, Handels A. G. Wega, were merely names in the minds of their own officers.

Most of these companies had been set up by Kreuger agents who were unknown even to his own associates. The whole and simple duty of these inconspicuous gentlemen was to keep their books as Kreuger should direct them. Bror G. B. Bredberg, for example, was a clerk and stockbroker who had been sent down to Zurich in March 1923, at a handsome salary, to obey orders. In Zurich with the assistance of Walter Ahlstrom and with two checks for 1.5 million Swiss francs each, he registered a company called the Finanzgesellschaft. A few days later Torsten Kreuger appeared and Bredberg with Torsten Kreuger and Ahlstrom moved east to Vaduz, capital of the minute principality of Liechtenstein where, with the same checks used to register Finanz, they registered the Union Industrie A. G. with Bredberg as board of directors, managing director, and accountant. After which creative act Torsten Kreuger removed 2,450,000 francs of the company's capital for the purpose, as he said, of acquiring match factories in Poland and Czechoslovakia. Continental was formed in much the same way but by Kreuger personally.

That company which was eventually to bleed American investors through International Match of $88 million was founded in Zurich in 1923 by Kreuger and a Swiss-American secretary named Hoffman with a capital of 60 million francs of which sum 1 million francs was in cash, 9 million in checks, and 50 million in a guaranty of Swedish Match executed by Kreuger himself. Hoffman was the board of directors. Once the company was registered, Kreuger and Hoffman left Switzerland with its capital in their briefcases and eventually Continental was transferred to Liechtenstein where the prince's finance minister obligingly made a deal to limit the company's taxes.

As to funds, none of these companies, as the accountants quickly found, had any real assets. The credit balance of 112,570,696.93 Dutch florins shown by Dutch Kreuger and Toll at the end of 1930 was a pure fiction and the reserve of 280,316,949.21 Dutch florins meant nothing since all cash received was immediately transferred to Kreuger and Toll. (The liquidators of the latter company found that Dutch Kreuger and Toll had "never earned real profits.") The mission of Dutch Kreuger and Toll was to "hold" nonexistent properties and to "owe" nonexistent debts so as to dress the balance sheets of the holding companies and persuade the investors of Europe and particularly of America to buy their stocks and bonds. Kreuger and Toll and Dutch Kreuger and Toll, for example, published a consolidated balance sheet. The accountants found 140 entries on the books of Dutch Kreuger and Toll affecting Kreuger and Toll which were not on the books of the latter company, and 74 on the books of Kreuger and Toll not on the books of the former. In the same way there were 68 entries on the books of Swedish Match affecting Kreuger and Toll balanced by no corresponding entries on the books of Kreuger and Toll. The aggregate of such one-sided credits and debits on the books of Kreuger and Toll, Continental, Swedish Match, and Dutch Kreuger and Toll alone was almost 3 billion kronor.

The method of operation may be gathered from the lurid testimony of Bredberg before the Stockholm police. Kreuger, he said, would turn up in Zurich now and then and give orders as to entries, handing over, in some cases, actual securities to be kept in the safe or handing over on other occasions written statements that the documents in question had been deposited for Finanzgesellschaft somewhere else. Also each year before closing the books Bredberg would visit Stockholm with a draft balance sheet which would be edited by Kreuger and by Kreuger's auditor.

During 1928 Bredberg, on instructions from Stockholm, credited

Kreuger and Toll with a total of 6 million francs Swiss debiting the Eddy Match Company. When he visited Stockholm early in 1929 he asked Anton Wendler, an accountant, what the Eddy Match Company was.

Wendler didn't know. But the entries stood nevertheless and eventually "Eddy Match" stood debtor on Bredberg's books in the amount of 31 million Swiss francs. Entries on the books of Union Industrie were of the same complexion.

In the same way Carl Lange emulated Bredberg's bookkeeping feats with Garanta and signed in 1925 at Kreuger's request a balance sheet showing assets of 46 million Dutch florins and a debt to International Match of 45 million Dutch florins—neither assets nor debt having, so far as he knew, any existence. And Sven Huldt of the Netherlands Bank for Scandinavian Trade did his bit in like manner. On December 31, 1926, and December 31, 1927, having been shown by Kreuger certain documents in unknown languages which he did not attempt to read, he signed a deposit receipt stating that the bank held a contract between International Match and the Polish State and a second deposit receipt crediting Continental with possession of a Spanish match monopoly and a certificate for installments paid by Spain to Continental showing a balance in Continental's favor of 200 million pesetas.

But perhaps the palm for bookkeeping ingenuity must go to one Victor Holm, director of Dutch Kreuger and Toll, who deposited on December 31, 1930, 34 million Dutch florins in the International Bank and Finance Company of Danzig, which bank was not formed until January 2, 1931!

The purpose of these various institutions in Kreuger's scheme of things was of course quite simple—to sell stock and bonds.

To do so, he required persuasive statements. To prepare persuasive statements he needed willing debtors and depositees. And to secure willing debtors and amenable depositees he needed the existence of a dozen-odd desk-drawer corporations. The administration of the scheme was also simple. It was merely necessary to keep the various spider webs from short-circuiting by an exchange of information between their personnel. And that Kreuger insured by establishing himself as the only point of common contact and by breaking up intimacies or friendships between his various employees as rapidly as they were discovered. All Kreuger agents signed a pledge of secrecy upon entering his employ and business intercourse between officers of Kreuger and Toll and Dutch Kreuger and Toll was strictly forbidden. With insulation assured the rest was bookkeeping.

Kreuger's policy as a stock seller was to show a strong earning capacity, high dividends nicely related to profits, insignificant current liabilities, and a fat surplus. And the fake companies provided the tools. But fake companies and glib bookkeeping are not enough to sell 17 issues of shares and bonds, with some issues amounting to $50 million over a period of nine years. There must also be expansion, industrial conquest—something to spread across the annual statements to capture the public imagination. And that material Kreuger found in Europe. In the old legends of Kreuger's life his enormous loans to governments against match concessions played a large and spectacular part. Kreuger was the man who had lent almost $400 million to the nations of the world at a time when Europe was starving for money. Biographers said, are still saying, on the one side that he showed the greatness of his heart in permitting Greece to repatriate her Levantines at the mere cost of a match concession, and, on the other, that he displayed the weakness of his judgment by overextending himself and by establishing, under color of concessions, foreign competitors to his own concern. But such criticism and such praise loses sight of Kreuger's objective. He was not interested in Levantines or competitors. He was interested in finding an occasion for an issue.

All the government loans were a glittering excuse—and a brilliant innovation as well. For Kreuger was the first banker to invent a device whereby a private loan to a foreign power could be insured against the aptitude of foreign powers to "forget" their private obligations. By the simple mechanism of tying up his loan with the grant of a match monopoly and making the royalties on the match monopoly (which he was to pay the borrowing government) security for the service of the debt (which the borrowing government was to pay him) he put it in his own power to pay himself. And thus provided not only for a banker's profit on the loan and a match maker's profit on the concession but for complete security for both. While, in addition, he advertised himself and his companies in a way, and with a prestige, which made the early sales of his securities child's play. Prestige explains the loans to France and Germany which carried certain valuable concessions but no absolute monopolies. And prestige justified them both. Kreuger's success in supplanting J. P. Morgan and Company as banker to the French made him, for a time, the unquestioned leader in world finance. And had the German loan not fallen foul of the depression of 1929 it is quite possible that Kreuger would today be alive and full of honors. After all it is no small thing for a private individual to lend $384 million to 15 countries including a loan of $75 million to France and one of $125 million to Germany. The Medicis did much less at the height of their power.

But not even government loans were enough for Kreuger's purposes. It was also necessary to expand in industry itself. And beginning in 1926 and 1927, Kreuger began to buy into iron and pulp and telephones and newspapers, even a gold mine. These purchases were all justifications. They were excuses. Only on that hypothesis is the German loan explicable. Only on that hypothesis can the web of fraudulent companies be understood. And only on that hypothesis can any estimate of the last phase of Kreuger's career be made. From 1923 on, his match industry made relatively small advances. Nonetheless, over the same period, Kreuger's companies numbered 250 million worth of shares in America alone.

History written by the accountants, then, turns the great success story of the Kreuger legends inside out. Instead of the Roi des Allumettes we are presented with the Prince of Promoters.

And instead of the victim of the Depression, the martyr of the economic wars, we are left with Ivar Kreuger, swindler, dead by his own hand. And dead with reason. For the reports of Price, Waterhouse and

Company make it clear that the tragedy of which the last expression was the army-type Browning and the tumbled bed was no product of the crash of '29.

All that is necessary to an understanding of the real causation of the tragedy is a reading of the books of International Match for the years 1924 and 1925 and 1926. What Kreuger was playing was nothing more subtle or more intelligent than the old Ponzi game. He was paying dividends out of capital. And trusting to more capital to make good the loss. And there was no possible outcome but disaster. The only question was: How long disaster could be deferred?

Already by the year 1928 Kreuger had himself begun to guess how long. The second issue of Kreuger and Toll "participating debentures" in that year was not fully subscribed and Kreuger gave his guaranty for 2.7 million kronor. By March of 1929 the guess had become a probability, for in that year the Kreuger and Toll debenture issue failed of subscription and Kreuger, taking over the balance, gave guaranties for 13.8 million kronor. And in November of the same year the probability had edged into the field of certainty for Kreuger had had to take over half the issue of 110,000 B shares of Kreuger and Toll and part of the debenture issue, giving guaranties totaling 85 million kronor. On these four issues Kreuger and Toll had actually received 101.7 million kronor less fresh capital than its statements showed. And without fresh capital the Ponzi game would never work. Moreover Kreuger himself had pledged his personal credit for the unsubscribed balance.

OCTOBER 1929 is the date of catastrophe. From that time on, and with an increasingly rapid fatality, events which Ivar Kreuger could no longer control beat in upon him and eventually beat him down. What Kreuger himself thought of his situation may be guessed from the fact that it was in the fall of 1929 with 101.7 million kronor of guaranties on his hands and 101,738,000 kronor of capital shortages on, or rather under, his companies' books that he undertook to lend the German government (which had not yet ratified the Young Plan on postwar debt and was moreover in ill odor thanks to the rise of Adolf Hitler) the enormous sum of $125 million—$50 million to be paid in August 1930, and the balance on May 29, 1931. Nothing in Kreuger's career has more amazed his many biographers than this suicidal loan made in the shadow of the great Depression to a nation with impaired credit by a man whose securities would not sell. But in fact nothing is more logical. Only by an act of desperate courage capable of restoring his slipping prestige could Kreuger ever extricate himself. And the German loan was precisely the act required.

Had the times changed, that act of insolent daring might have succeeded. As it was it came within a stone's throw of success. The French, instigated by some divinity, redeemed their loan in April, freeing $75 million of much-needed cash. And the August 1930, installment of $50 million was duly paid. But as the 29th of May, 1931, drew on it became more and more apparent that there was to be no further intervention of a god. Unless Kreuger himself should do the intervening. And Kreuger had nothing with which to intervene. Not even the vast sum of 432 million kronor, which, as Price, Waterhouse found, he had appropriated from his five principal companies, could save him. Of that sum, 101,738,000 had gone into the purchase of unsubscribed portions of his own issues. Other millions had gone into supporting operations. Millions more were being poured into old borrowings to expand the shrinking collateral. Millions had been paid out in dividends, thrown into unsound investments, and tied up in long-term loans. Short of a miracle, the jig was up.

IT WAS Kreuger who performed the miracle. And out of the emptiest hat. Or rather out of the Italian coat-of-arms on the flap of an old envelope, a little ink, and 46 embossed and printed sheets. The envelope came from Kreuger's drawer. The printed sheets were provided by an honest Stockholm printer. And the ink Kreuger himself applied sitting late in the great office at the Match Palace laboriously and clumsily forging the signatures of Signori Mosconi and Boselli to £28,668,500 of worthless Italian bonds. Pencil tracing showed under some. Boselli's name was misspelled in three various ways. Mosconi, who signs himself with an apparent N, is made to sign with a clear M. And the brief Italian phrases were, on certain of the bonds, not even good Italian. Nine million pounds of these bonds were wedged into the statement of Kreuger and Toll for 1930, a loan was arranged with the Skandinaviska Kredit A.B. And the German installment was paid.

The crisis was passed. But another crisis immediately replaced it—the July dividends. To meet them Kreuger determined upon what was to him the most desperate act of his career—the sale of the controlling interest in Ericsson. It was as though Napoleon had offered to partition his empire. But Kreuger had no choice. He went to America in the summer of 1931, arranged for an exchange of stock between I. T. and T. and Ericsson and the payment by the former of $11 million and, in August, borrowed $4 million more from U.S. banks for his immediate needs. From New York he returned to Stockholm. Kreuger and Toll must have 40 million kronor. There was no collateral—only stock in the Boliden gold mines and that stock was already pledged to Skandinaviska. There was only one way out, to "borrow" International's $50 million of German bonds, pledge them with Skandinaviska, free the Boliden stock, pledge the Boliden stock with the Riksbank, tell the Riksbank that Kreuger and Toll was in danger, and force the Riksbank to lend him the 40 million kronor. And that he did. The "borrowing" of International's $50 million was covered by £19 million of the forged Italian bonds. And the public was told that Kreuger and Toll's indebtedness would be down $20 million in September.

But there was no truce with fate. Danger now threatened in New York. I. T. and T. was threatening to check the Ericsson books. On December 22, 1931, Kreuger reappeared in New York. Boliden was the card. Largely out of his own head, he dictated the annual report of Kreuger and Toll for 1931, painting a picture of the Boliden mines which was calculated to sweep another score of New York millions into his empty tills. But New York in January 1932 was in no mood whatever to respond. And while he waited, while he listened, while he talked, the blow had fallen. The game was played. I. T. and T.'s auditors in Stockholm had discovered that an asset item of 27 million kronor cash on the books of Ericsson was really only a claim against Kreuger companies in that amount. There was no adequate explanation. The catastrophe was complete.

Kreuger had not only squeezed the last sponge of credit dry. He had also played the market. He had been playing it for two years, using the funds of Kreuger and Toll and the services, under one name or another, of most of the brokerage houses of New York. Millions of dollars were gone, in support of a fatally falling market.

There on the 21st of February was Kreuger in New York, his credit gone, his Ericsson contract rescinded, his reputation impugned, losing millions on a falling Stock Exchange, issuing falsely comforting statements, borrowing a last feeble $1.2 million from Swedish banks to pay interest on debentures, pledging 350,000 shares of Diamond Match to extend his $4 million loan and trying to make sense while the men from Lee, Higginson called to advise him to take a rest. The telephone was going day and night. The housekeeper, Hilda Aberg, was buying an alarm clock to waken him for transatlantic calls past midnight. People were coming in to see him at all hours. He began smoking—lighting cigarettes rather—and playing solitaire sitting at his desk. He was more and more nervous. One day he came in with a package 40 inches long. He stood it in a corner in his bedroom.

The night before he left he was telephoning and telegraphing and sending messengers with wrong addresses and saying, What is it? What is it? At 2:30 in the morning Hilda woke up and the lights were on and he had gone. In the morning there was some candy on the table from a night-owl tearoom over on Lexington Avenue. Hilda went in to waken him at 8. He was lying on the bed fully dressed, only his coat off and his shoes beside him on the blankets. He refused to change his clothes. When he came out to breakfast there was shaving cream smeared on his tie. Hilda went in to make his bed when he was gone.

There was a slip of paper on the table by the bed. It said: "I am too tired to continue." Telegrams came in. The telephone was ringing all day long, but he was not there. He was not there or at his office. The next day when he was gone Hilda opened the tall package 40 inches long. It was a loaded rifle.

Kreuger sailed the 4th of March on the *Ile de France*. The bankers let him go. Why they let him go, why they did not suspect him, why for eight years they had not suspected him, they themselves have never cared to say. Durant accompanied him. On the 10th, the ship landed in Havre. There were cables for Kreuger and a delegation of French bankers. One of the cables was from Herbert Dillon of Eastman, telling him that selling had increased and asking for additional security and for explicit information about Kreuger and Toll's finances.

As for the bankers, they had come down in answer to a radio from Kreuger inquiring if he might borrow 20 million francs. Their house, a private bank, had long been angling for his business. They waited feverishly, their fountain pens bursting with ink, their checkbooks eager in their pockets. Kreuger received them in his compartment on the train. Unfortunately he had changed his mind. He did not need the 20 million francs and he had made it a rule never to borrow money that he did not need. Their faces fell. "However," said Mr. Kreuger, "I do not wish to give you your trip for nothing. I am myself a little short of cash. I will take 5 million francs." The gentlemen were delighted.

The 5 million francs was delivered to 5 Avenue Victor-Emmanuel III. The note was to be signed the next day—any time—at his convenience.

The early boat train reached Paris at noon on Friday and at 2:30 in the afternoon there was a meeting in Kreuger's apartment. Kreuger seemed to follow the discussion at first but later his mind appeared to wander. Feeling in the room grew tense. An accountant who had never dared to question Kreuger's will finally managed the courage to say that there were some who could not understand where the money for the Italian bonds had come from. Kreuger made no reply. Desperate, the accountant pushed the question: "Are they authentic?" Kreuger, walking absently up and down the room, stopped and gave him a long look. "Yes," he said.

At a meeting later that day with Oscar Rydbeck, head of the Skandinaviska bank, Kreuger explained that his difficulties were due to his illness and to the bear pool operating in Paris with the stolen shares. Rydbeck asked if the Italian bonds might not serve as basis for a loan. No, for Kreuger had bound himself neither to sell nor pledge them ... But would not the Italian government buy them in? ... Kreuger would have to go to Rome for that himself... Then why not go? ... It would take so long a time ... All the more reason then to start at once ... The subject was dropped.

AT FIVE, his friend Krister Littorin drove Kreuger to the Avenue Victor-Emmanuel and left him there in the salon in the gathering dusk. Littorin then went on alone to the Hotel du Rhin where he was shown a statement of expected earnings for 1932 and 1933 that was clearly wrong. Large demands, two bankers told him, were to be made the next day by brokerage houses in New York.

At 10 the next morning Littorin went to Kreuger's flat. He had known Kreuger a long time. He was very fond of him. He stood in the door of the salon looking at the white-lipped, smiling face. He spoke as gently as he could of the earnings statement. Kreuger was also quiet in his chair: "It was probably not a good idea to give that statement ..." Littorin was moved: "Whatever you have done," he said, "whatever you have said, and whatever you have written, you should understand that you are surrounded by true friends who wish you well ..." He stood there waiting in the door. He turned to go. Ivar would not forget the meeting at 11? Ivar would not forget.

The door closed. Minutes passed. Miss Bokman, Kreuger's secretary, came, sat down, talked briefly, left again. At 11 the bell of Ste. Clotilde echoed in the rue Las Cases and down the Boulevard St. Germain. The doors of the Salle de l'Horloge were shut against the crowd. The room at No. 5 was very still. Through the closed windows the passing cars and the children's voices under the plane trees sounded far away and faint. Kreuger laid three brief letters on the desk. To one he pinned a telegram. The telegram had come from Stockholm: Kreuger was to meet the Bank of Sweden's representatives in Germany the following day. The doors of the apartment were all closed. Kreuger drew the bedroom blinds evenly and neatly to the sill. He smoothed the unmade bedclothes and lay down. The street sounds had grown fainter through the darkened blinds. Looking up he saw the fat, gold stucco cherubs in the ceiling corners of the room. Odd witnesses! He turned his black coat back and laid aside the leather-covered large gold coin above his heart.

For a long time he had worn it there as fetish or as guard against some shot, some madman. Kreuger snapped a cartridge in the army type, the 9 mm. He placed his feet together neatly side by side. He shot himself an inch below the heart.

◆

AFTERMATH

So, how much vanished? The answer starts at $250 million and goes up to $400 million (about $10 billion in current dollars). These are guesses; what can be said with certainty is that when Kreuger's U.S. operations were declared bankrupt in August 1932, it was the largest to that date.

In the wake of all this, Congress scheduled hearings on stock market practices in January 1933. For two days, it focused on Kreuger's actions in the U.S., particularly a $50 million float in 1931 in which he substituted Yugoslavian bonds for French ones, eroding the quality of the collateral. As a result of this particular debacle, Congress eventually passed the Trust Indenture Act in 1939, which regulates the use of collateral in borrowings. In general, there is no doubt that the Kreuger story played a large role in the creation of the SEC.

Winding up the Kreuger enterprises took years; the bankruptcy trustees in the U.S. issued their final report in 1945, and eventually U.S. investors got back about 30 cents on the dollar. The genuine Kreuger assets were able to resume business; some descendants operate still.

4

THE ADELPHIA STORY

*Once the country's sixth-largest cable company, Adelphia was
once the pride of Coudersport, Pennsylvania. Then it wasn't.*

---

by DEVIN LEONARD

August 12, 2002

Dale Cowburn was allergic to bee stings. He carried medication at
all times in case he encountered an angry swarm. Last summer,
however, while he was working in his barn, Cowburn was stung twice
on the head. He had a heart attack and died on the spot.

The news traveled quickly through Coudersport, Pa., the town of
2,600 near the New York border where Cowburn had lived. One of
the locals moved by his death was John Rigas, chairman and CEO of
Adelphia Communications, the nation's sixth-largest cable television
provider, a company with $3.6 billion in annual revenues and
headquarters in—of all places—this rural town. Rigas knows about
bees. He owns a farm outside town that sells Christmas trees, maple
syrup, and honey. Soon after Cowburn's death, there was a knock on
the door at his house. It was Rigas's beekeeper. He'd been sent to
destroy the offending insects.

More than just the town's richest man, Rigas was a 76-year-old worth billions. He owned the Buffalo Sabres hockey team. He hobnobbed with Ted Turner. But the silver-haired cable mogul told people in a humble whisper that he was just a small-town guy who loved helping his neighbors. He sent busloads of children to Sabres games. He used Adelphia's corporate jet to fly ailing people to faith healers and cancer treatment centers.

Townspeople flocked to the Masonic temple every year for Adelphia's Christmas party. In 2001, there were two towering Christmas trees and the Buffalo Philharmonic played "The Nutcracker." That was really something for a town like Coudersport. "Each December the Rigas family brings their world to us, and I am grateful" wrote a columnist in the local paper.

John Rigas was also revered in the cable business. He was one of the pioneers who had started stringing wires and urging customers to throw away their rabbit ears in the early 1950s. He was inducted into the Cable Television Hall of Fame in 2001. In a celebratory video, Decker Anstrom, CEO of the Weather Channel, said, "If there's one person I'd like my son to grow up to be, it would be John Rigas."

Then, in the blink of an eye, John Rigas lost everything—his company, his reputation, even the affection of his beloved Coudersport. Last March, Adelphia disclosed it was on the hook for $2.3 billion in off-balance-sheet loans the Rigas family had used mostly to buy company stock. Rigas resigned, as did his three sons—Michael, Tim, and James—who held top executive positions and sat on the board with their father. (The Rigases refused to talk to FORTUNE.)

The independent directors now running the company say they discovered that under the Rigases, nothing was as it seemed. They say Adelphia inflated subscriber numbers. Routine expenses like service calls had been booked as capital items, inflating Adelphia's reported cash flow. But what was perhaps most unsettling was the unabashed manner in which the Rigases had helped themselves to shareholder dollars.

Adelphia financed the family's $150 million purchase of the Sabres. It paid $12.8 million in 2001 for office furniture and design services provided by Doris Rigas. Even John Rigas's good works were tainted. Adelphia paid a Rigas family partnership that owns the Sabres $744,000 for "luxury-box rentals, hockey tickets, and other entertainment costs." That means shareholders probably picked up the tab for all those children who went to games. The same goes for the beekeeper's visit.

As Adelphia slid toward bankruptcy—it filed for Chapter 11 protection in June 2002—the entire cable industry was affected. The stock of competitors like Comcast and Charter fell because Wall Street feared they might have similar secrets. Investors dumped shares of entertainment companies like Disney, afraid that Adelphia wouldn't pay its programming bills.

Citizens of Coudersport no longer speak so worshipfully about John Rigas. But even now there are people who praise him as a principled man who refused, for instance, to allow porn channels on his cable systems. The John Rigas they describe believed in small-town values: strong families, hard work, church on Sunday. That's why, they say, he remained true to Coudersport. But surely there was another reason. There were things John Rigas and his sons got away with in Coudersport that would never have been tolerated anywhere else.

John Rigas didn't impress anybody much when he first arrived in Coudersport in 1951. The son of a Greek immigrant who ran a hot dog restaurant in nearby Wellsville, N.Y., Rigas was a character. He was 5 feet 5 inches tall. He had a gap-toothed smile, a wandering left eye, and a lot of energy. His father had tried to entice him to work at the restaurant when he came home with an engineering degree from Rensselaer Polytechnic Institute in 1950. But after a few months at the grill, John borrowed money and bought the Coudersport movie theater for $72,000. He sold tickets, made popcorn, and sometimes slept over when he was too tired to drive home.

Back then Coudersport didn't seem like a place anybody would go to make a fortune. It was a one-stoplight town in the Allegheny

Mountains, far from any major highway. Main Street was four blocks of low-slung brick buildings. It wasn't quaint; there was a hard edge, even a sense of desperation in the air. Each spring when diplomas were passed out, the locals muttered, "Say goodbye to another graduating class at Coudersport High."

People who stayed behind weren't sure what to think about a man like John Rigas, who wore his ambition on his sleeve. "It's the same plague you see in other small communities," says Bruce Cahilly, a local attorney who befriended Rigas early on. "People who have more talent and expertise are perceived as threats." So John was snubbed when he moved to town with Doris, a former high school English teacher from a poor family in the Finger Lakes area. John was wounded, but he seemed determined to win everybody over. He stayed until midnight talking to moviegoers after the lights went up. He stopped people on Main Street to ask about their children. He began attending the Episcopal church preferred by the town's business leaders, even though he'd been raised in the Greek Orthodox faith.

With Doris's prodding, John also pursued other business opportunities. In 1952 he overdrew his bank account to buy the town cable franchise for $300. A doctor and a state senator agreed to put up $40,000, and John was in the cable business. He wired up Coudersport. Four years later he and his brother Gus did the same in Wellsville.

By the mid-1960s Rigas could afford to build a house just outside town with a pool for his four children. He was invited to sit on the board of the local bank. For a man who wanted to be accepted, the offer meant a great deal. Besides, he could always use a loan.

John Rigas and his sons would become famous in the cable industry for taking huge risks and leveraging Adelphia to the hilt. That would not have surprised anybody in Coudersport. After wiring the town John acquired more rural cable systems in New York and Pennsylvania, and he bragged to friends about how much debt he was taking on to finance the deals. "Hey, I just borrowed $10 million," John blithely told Henry Lush, a local furniture-store owner. His secretary was forever going to the bank and moving funds from account to account so that her boss could stay ahead of creditors. People who tried to collect debts discovered it was no simple matter. Bruce Cahilly once drove out to John's house to seek payment for some legal work. When all else failed, he grabbed two five-gallon cans of blue pool paint from the garage. "That's just as well," John shrugged. "Doris doesn't like blue. She wanted green."

A lot of people in Coudersport would have been satisfied with a house, a pool, and a seat on the bank board. But John kept pushing himself. He and Doris drove their children just as hard. They raised Michael, Tim, James, and Ellen, their youngest, to be model students. No smoking, no drinking, no hitchhiking across the country like their cousins in Wellsville. Doris, locals say, seemed to feel that the family was too good for Coudersport and drove her children to outshine their classmates.

One by one the Rigas children went off to elite colleges. Michael, the oldest, went to Harvard and then on to Harvard Law. Friends recall that he was smart and ambitious but monkish, usually spending Saturday nights studying. Tim, the second child, was equally bright. He got a bachelor's degree in economics from Wharton, and he had a social life too. He played intramural volleyball and belonged to a singing group called the Penny Loafers. James, the youngest of the boys, went to Harvard and then to Stanford Law School. He drank beer and played pinball, but he impressed everybody as a straight arrow. "He was the last person you would have thought would have gotten into trouble," says Steven Durlauf, a Harvard classmate.

For all their winning qualities, there was something odd about the Rigas boys. Unlike their father, they were awkward socially. When they attended their cousins' weddings in Wellsville, they stood in their tuxedos against the wall, arms crossed. "They didn't mingle," a Rigas family member says sadly. "They just stood there. Somebody said, 'They must be the bouncers.' "

The boys clearly preferred being with their immediate family in

Coudersport. Not long after getting their degrees, Michael and Tim moved back in with their parents. Neither married. James spent a year and a half in San Francisco after Stanford, working at Bain & Co., but then he too returned to Coudersport, where he married and got a place of his own in town. "John just controlled everything with those boys," laments a relative. "He wouldn't give them any rope." (Ellen went to Harvard and then pursued a career in music and film production in New York.)

All three sons went to work for their father. John couldn't have been happier. Adelphia was still a shoestring operation: John ran the company out of an office over a hardware store with three secretaries and a lineman. Once his sons joined the business, things changed rapidly. In 1981, Adelphia moved into an old church around the corner. People wondered what John was going to do with all that extra space. In 1985, Adelphia went from 53,538 subscribers to 122,500 after it acquired a cable system in Ocean County, N.J. When the Rigases took Adelphia public the next year, it had 370 full-time employees and deals on the table that would increase its subscribers to 253,767. By the mid-1990s Adelphia had moved into the old Coudersport High School building on Main Street, where the boys had gone to school. It was an odd place, perhaps, for what was now one of the nation's ten largest cable companies, managing 1.2 million subscribers. But the Rigas systems were the envy of their peers. They were clustered together in six areas—western New York, Virginia, Pennsylvania, New England, Ohio, and coastal New Jersey—making it easier for Adelphia to control costs. That allowed Adelphia to enjoy 56% operating cash margins, the highest in the cable industry.

John and the boys came to be considered savvy businessmen. John was the resident wiseman, but he was also obsessed with details. He knew every inch of his cable systems; he looked at every résumé that came in. Michael was responsible for the daily operations of the cable systems. Tim was CFO. James supervised Adelphia's push into new technologies, including telephone service.

Yet as the cable industry grew up, the Rigases operated as if they were a million miles away from prying investors. Says Tom Cady, a former Adelphia sales and marketing executive: "Decisions were made at the dinner table rather than in a boardroom or somebody's office." John and his sons showed up late for meetings so often that people joked that the family operated "on Rigas time." They were famous for not returning calls from analysts. Occasionally, when they spotted a cable acquisition they really liked, they simply kept it for themselves.

What's more, the Rigases structured Adelphia so that there were no checks and balances at the top. Adelphia issued class A shares with one vote each to the public, but the Rigases retained all the class B stock with ten votes per share. Therefore they got to pick the board of directors. John, the three boys, and Ellen's husband, Peter Venetis, held five of the nine board seats. They filled the other four with John's friends and business associates. Who else would want to travel to Coudersport for meetings anyway?

By all accounts Tim Rigas ran the financial side of the business like a Saudi prince. He was CFO, and he was also the chairman of the board's audit committee, which oversaw the CFO's work. To anybody who'd followed John Rigas's career, what happened with Adelphia's financing was predictable. The small-town businessman who had boasted about his stomach for leverage now saddled Adelphia with outlandish amounts of debt. In 1996, Adelphia's debt was 11 times its market capitalization, an off-the-chart number. (By contrast, Comcast's ratio was 1.28; Cox Communication's was 0.45.) Bond-rating agencies constantly subjected Adelphia to credit reviews. Shareholders paid a price. A Salomon Smith Barney analyst noted that Adelphia's debt "has caused the stock to trade at the steepest discount to estimated net asset value of any cable operator."

Stranger still, Adelphia began commingling revenues from its own cable operations, family-owned systems, and loan proceeds in an account referred to internally, according to documents filed recently with the SEC, as the "cash-management system." It was a lot of money. After Adelphia made a series of acquisitions in 1999, its annual revenues reached $3 billion. From time to time the Rigas family dipped into the account for personal business. The company says the Rigases tapped the account earlier this year to pay $63 million in margin loans. They used $4 million from the account to buy Adelphia stock. Another $700,000 went to pay for Tim's membership at the Golf Club at Briar's Creek on John's Island, S.C.

The independent directors now running the company say neither the unusual account nor the family's withdrawals were approved by the board. The Rigas family spokesman insists that none of it was hidden from the directors.

The Rigases didn't particularly care if investors shied away from Adelphia's stock or if bond-rating agencies called their debt junk. They cared about Coudersport. As Adelphia prospered, John Rigas became the town's biggest benefactor. He hired many locals and paid them well. Employees built suburban-style houses. The newspaper store started selling fancy coffee. A gym opened on Main Street.

John combed the local papers and sent checks to down-on-their-luck families. "I'd always know when he did that because I'd get calls saying, 'Thanks for the article. I just got a check from John Rigas,' " says John Anderson, managing editor of the *Wellsville Daily Reporter.* People seeking favors camped out in Rigas's favorite restaurants, waiting for the CEO to arrive for lunch. He rarely turned anybody down.

Coudersport treated the Rigases like royalty, and they behaved accordingly. John now traveled in a Gulfstream jet, which Adelphia purchased from King Hussein of Jordan. At the Adelphia Christmas party one year, the orchestra played selections from the musical *Camelot.* It was John's favorite music, the conductor told the audience.

Doris rarely ventured into town, sending servants to do her shopping. When she was seen, she was in one of her Toyota minivans, an employee behind the wheel. But everyone felt her presence. The Rigases accumulated a dozen or so houses in Coudersport and the surrounding area. Doris had most of them painted brown and surrounded by split-rail fences. She also helped design Adelphia's buildings, including its brick-and-marble headquarters on Main Street, which locals call the "mausoleum."

The boys, for their part, seemed to owe their allegiance more to the family empire than to the town. Michael was the only one who showed interest in community service. He worked 16-hour days and still attended Coudersport Rotary Club meetings. Tim, too, worked hard, jetting around the country negotiating acquisitions. He dressed well, had lots of girlfriends, and belonged to nearly 20 golf clubs. But when he was home, Tim would take John to church and Doris to her favorite restaurant, the Beef 'N' Barrel.

James seemed more interested in having his own fiefdom. He spent most of his time running Adelphia Business Solutions, a telephone service company spun off from the parent. He flew coach and stayed in midrange hotels. (Sources tell FORTUNE that of all the sons, James was the least involved in Adelphia's financial weirdness.) Yet he, too, behaved like royalty at times, building a baronial house on a hill above town. Even Ellen lived in high style—on the company tab. The company says she and her venture capitalist husband lived rent-free in a Manhattan apartment owned by Adelphia. The corporation also put up $3 million in production money for *SongCatcher,* her critically acclaimed film about a musicologist. (Ellen Rigas and her husband have paid the back rent on the apartment to Adelphia.)

It struck some of the locals that the Rigases were rather free with shareholder money. Teresa Kisiel, Coudersport's tax collector, couldn't help noticing that Adelphia paid its real estate taxes and those of the Rigas family with a single check. It was no secret that shareholders were footing the bills for a planned golf course. Sometimes people in Coudersport even wondered whether all the spending was legitimate. But the thought would pass. "He's our Greek god," Shirlee Lette, a local newspaper columnist, told a visiting reporter.

Oren Cohen thought there was something about the family's spending that didn't add up. Then a high-yield-bond analyst for Merrill Lynch, Cohen had followed Adelphia for a decade. He'd noticed that the Rigases were buying their own stock aggressively, but he couldn't figure out how they were paying for it. They didn't appear to have the cash themselves. John Rigas made $1.4 million in 2000. Michael, Tim, and James each took home $237,000.

The Rigases didn't have any sources of income outside Adelphia. They never sold their stock, and it didn't pay a dividend. Cohen was pretty sure their private cable systems weren't throwing off cash. John couldn't be selling that much honey at his farm. But every time Cohen tried to get an explanation, Adelphia rebuffed him.

Last February, Cohen noticed that the Rigases had bought or were committed to buying $1.8 billion of Adelphia stock and convertible bonds. At the time of the purchases the stock had been trading at about $40 a share. Now it was at $20. If John and his sons were using borrowed money, the Rigases were in trouble. It was time to call Adelphia again. "It seems to me the Rigases are $900 million or $1 billion in the hole," Cohen said to the head of investor relations. "How's this stuff being funded?" He got the brush-off.

On March 27, Cohen nearly shouted for joy when he spied a footnote on the last page of Adelphia's quarterly earnings press release. It said Adelphia was liable for $2.3 billion in off-balance-sheet loans to the Rigas family. Near the end of a conference call that day, Cohen pressed Tim Rigas for details. Tim muttered something about family stock purchases and said he would provide details later.

That might have sufficed in the past, but it was just months after the disclosure of off-balance-sheet debt at Enron had led to the largest corporate bankruptcy in history. Adelphia's stock tumbled 35% in three days. The SEC began an investigation.

Things in Coudersport quickly spun out of control. John issued a statement acknowledging that "shareholders are looking for greater clarity and transparency." The stock continued to fall as Adelphia announced it would be restating earnings for 1999, 2000, and 2001. The company delayed filing its 2001 annual report to sort out its books. On May 15, John resigned as chairman and CEO.

Rigas was succeeded by interim CEO Erland Kailbourne, a retired Fleet Bank executive and Adelphia "independent" director. Kailbourne was a consummate Rigas family insider, an old friend from Wellsville, and a lot of observers suspected that John might still pull strings.

But the truth is, the independent directors were livid. They'd signed off on the lending agreements, but they thought the Rigases were buying more cable systems, not taking out what were essentially margin loans to buy Adelphia stock. John had made them look like fools. Kailbourne and the three other independent directors hired David Boies, the attorney who led the case against Microsoft, to look into Adelphia's books.

John did not object. Neither did Michael, Tim, or James, who resigned soon after their father. Boies sent in forensic accountants, who discovered that a $167 million bond purchase by the family hadn't been paid for. They also unearthed what appeared to be evidence of fraud. FORTUNE has learned that five members of the accounting department who worked under Tim Rigas are now cooperating with federal prosecutors.

The independent directors also discovered that even after the disastrous March 27 conference call, someone in the family withdrew $175 million from Adelphia's cash-management system to cover margin loans.

Adelphia's stock was soon worth pennies. The company was delisted by the Nasdaq because it didn't file its 2001 annual report. That triggered the default of $1.4 billion in Adelphia convertible bonds. Bankruptcy was all but certain. The company desperately needed a loan to stay afloat. But Wall Street wasn't about to lend it any more money as long as the Rigases were around. The family still held 100% of the company's class B voting stock. Technically they still controlled Adelphia.

The problem was that John Rigas didn't think he'd done anything wrong. The day after he resigned as chairman and CEO, he startled the independent directors by showing up at a directors' meeting. Surely, he told them, this mess could be sorted out and things would get back to normal. No, John, said his old friends, you and the boys have to go. Lawyers from Boies's firm tried to negotiate a severance package with

John but couldn't reach an agreement. Finally the independent directors gave the Rigas family an ultimatum: Turn over your voting shares to us, or we'll resign and go public with everything we've uncovered. After an all-night negotiating session on May 22 in Coudersport, the Rigases finally relinquished control at 5 a.m. Adelphia got a $1.5 billion bank loan.

If John Rigas showed up on Main Street in Coudersport tomorrow, some people would avoid him. Others might curse him. But the vast majority would pat him on the back and tell him to keep his chin up. They remember the checks, the Christmas parties, all the nice things he's done. Rigas knows that. But he hasn't been seen in town since everything fell apart at Adelphia. His friends say his health isn't good, and that must be part of it. But maybe there's another reason: He'd have to look everybody in the eye.

◆

AFTERMATH

In late July 2002, federal agents staged a dramatic early-morning arrest and perp walk for John, Timothy, and Michael Rigas at their Manhattan apartment. Two other Adelphia executives, former vice president for finance James Brown and former director of internal reporting Michael C. Mulcahey, were arrested the same day in Coudersport. The five were indicted on charges including bank fraud, conspiracy, securities fraud, and wire fraud. Brown pleaded guilty and began cooperating with the prosecutors.

In April 2004, the case went to trial, with Brown as the star witness. He testified that Tim Rigas doctored Adelphia's financial statements and implicated John and Michael Rigas in the company's false filings. In July, the jury found John and Tim Rigas guilty of conspiracy, securities fraud, and bank fraud. (An appeals court overturned their conviction on one count of bank fraud in 2007.) Mulcahey was acquitted of all charges, though he was later barred for life from serving as an officer or director of a public company in a separate case brought by the SEC. Judge Kevin Castel of the US District Court (Southern District of New York) said of him in November 2006: "Because Mulcahey's securities law violations were repeated, varied, and knowingly perpetrated, and because a strong likelihood exists that his violations will recur if not enjoined, the Court imposes a permanent officer and director bar against Mulcahey."

The same jury acquitted Michael Rigas of conspiracy and wire fraud but deadlocked on the remaining charges, forcing the judge to declare a mistrial. Michael Rigas pleaded guilty in 2005 to making a false entry in company records and received two years' probation.

The other family members were not as fortunate. John Rigas and Tim Rigas began serving their sentences in August 2007 at a low-security federal prison in North Carolina. In 2008, a district judge reduced both father and son's prison sentences by three years based on the 2007 reversal: John Rigas's to 12 years and Tim Rigas's to 17. The Rigases appealed to the U.S. Supreme Court, which turned them down in March 2008. Another appeal, to the Third Circuit, is pending

The company also suffered. Adelphia filed for bankruptcy in 2002. In 2005, it paid $715 million to settle fraud charges with the U.S. Justice Department and the SEC; at the time, this was the second-biggest accounting-fraud case recovery (after WorldCom, which paid $750 million). As part of the agreement, the Rigas family surrendered $1.5 billion in assets to Adelphia, including cable systems, company common stock, and real estate. The following year, Comcast and Time Warner took over Adelphia's cable properties in a $17.6 billion deal. Adelphia re-emerged from bankruptcy in early 2007 with a plan to liquidate assets, pay its creditors, and cease operations. Its former headquarters—the brick-and-marble "mausoleum" on Coudersport's Main Street—was sold at auction for $3.4 million later that year.

5

THE LOOTING OF IOS

For decades, Robert Vesco was an international
man of mystery. Here is how it all started.

by ROBERT A. HUTCHISON

March 1973

When Robert Lee Vesco flew into Geneva one day in June 1970, he was the all-but-unknown 34-year-old chief executive of a modest-size company called International Controls Corp. But a number of frantic people in the tranquil Swiss city were all too ready to accept Vesco for what he proclaimed himself to be: the savior of Investors Overseas Services.

The transnational mutual fund empire built by Bernard Cornfeld urgently needed help when Vesco arrived, accompanied by Dr. Milton Meissner, a tall, soft-spoken New York management consultant who had once helped run Mexico's electrical-power industry. Vesco and Meissner were astonished by the chaos that greeted them at IOS's lakeside headquarters. Cornfeld had been deposed as chairman a month before and, according to Vesco, "was jumping out of boats and trying to crash gates and a few other odds and ends."

Such pandemonium suited Vesco perfectly. As later events revealed, his main objective was to save International Controls from impending disaster. Sales and income were sagging, and the cost of servicing a staggering long-term debt (which exceeded shareholder equity) was eating up more than 20% of the company's gross profits.

The IOS directors, who had been shut in their velvet-draped Bella Vista boardroom for over a month of nonstop crisis meetings, had no way of knowing that International Controls was also hard pressed. When Vesco made his offer of emergency financing, he declared that "it is not our intent to assume control of IOS, but simply to benefit by what may be an attractive investment opportunity." After two months of deliberations, the directors accepted his proposal.

Vesco and his lieutenants lost no time in focusing on three of IOS's richest mutual funds: the Fund of Funds, Venture Fund (International), and IIT—an International Investment Trust. In mid-June 1970, those three "dollar funds" had combined assets of $1 billion. By early 1972— after a tide of shareholder redemptions—there was only about $427 million left, and more than half of that allegedly has been diverted into dubious investments or has simply vanished. Another IOS entity— Investment Properties International Ltd. (IPI), a closed-end real-estate investment company with $135 million in assets—also fell into Vesco's hands and has since been turned over to a Bahamian company controlled by two of his associates.

QUESTIONS BEFORE THE COURT

Last November Vesco was named as the central figure in one of the largest securities fraud complaints ever filed by the U.S. Securities and Exchange Commission. No less than 42 individuals, corporations, mutual funds, and banks are accused of having bilked IOS companies and the three "dollar funds" of more than $225 million.

The 17,000-word document reads like a Hollywood thriller. Its allegations trace a global web of deceit and purport to show how he and his associates created a Sargasso Sea of offshore companies for the purpose of moving money out of IOS and its funds and into legally impenetrable waters.

Vesco and the other defendants have denied all the charges. They will also argue that many of the alleged acts are not within the court's competence, having taken place in the Bahamas, Costa Rica, Luxembourg, the Netherlands Antilles, and Panama.

In establishing their case, government attorneys will have to answer two salient questions: First, how did Vesco parlay a collection of modest manufacturing companies, name dropping, and audacity into control of the world's largest offshore financial complex? Second, how did the Vesco group siphon off the assets of IOS and its funds to the detriment of investors?

The answers to these questions lie deep in the histories of Vesco and Cornfeld. Both men are intensely ambitious and impatient of legal restraints. Cornfeld, a former social worker who grew up in Brooklyn, created IOS with the simple notion that millions of well-to-do people all over the world would invest in mutual funds that were sold hard and offered freedom from tax collectors' surveillance. To guarantee that freedom, Cornfeld based IOS Ltd., in Switzerland, where tax evasion is not a criminal offense. And he was careful to incorporate both the parent IOS Ltd. and its fund management subsidiary, Transglobal Financial Services Ltd. (formerly Investors Overseas Services Management Ltd.), in Canada, knowing that Canadian regulatory agencies exercise little influence over nonresident corporations that conduct their affairs elsewhere. Unwittingly, however, Cornfeld had created a business that was uniquely ripe for manipulation, too.

Vesco is also a man of humble origin who understood the cupidity—and innocence—of people who want to get rich quickly. A self-taught engineer, he started his career as a freelance promoter at 24. Seven lean years later, in 1966, he pieced together his first deal of consequence by merging two little companies into the Florida-registered shell of Cryogenics Inc., whose public ownership made it a suitable vehicle for Vesco's operations. This corporate hodgepodge he renamed International Controls Corp. At the time he said that his purpose was to transform the company into a "fabulous moneymaking machine."

Three years later he had transformed sales of less than $400,000 and no profits into a corporation with sales of $101 million, earnings of $4.7 million, and stockholders' equity of $41.7 million. An important element in this performance was Vesco's victory in a bitter battle for control of Electronic Specialty Co. of Pasadena, Calif., a manufacturer of aircraft parts and electromechanical components four times the size of International Controls. In the process, however, he entangled himself in a lawsuit that drew the SEC's attention.

The affair left Vesco with a tarnished image. He became known as a shifty customer, aggressively acquisitive, and very hard-hitting—in short, a man to be wary of. International Controls' stock never really performed. It briefly hit a high of almost $51 in mid-1968 but thereafter declined steadily and was last traded at $3 before being suspended when the SEC brought in its fraud complaint last November.

For some time Vesco had studied the Cornfeld operation, pondering the possibilities of combining offshore banking and mutual fund management with his own operation. IOS was in the throes of a crisis of confidence, engendered by a somewhat illusory cash shortage. Actually, substantial liquid assets were available, but the IOS board was dominated by sales executives with little financial sophistication who seriously feared that they could not meet the next payroll. The world's leading banks were not interested.

BIG NAMES, BIG TALK

Vesco employed audacity and show to impress the directors. He said—quite accurately—that both the world's largest bank (Bank of America) and the world's largest insurance company (Prudential) were International Controls' prime lenders. But he went one step further, saying that he was acting as the Bank of America's front man in Geneva. The IOS directors believed him at the time but asked for confirmation that International Controls had $5 million to lend. Vesco coolly instructed his New Jersey headquarters to transfer all available corporate cash to the company's account at Bank of America. He then asked the bank to cable him in Geneva confirming the balance.

The return telegram made Vesco hopping mad. International Controls, the bank said, had a cash balance of more than $3 million—but that money was not available for withdrawal. Furthermore, it warned, the intended transaction with IOS appeared to violate the loan agreement International Controls had with the Bank of America.

Vesco then turned to Butlers Bank, a small private bank in Nassau with a net worth of $5.2 million. Butlers, run by an American named Allan Butler, was having difficulty meeting trade creditors' notes. By helping Vesco gain control of IOS, the bank obviously could expect to gain a lot of new business.

Butlers cabled on August 25, affirming that International Controls held $5 million on account. The IOS directors presumably did not learn, however, that the money was a back-to-back deposit against a loan to an International Controls subsidiary. Other gestures on Vesco's behalf earned the bank and Allan Butler the dubious distinction of being listed as defendants in the SEC suit.

Sir Eric Wyndham White, the chairman of the IOS since Cornfeld was ousted, advised the IOS board to accept Vesco's offer of "interim financing." He told the uneasy directors that "one of the leading banks in the world" had indicated that, although Vesco was a hard businessman to deal with, he was a person of impeccable integrity who had "gone against the financial establishment in the U.S. and won." Six days later the final agreement was signed. The cash was promised in two weeks.

Thus Vesco had International Controls lend IOS $5 million—which International Controls itself had to borrow. Then, in a masterly touch of financial hocus-pocus, he arranged for IOS to collateralize the loan by maintaining cash deposits in segregated accounts at Butlers Bank. In effect, IOS had "rescued" itself with its own money. This demonstrated that Vesco already knew something about IOS that its own directors apparently did not: The company may have needed a lot of things, but money was not first among them.

The loan agreement's terms put Vesco in a commanding role, in spite of the fact that he and his associates had no equity position in IOS. Vesco became a member of the board of directors and chairman of a newly formed finance committee that had veto power over "any action of financial significance." He quickly moved to stamp out any internal resistance. Employees who opposed him feared for their jobs.

Cornfeld, who had about 15% of the preferred stock, was stirring up trouble with excited warnings that Vesco was a financial hoodlum out to bleed the company dry. But by accepting the title of chairman of IOS's sales subsidiary, he had fallen into a trap. Any operational role given to Cornfeld without approval from International Controls technically violated the complex 110-page loan agreement. Vesco used this as a pretext for calling the $5 million loan in default. At the December 1970, executive-committee meeting, members recall, Vesco angrily announced that Cornfeld would either have to sell his stock or find the necessary cash to meet IOS's obligations to International Controls.

When the meeting ended, Vesco drew Cornfeld into one of the Louis XVI salons adjoining the IOS boardroom and asked him how much he wanted for his stock. "Around a dollar a share," Cornfeld says he replied. "How much do you want?" he asked Vesco, meaning the price International Controls would exact for withdrawing from IOS affairs. Vesco's answer was that IOS would have to retire the $5 million loan forthwith, thereby incurring penalties that would raise the cost to about $9.5 million. That discussion ended in stalemate.

A few weeks afterward, Vesco phoned Cornfeld in California with news that he had a hidden purchaser for Cornfeld's stock at 65 cents a share. Cornfeld rejected the offer, and several days later Vesco said the purchaser was prepared to go as high as 92 cents a share. In negotiations that followed, Cornfeld says, he got the strong impression that the purchaser was the Union Bank of Switzerland, one of the three biggest Swiss banks.

From a Bank Cantrade subsidiary, associates of Vesco had acquired a dummy corporation with the unlikely name of Linkink Progressive Corp., registered in Panama. Vesco eventually identified Linkink as the prospective purchaser, suggesting—Cornfeld recalls—that the company was controlled by a number of banks. Actually, Linkink was owned by still another Panamanian shell company called Red Pearl Bay S.A.

While negotiations were going on, the Cornfeld camp began to suspect that Vesco was trying to use money from one of the IOS funds to buy Bernie's stock. The suspicion was based on the fact that Meissner, whom Vesco had installed as his front man in Geneva, had requested the transfer of $6.2 million from IOS's IIT fund to a numbered account at Manufacturers Hanover Trust Co.'s branch in Frankfurt.

In this atmosphere of mistrust and intrigue, the deal was signed in the early hours of January 16, 1971. Cornfeld, with his usual coterie of girls, quickly boarded a jet for Cuernavaca, Mexico.

The Cornfeld buyout left Vesco in the driver's seat. International Controls took its first equity position in IOS by starting to purchase insiders' preferred stock. Many of the old guard vanished; Vesco became chairman of the board.

Canadian authorities and the shareholders of IOS were never told whom Linkink actually represented. Three months later, Linkink, along with the six million Cornfeld shares, was sold by Red Pearl Bay to a Canadian subsidiary of International Controls. The purchase price was 50,000 shares—less than 1%—of the Canadian subsidiary's outstanding common stock. At the end of that year the same 50,000 shares were bought back from Red Pearl Bay by International Controls for $50,000. In effect, ICC ended up with Cornfeld's $5.5 million worth of IOS stock for an outlay of $50,000.

By mid-1971, Vesco was beginning to take seriously his role as a major figure in international finance and to indulge his penchant for self-important gestures. Always fond of dropping famous names, he had acquired the services of a man who bore one: James Roosevelt, son of the late President. Roosevelt, was brought into IOS by Cornfeld and remained with Vesco long enough to be included as a defendant in the SEC action. Vesco also hired Donald Nixon, the President's nephew, and Regina Cahill, daughter of New Jersey's Governor William T. Cahill.

To add further to his image of success, Vesco had an International Controls subsidiary buy a Boeing 707 from Pan Am for a reported $1.2 million and spend almost as much again to have it fitted out with a luxurious interior and a communications system that would enable Vesco to hold mid-air conferences. With Cornfeld out of the picture, Vesco thought his problems were over. But eight sales captains from the old guard launched a proxy contest before the 1971 annual meeting. Narrowly defeating the dissidents, Vesco moved quickly to "restructure" IOS. The plan finally settled upon was largely drafted by his newly appointed lieutenant for offshore financial affairs, a Canadian named Norman LeBlanc. A former Coopers & Lybrand partner who had handled the initial six-month investigative audit of IOS for Vesco, LeBlanc had gone on to become IOS's financial vice president. LeBlanc's plan called for two major modifications in IOS's corporate structure:

First, IOS Ltd. was turned into a holding company by the transference of its operating functions to the fund management company. That company had already been combined with the sales company and renamed Transglobal Financial Services. IOS owned 80% of Transglobal.

Second, all IOS's European and Bahamian banking operations were spun off to a newly formed holding company, International Bancorp Ltd. IOS shareholders first learned of this massive restyling of assets through newspaper reports of a stock and debenture dividend: one share of International Bancorp common and $1 face amount of Bancorp debentures for every ten shares of IOS common and preferred stock.

A follow-up letter to shareholders revealed that 30% of the International Bancorp stock had been traded for what looked like nebulous assets. In effect the IOS board of directors was dealing a 22% slice of the banking pie directly to International Controls, 48% to the other IOS shareholders, and the rest to banker Frederic J. Weymar, a close Vesco associate, in exchange for the stock of a new bank, Bahamas Commonwealth Bank. Its major assets were its grand name and a dubious loan portfolio.

Weymar, who was then appointed International Bancorp's president, was well versed in the complexities of international banking. A former chairman of Bache & Co.'s German subsidiary, he had been asked to resign in 1968 on grounds of poor management. Soon after, he joined Butlers Bank in Nassau.

How Weymar acquired Bahamas Commonwealth Bank was not disclosed to IOS stockholders, but the information would hardly have reassured them. According to the SEC, Weymar had purchased the banking shell from Butlers Bank only days before International Bancorp's creation. He paid a total of $1.8 million for the shell—Bahamas Commonwealth's initial capitalization—but only $300,000 was in cash, the remainder in promissory notes. He then exchanged the Bahamas Commonwealth paper for International Bancorp equity listed on its books at roughly $5 million.

Weymar brought with him from Butlers Bank a loan portfolio of an unstated amount, which included a mortgage of "a couple of hundred thousand" dollars to Lynden Pindling, Prime Minister of the Bahamas, and another to Paradise Bakeries, a Bahamian bakery owned by Pindling's relatives. Other loans soon extended by Bahamas Commonwealth included $100,000 to Richard Clay, a director of the new bank, for the purchase of a house in New Jersey. IOS Director James Roosevelt borrowed $150,000, collateralized in part by a collection of his father's memorabilia.

A NIGHT IN A GENEVA JAIL

At the end of November 1971, Vesco flew back to Geneva to appear before the dean of the city's examining magistrates, Judge Robert Pagan, in a criminal action against him, Meissner, and Ulrich Strickler, a Swiss management consultant. The complaint, by former IOS sales manager David Tucker, alleged that Vesco and the others had illegally removed 56,000 IOS Ltd. preferred shares from Tucker's account at Overseas Development Bank in Geneva and sold them to the same Canadian subsidiary of International Controls that held the Cornfeld stock. This incident was alleged to have taken place four days before the 1971 annual meeting in Toronto, so that Vesco could vote the shares.

It had been Tucker's misfortune to have a large-dollar loan outstanding at Overseas Development Bank, the IOS bank in Geneva, collateralized by his stock. Although Tucker was making regular payments on the loan, his stock was "inadvertently" included among 135,000 shares that Vesco and Strickler, on a visit to the bank the Saturday before the annual meeting, had removed from the vaults.

Tucker, informed that his collateral had been sold that same Saturday afternoon at 22 cents a share, threatened to report this "theft" to the Geneva police. Realizing that perhaps the boundaries of legality had been overstepped, Vesco ordered the Tucker sale rescinded and the shares returned in time for Tucker to vote them at the Toronto meeting. Nevertheless, two weeks later Tucker brought suit in Geneva, alleging improper business conduct, fraud, and attempted embezzlement.

In the investigative hearings that followed, Judge Pagan concentrated on the fact that Vesco and Strickler, with the support of Meissner, had physically removed the 135,000 shares, Tucker's included, when the bank was closed for business. For about two hours Vesco tried to impress upon the crusty old judge his importance, his international connections, and the value of his time. An exasperated Pagan finally signaled for a *gendarme,* turned to Vesco, and ordered him arrested. Vesco could not believe his ears. A bail hearing was set for the following afternoon. Meanwhile the three executives were doomed to spend the night in Geneva's almost medieval St. Antoine Prison.

The news spread shock and consternation among the remaining IOS troops—there were then still about 700 in the Geneva area, down from a pre-crisis high of about 2,600. The next day the prosecutor agreed to the three men's release on $175,000 bail.

The Boeing, with the boss aboard, left Geneva the following day, never to return. Meissner moved to France and for months ran IOS from a hotel room in the gambling resort of Divonne-les-Bains. Strickler was transferred to Munich, also out of Judge Pagan's reach.

Tucker was induced to drop his complaint by a high-powered team of lawyers imported from Washington and New York. This left the door open for the prosecutor to close the file and refund the bail money. Which is what happened, three months later.

Vesco soon changed his plans for a restructured IOS. The $5 million loan from International Controls was repaid. And in accordance with the loan agreement, IOS issued six million common shares to an International Controls subsidiary as a premium for having provided the "emergency" financing. This boosted the Vesco group's share of IOS to 38%—just in time for the second spinoff. This time most of IOS's insurance operations and substantially all of IOS Real Estate Holdings Ltd. were transferred to another newly formed Bahamian shell company, Value Capital Ltd.

Meissner stated that the assets handed over to Value Capital had a book value of $1.3 million. In return, 62% of Value Capital's stock went to IOS shareholders as a pro rata dividend. The rest was distributed to International Controls. Four days later the same assets were written up in Value Capital's books to $20.8 million. The auditors, now concerned, refused to endorse this extraordinary piece of accounting.

Almost ignored in the year-end excitement was a letter IOS sent out to its estimated 300,000 remaining fund holders under the IOS Investment Program. They were informed that "certain procedural changes" would affect future payments into their investment accounts. The first was a shift in the custody of cash for the major IOS dollar funds from Credit Suisse, Zurich, to Overseas Development Bank, Luxembourg.

A new Swiss law had been rushed into force earlier that year prohibiting the solicitation of sales by non-registered investment companies either inside Switzerland or from a Swiss base. Since IOS could not meet the stringent registration requirements, the company was forced to remove all client-oriented functions from Switzerland. Only the Netherlands seemed to offer the right degree of regulatory tolerance. The "dear clients" were therefore told to make their future checks or bank drafts payable to ODB Luxembourg and send them to a post office box in

Amsterdam. IOS still received an estimated $1 million monthly from existing contractual plan clients. Payments mailed to the box were transferred to a floating account at ODB Luxembourg.

Next, the custody of securities owned by the IOS funds was switched from the irreproachable Bank of New York to a bank one-fifth its size —Vesco's long-time New Jersey banker, American National Bank & Trust. The bank had previously acted as registrar and transfer agent for International Controls' common stock. And its senior vice president, Wilbert Snipes, had been a director of International Controls since 1966.

With the creation of a new offshore combine from the ruins of IOS well under way, Vesco resigned from the hot seat in Geneva, hoping to remove himself from the SEC's gaze. On April Fools' Day 1972, International Controls announced that a Bahamian company, Kilmorey Investments Ltd., had purchased International Controls' 38% interest in IOS Ltd. The four owners of Kilmorey were close Vesco associates and members of IOS management. LeBlanc, Meissner, Strickler, and Stanley Graze, the IOS fund manager, ostensibly paid $2.8 million in cash and notes for the 23.6 million IOS common and preferred shares held by two International Controls subsidiaries. But this was never substantiated, the SEC later alleged in its complaint.

International Controls was left with its 22% interest in International Bancorp and 38% interest in Value Capital. But storm warnings were still flying in Washington. So last June 1, LeBlanc resigned from IOS and sold his shares in Kilmorey "at a profit" to Ulrich Strickler. During the next two days LeBlanc went through a series of financial gyrations that enabled him, for a total cash outlay of only $2,000, to acquire a controlling interest in the most valuable pieces of the former IOS empire—an enterprise that three years previously had valued its stockholders' investment at almost $100 million. And he did not assume any of the liabilities of IOS itself.

For $1,000 each, LeBlanc bought two empty shell corporations, Global Holdings Ltd. and its operating subsidiary, Global Financial Ltd., both based in Nassau. The same day Global Financial issued its note to

International Controls for $7.35 million, the announced purchase price for the two former IOS properties. It then took title to International Controls' share of Value Capital and International Bancorp.

At the ICC board meeting the day before, Vesco had assured the directors that LeBlanc's offer was fair, that LeBlanc would honor his obligation, and that there was absolutely no connection between himself and LeBlanc. The board had little choice. No other purchaser was on the horizon and the company urgently needed the injection of new income to bring color back into its paling balance sheet. With sales sagging to around $70 million, ICC was operating at a loss.

Also as fast as possible, $20 million was diverted from IOS's Venture Fund (International) and invested in the two LeBlanc dummy corporations. This represented more than 40% of Venture Fund's assets, so the diversion severely restricted the redeemability of the fund's shares. No sooner had the Venture money come into the two Globals than LeBlanc paid off the full $7.35 million note, permitting International Controls to claim a profit of $1.7 million on its 17-month IOS investment.

TROUBLE IN THE BOARDROOM

Although not externally visible, a split had developed inside the International Controls boardroom. Vesco, under pressure, resigned as chairman "to clear his skirts with the SEC." Before long, though, he came back on the board. His $120,000-a-year employment contract was altered to read "consultant," but he kept the same substantial perks— liberal expense accounts, jet plane, limousine, legal indemnification, office, and free lodgings.

With International Controls clear of the IOS wreckage, what the SEC called the final phase of Vesco's two-year-old pursuit—the looting of the funds—began in earnest. This operation, until interrupted by the SEC, netted some $235 million (roughly half their combined assets) and another $135 million from a closed-end investment company— whose assets had been dumped into a mystery Bahamian corporation,

Property Resources Ltd., of which Clay and LeBlanc were directors. At least $110 million of the "misappropriated" cash has never been accounted for, according to the SEC. The SEC was able, however, to trace a $1 million loan from Fund of Funds to Conservative Capital Ltd. Conservative's sole asset was a flooded Quebec gold mine that hadn't been worked since 1960.

PLANNING A FINANCIAL HAVEN

Vesco was spending much of his time in San Jose, the capital of Costa Rica, negotiating permission to establish an international free zone that would transform the country into the world's newest haven for flight capital. The zone would consist of a financial and business district and one or more residential areas administered by a seven-member council appointed by a board of governors. Under the proposed charter, Costa Rican nationals would be excluded from working or residing in the zone except by permission of the council.

President Jose Figueres's parliamentary opponents vigorously attacked the plan, fearing that the zone would become a base for financial piracy. Figueres had defended the project, claiming it would bring in healthy new capital and assist in economic and social development.

As part of the intended relocation, crateloads of office furniture were shipped from IOS's unused offices in France to San Jose. When critics in Parliament asked why Vesco's jet had been permitted to offload cases of goods at San Jose's international airport without customs clearance, Figueres later replied that the cargo was only "toys for poor children."

IOS was on the brink of insolvency last October when its sale for $5.7 million to a group of Spanish grandees fell through. The Spaniards were said to be fronting for Alberto Alvarez, the Cuban exile associated with Costa Rican President Figueres, but they had second thoughts because of the SEC action. Meanwhile, IOS management suspended redemptions of shares in the dollar mutual funds. Canadian and Luxembourg authorities also froze the assets of IIT pending the outcome of this month's trial.

VESCO'S COSTA RICAN MONTICELLO

Last December a group of "independent" directors attempted to pry loose IOS's seven closely regulated Canadian funds, with assets of $210 million. A controlling interest in the London-based insurance operation, International Life Insurance Co. (U.K.) Ltd., was sold to Keyser Ullman Ltd., the British merchant-banking group, before the end of the year. IOS's only remaining assets were its ten million shares of Transglobal Financial Services, largely tied up in litigation, and some attached real estate in Geneva and France. Its liabilities included a collection of some 250 lawsuits around the world.

Vesco has spoken publicly only through lawyers. He denied any wrongdoing, and contended that he does not control IOS, the funds, or the men who run them. Privately, he told neighbors that he intends to move his family to San Jose. Vesco has already rented a three-story suburban mansion that for 20 years had been the residence of U.S. ambassadors to Costa Rica. Set in an imposing park, the house is a copy of Monticello.

In spite of such trimmings, San Jose—a little city with narrow, noisy streets, no stock market, and less than a dozen banks—is a world away from Wall Street, the City of London, and the financial centers of Switzerland where Vesco had hoped so ardently to be accepted.

He wanted to get there too fast. Had he taken his time, offshore regulation being what it was, he might have succeeded. Georges Carlweiss, a Geneva banker whom Vesco once gave as a reference, has observed: "Finance can be like driving a car. If you drive slowly and have an accident, it's not likely to be very serious. But if you miss a bend at 220 kmph and shoot off the road, it's pretty damn near certain to be fatal." Vesco, Carlweiss added, had been driving dangerously fast for a very long time.

◆

AFTERMATH

After fleeing to Costa Rica in 1973, Vesco spent roughly the next ten years there and in the Bahamas, Nicaragua, and Antigua. Despite the ambiguity of his legal status, he stayed true to his lavish lifestyle. He kept his Boeing 707, equipped with a dining room, mahogany conference table, and sauna. The piece de resistance was a discotheque, complete with dance floor and strobe lights.

By 1982, Vesco felt U.S. pressure bearing down, and he went to Cuba, where Fidel Castro agreed to harbor him from the Yanqui oppressors. The Cubans, thinking they had an accomplished business mind in their midst, asked Vesco to help turn Cayo Largo island into a tourism center. But the project didn't get very far, in part beause Vesco began charging exorbitant personal bills. There were also reports that he had become involved in drug trafficking.

In 1995, Vesco's situation unraveled when Cuban authorities charged him with "fraud and illicit activity" in connection with the marketing of a drug that supposedly cured cancer. Vesco was sentenced to 13 years in prison, and vanished from sight. The former enforcement director of the Securities Exchange Commission, Stanley Sporkin, commented during this period, "In a way, he has given himself a life sentence. He is probably getting a greater sentence now than if he had stayed in the United States. If he had stayed, he would be free now, back home." The SEC's case against Vesco remained open.

In May 2008, reports surfaced that he had died of lung cancer the previous November.

BAD DEALS

6

THE INCREDIBLE
ELECTRICAL CONSPIRACY

---

by RICHARD AUSTIN SMITH
April and May 1961

Some corporate sins are easy to understand—the result of a moment of temptation, or a bad apple or two gone rotten. Other cases are harder to fathom. How, for example, could dozens of skilled professionals from 29 companies convince themselves that they weren't doing anything wrong when they were meeting secretly, under false names, to fix prices and rig bids? And how could this go on for the better part of a decade? As the Justice Department's head of antitrust put it at the time, "These men and companies have in a true sense mocked the image of that economic system which we profess to the world." In a two-part series, FORTUNE detailed the story behind the story of what was then the biggest criminal case in the history of the Sherman Act. What follows is a combined and condensed version of those articles.

In a Philadelphia federal court in February 1961, the great price-fixing conspiracy in the electrical-equipment industry came to a climax with jail sentences for seven executives and fines of nearly $2 million levied against 29 corporations. Behind us now are the ruinous days of the 1954-55 "white sale," the bitter meetings, the regimen of concealment. Ahead is exposure. Here is the story of how the Antitrust Division broke the case and what went on at General Electric from the time a principal conspirator realized the game was up until the corporation threw in its hand 14 months later.

Shortly before ten o'clock on the morning of September 28, 1959, an urgent long-distance call came in to GE's transformer division at Pittsfield, Mass. It was for Edward L. Dobbins, the divisional lawyer, and the person on the line was another attorney, representing Lapp Insulator Co. He just wanted to say that one of Lapp's officers had been subpoenaed by a Philadelphia grand jury and was going to tell the whole story. "What story?" asked Dobbins pleasantly, then listened to an account that sent him, filled with concern, into the office of the division vice president, Raymond W. Smith.

At that time, Smith was a big man in GE, veteran of 28 years with the corporation, and one of President Robert Paxton's closest friends; he was also a big man in Pittsfield, where the transformer division employs 6,000 people out of a population of 57,000, director of a local bank, active member of the hospital building board. Smith heard Dobbins out, his six-foot-five frame suddenly taut in the swivel chair and a furrow deepening on his forehead; he got up and began pacing back and forth. "It's bad," he said, "very bad." Then he added, shaking his head grimly, "You just don't know how bad it is!"

The story Dobbins heard was that Paul Hartig, one of Ray Smith's departmental general managers, had been conspiring with Lapp Insulator and a half-dozen other manufacturers to fix prices on insulators. Such news was unsettling enough to any boss, but Smith's alarm had its roots in something deeper than the derelictions of a subordinate. He was himself "Mr. Big" of another cartel, one involving

$210 million worth of transformers a year, and he didn't need the gift of prescience to sense the danger. Smith concluded that he had no choice but to report the trouble to Arthur Vinson, vice president of the apparatus group, in New York.

By coincidence, GE Chairman Ralph Cordiner showed up in Pittsfield the next day. He had come, ironically enough, to hear an account of the new market approach by which the transformer division expected to beat the ears off the competition. GE had worked out a method of cutting the formidable costs of custom-made transformers by putting them together from standard components. Told of Hartig's involvement in the insulator cartel, Cordiner reacted with shock and anger.

Up until then he had reason to think his general managers were making "earnest efforts" to comply with both the spirit and the letter of the antitrust laws. Upon becoming president of GE in 1950, Cordiner had decentralized the conglomerate's management. This philosophy was new; at the same time, Cordiner specifically prohibited meeting with competitors on prices, bids, or market shares.

That needed to be said. Though it was company policy under something called General Instruction 2.35 to "conform strictly to the antitrust laws," GE's behavior had not always been so forthright. In 1947, less than a year after lawyers toured the company to put everyone on notice that it was illegal to discuss prices with competitors, GE officials quietly rejoined the cartel in the transformers industry. "Word came down to start contacting competitors again," recalls Clarence Burke, an executive in the heavy-equipment division. "We were cautioned at this time not to tell the lawyers what we were doing and to cover our trails in our expense-account reports."

Burke's division was hardly alone. In the decade from 1940-50, GE had been involved in 13 antitrust cases, the offenses ranging from production limitations and patent pooling to price fixing and division of markets. Moreover, there was a powerful school of thought within the company that didn't see a problem with any of this. Though senior executives were required to initial the company's antitrust directives, for many this was simply a matter of form. "When anybody raised a question about that," says Burke, "they would be told it doesn't apply now."

This collusionist school held that competition, particularly price competition, was for the birds. Getting together with competitors was looked on as a way of life. It was considered easier to negotiate market percentages than fight for one's share, less wearing to take turns on rigged bids than pay the rugged individualist. Admittedly, all of them knew they were breaking the law—Section 1 of the Sherman Act is as explicit as a traffic ordinance. Their justification was on other grounds. "Sure, collusion was illegal," explained an old GE hand, "but it wasn't *unethical.*" There can be no doubt that the collusionists' influence was formidable and pervasive, even after Cordiner sent out company Directive 20.5 in 1954, restating GE's position on antitrust.

It was no wonder, then, that Cordiner was upset by what he heard about the insulator department. And this was only the beginning. GE's general counsel, Ray Luebbe, was brought into the case, and within a matter of days Paul Hartig was in Luebbe's New York office implicating Vice President Ray Smith. Smith made a clean breast of things, detailing the operation of the transformer cartel. The essentials: Bids on government contracts were rotated to ensure that GE and Westinghouse each got 30% of the business, the remaining 40% being split among four other manufacturers; book prices were agreed upon at meetings held everywhere from Chicago's Drake Hotel to the Homestead at Hot Springs, Va.; secrecy was safeguarded by channeling all phone calls and mail to the homes, and destroying written memoranda upon receipt. Then Smith implicated a second GE vice president, 41-year-old William S. Ginn, head of the turbine division, as an important man in two cartels—one in transformers and one in turbine generators. The corporation was thus plainly implicated in four cartels.

The Justice Department was also looking for answers. The tactics of the Antitrust Division, led by Robert A. Bicks, were based on using the Philadelphia grand jury to subpoena documents, and then, after study of these, to subpoena individuals—the corporation executives who would logically have been involved if a conspiracy existed. The ultimate objective was to determine whether the biggest electrical manufacturers and their top executives had participated in a cartel, but the approach had to be oblique. As William Maher, head of the division's Philadelphia office, put it: "The idea is to go after the biggest fish in the smallest companies, then hope to get enough information to land the biggest fish in the biggest companies."

In mid-November a second Philadelphia grand jury was empaneled, and Justice Department attorneys began ringing doorbells across the land. As the trust busters took more testimony, the industry grew apprehensive. The grapevine, probably the most sensitive in American business, began to shiver with talk that the feds were onto something—and that jail impended for the guilty.

Back at GE, Cordiner had issued instructions that all apparatus general managers were to be interviewed by company attorneys about participation in cartels. Most of the guilty lied, gambling that the exposures would not go any further. Cordiner, accepting their stories, began to formulate GE's defense. It would have two principal salients. First, the company itself was not guilty of the conspiracies; what had occurred was without the encouragement or even the knowledge of the chairman, the president, and the executive office. GE's corporate position on antitrust compliance was a matter of record, embodied in Directive 20.5. Second, those employees who had violated Directive 20.5 were in for corporate punishment. "Stale offenses" were not to be counted, but a three-year company "statute of limitations" would govern liability (the federal limitation: five years).

Punishment of necessity had to go hand in hand with a corporate not-guilty stance. If GE's defense was to be that the conspiracies had taken place in contravention of written policy (Directive 20.5), then unpunished offenders would be walking proof to a jury that 20.5 was just a scrap of paper. On the other hand, here was a clear management failure to detect over almost a decade the cartels that were an open secret. As GE was to learn, lots of people who approved of punishment for the offenders did not think this permitted GE to wash its hands of responsibility. Westinghouse's president, Mark W. Cresap Jr., spoke for many executives both inside the industry and out when he stated his position in January 1961: "Corporate punishment of these people ... would only be self-serving on my part ... this is a management failure." Aside from the moral question, the legal basis of GE's not-guilty stance was shaky. Distinguishing between an "innocent" corporation and its "guilty" executives would be tough, for Cordiner himself had given the general managers clear pricing powers.

The Cordiner position had another weakness: It was based on the assumption that GE was involved in, at most, four cartels. Thus when wider involvement came to light—the four cartels multiplied into 19 and accounted for more than 10% of GE's total sales—the company found itself in the ludicrous position of continuing to proclaim its corporate innocence while its executives were being implicated by platoons.

INSIDE THE SWITCHGEAR CARTEL

All cartels are not alike; to get a broad sense of what one looks like, here is a close look at on the most important and long-lived versions.

In 1951, George Burens became the new boss of the switchgear operation. Burens had started out at GE as a laborer; he had the additional disadvantage of being a junior-high-school man in a corporate world full of college men, but during the next 30 years he had steadily risen by sheer competitive spirit. "He had grown up hating competitors" was the way a colleague put it. "They were the enemy." So it was more than a little ironic that his new job put him in charge of the division with probably the oldest conspiracy then extant. The conspiracy was in circuit breakers, and it had been operative over the span of a quarter-century.

Reporting to Burens from this division was Clarence Burke, who got the job when his predecessor made the mistake of taking General Instruction 2.35 at its word, and therefore refused to talk with competitors. "I had no objections," said Burke. He had persuaded himself that what he was doing in defiance of the letter of the antitrust directive was not done in defiance of its spirit.

Burens arrived on the scene in September 1951 and busied himself with splitting switchgear into three independent companies (high, medium, and low voltage), each with a general manager and himself as GM of the entire division. He was content for a time to let his new departmental GMs, including Burke, run the conspiracy. And some conspiracy it was.

Some $650 million in sales was involved, according to Justice Department estimates, from 1951 through 1958, and broken down into sealed- and open-bid categories. The sealed bids ($15 million to $18 million a year) were done with public agencies; the goal was to rotate that business on a fixed-percentage basis among the four participating companies, who represented all the circuit-breaker manufacturers in the U.S. GE got 45% of the business; Westinghouse 35%, Allis-Chalmers 10%, and Federal Pacific 10%. Every ten days to two weeks, there were meetings to decide whose turn was next. This was determined by the "ledger list," a table of who had got what in recent weeks; after that, the only thing left to decide was the price that the company picked to "win" would submit as the lowest bid.

Above this group was another whose purpose was to maintain the book prices and market shares in the private-sector market ($55 million to $60 million a year). A different executive would have the "duty" over each 30-day period. His job was to initiate a weekly intercompany memo detailing the jobs coming up that week, the book price each company was setting, and comments on the general level of equipment prices.

The two conspiracies had their own lingo and their own procedures. The attendance list was known as the "Christmas-card list," meetings as "choir practices." Companies had code numbers—GE was 1, Westinghouse 2, Allis-Chalmers 3, and Federal 7—which were used when calling a conspirator at home for price information. ("This is Bob. What is 7's bid?") At the hotel meetings, the conspirators did not list their company name when registering and did not eat breakfast with each other. The GE men observed two more precautions: never to be the ones who kept the records, and never to tell GE's laywers anything.

But things were not always smooth even inside this well-oiled machine, for the conspirators had no more compunction at breaking the rules of the conspiracy than at breaching the Sherman Act. One of the many ironies of the whole affair is that the conspiracy couldn't entirely suppress the competitive instinct. Every so often some company would decide that cutthroat competition outside was preferable to the throat-cutting that went on in the cartel; they would sit out the conspiracy for a couple of years.

In May 1953, for example, Clarence Burke took GE out of the high-voltage switchgear cartel. "No one was living up the agreements, and we at GE were being made suckers," he says. The GE boycott continued through 1954; even so, the three remaining cartel members would tell GE the prices they had decided on and express the heartfelt hope the company would honor them—which it did, pretty much.

This was the situation in mid-September 1954, when President Ralph Cordiner issued Directive 20.5, which blanketed the subject of antitrust with every conceivable admonition. Despite what was happening all around him, Cordiner probably meant every word of it. No corroborated evidence has ever come to light that he knew of GE's various cartels and conspiracies; quite the opposite. As Burke put it, "Cordiner was sincere but undersold by people beneath him who rescinded his orders."

The industry had a bad year in 1954, and when Westinghouse beat GE out of a big turbine order, Robert Paxton, executive vice president for industrial products, swore it would not happen again. Thus, when the next big job came along, GE was determined not to be underbid. Westinghouse and others wanted the job, too, and the price breaks came so fast it was difficult to keep track of them; one day the price was 10% off book, the next 20%, finally 40%. So began the celebrated "white sale" of 1954-55. Before it was over, the electrical industry was discounting prices as much as 40% to 45% off book.

GE, with its broad product lines, was not hit as hard by the white sale as some smaller companies, but it was just as anxious to call a halt. The word went out from headquarters that prices had to be got back up, and stability restored.

At the switchgear division, the pressure was so great that George Burens, the lifelong believer in tough competition, underwent a remarkable conversion. He decided to crank up the old cartel. By January 1956, GE, Westinghouse, Allis-Chambers, and I-T-E were back in business. Every month, one company conspirator would write a memo to the others, listing every pending job and stating the calculated book price. Then the conspirators would reassemble and compare calculations to forestall any chiseling. There were nine such meetings in 1956, held in various hotel suites. Into early 1957, the arrangement worked well.

Then, as usual, it cracked. Westinghouse tried to make a private deal with Florida Power & Light; when GE heard about the offier, it broke ranks. With the big guys cutting their own deals, Allis-Chalmers offered Potomoc Electric 12% off and Westinghouse 20% off to Atlantic City Electric, and it was the bad old days of the white sale all over again. In the winter of 1957-58, recalls Burke, "prices were 60% off book." That was the end of that cartel.

It did not, of course, mean the end of the other conspiracies GE was involved in. Far from it. Each general manager of a division or department took a strictly personal view of his participation in any cartel. Thus while circuit breakers was at daggers drawn, industrial controls was enjoying an amiable conspiracy. Power transformers and turbine generators were going nicely, too. Even the circuit-breaker-switchgear conspiracy started up again in 1958. Burens resisted getting back into this particular rat race, but the pressure—from both the market and from within the company—was too great. It took ten hours of angry argument, but eventually GE agreed to a 40.3% share of the public-sector business; Westinghouse, 31.3%; Allis-Chalmers, 8.8%; I-T-E, 4%, and Federal Pacific, 15.6%.

So began the final circuit-breaker cartel, born in recrimination and continued in mistrust. Nine months later, Edward Dobbins got that life-changing long-distance call.

THE AX FALLS

This, then, is the context in which GE was working when it decided how to deal with the government's charges. GE's posture was officially established in November 1959, and management moved to put it into effect. Ray Smith was told he was going to be punished. He forfeited his job and his title too. There was a spot for him abroad, at substantially less money, if he wanted to try to rebuild his career. Smith, 54, decided to take his severance pay and resign.

It was probably a wise move. Those conspirators who didn't quit had a very rough go of it. Initial punishment (demotion, transfer, pay cuts) was eventually followed by forced resignation. But the extra gall in the punishment was the inequality of treatment. William Ginn had been implicated at the same time as Ray Smith, and his case fell well within GE's statute of limitations. Yet he was allowed to continue in his $135,000 job as vice president of the turbine division—until he went off to jail for that conspiracy, loaded with the biggest fine ($12,500) of any defendant.

Widespread resentment over this curious partiality to Ginn and over the meting out of discipline generally was destined to have its effect: Willing GE witnesses soon began to turn up at the trust-busters' camp; among them was an angry Ray Smith, who claimed he had been acting on orders from above. His mood, as a government attorney described it, was that of a man whose boss had said: "I can't get you a raise, so why don't you just take $5 out of petty cash every week. Then the man gets fired for it and the boss does nothing to help him out."

There was, however, an interval of some three months between Smith's resignation in November and his appearance in Philadelphia with his story. And eventful months they were. The first grand jury was looking into conspiracies in insulators, switchgear, circuit breakers, and several other products. The second grand jury was hearing four transformer cases and one on industrial controls. With a score of

Justice men working on them, cases proliferated, and from December on lawyers began popping up trying to get immunity for their clients in return for testimony. But what Bicks and company still needed was decisive data that would break a case wide open. In January 1960, the trust busters hit the jackpot in switchgear.

The breakthrough came via a blond young man named Nye Spencer, I-T-E Circuit Breaker's sales manager for switchgear. When antitrust investigators came calling, armed with subpoenas, he had decided he wasn't about to commit another crime by destroying the records so carefully laid away in his cellar.

There were pages on pages of notes taken during sessions of the switchgear conspiracy—incriminating entries like "Potomac Light & Power O.K. for E" and "Before bidding on this, check with GE"; neat copies of the ground rules for meetings of the conspirators: no breakfasting together, no registering at the hotel with company names, no calls to the office, no papers to be left in hotel-room waste-baskets. Spencer, it seems, had been instructed to handle some of the secretarial work of the cartel and believed in doing it right; he'd hung onto the documents to help in training an assistant. But the most valuable windfall from the meticulous record keeper was a pile of copies of the "phases of the moon" pricing formula going as far back as May 1958.

Not much to look at—just sheets of paper, each containing a half-dozen columns of figures—but they immediately resolved the enigma of switchgear prices in commercial contracts. One group of columns established the bidding order of the seven switchgear manufacturers— a different company, each with its own code number, phasing into the priority position every two weeks (hence "phases of the moon"). A second group of columns, keyed into the company code numbers, established how much each company was to knock off the agreed-upon book price. For example, if it was No. 1's (GE's) turn to be low bidder at a certain number of dollars off book, then all Westinghouse (No. 2) or Allis-Chalmers (No. 3) had to do was look for their code number in the second group of columns to find how many dollars they were to bid above No. 1. These bids would then be fuzzed up by having a little added to them or taken away by companies 2, 3, etc. Thus there was not even a hint that the winning bid had been collusively arrived at.

With this little device in hand, the trust busters found they could light up the whole conspiracy like a switchboard. The new evidence made an equally profound impression on the grand juries. On February 16 and 17, 1960, they handed down the first seven indictments. Forty companies and 18 individuals were charged with fixing prices or dividing the market on seven electrical products. Switchgear led the list.

These initial indictments brought about two major turning points in the investigation. The first was a decision by Allis-Chalmers to play ball with the government; it turned over thousands of documents. Further, the testimony of Vice President J. W. McMullen, and others was so helpful that a number of new cases opened up. The Justice Department added five new major indictments—power transformers, power switching equipment, industrial controls, turbine generators, and steam condensers.

The second major turning point came through a decision in March by Chief Federal Judge J. Cullen Ganey, who was to try all the cases, that the corporations and individuals would either have to plead guilty or stand trial; he would not accept pleas of no contest. At the arraignment in April, Allis-Chalmers and its indicted employees promptly pleaded "guilty"; most others, including GE and its employees, pleaded "not guilty." They intended to take their chances before a jury.

Around the time of Judge Ganey's decision, Bicks and company got what seemed to be another windfall—a link to the very top of GE. Vice President George Burens, head of GE's switchgear division, and his three departmental general managers (Clarence Burke, H. F. Hentschel, and Frank Stehlik)—all of whom had been indicted that February—trooped down to Washington and claimed the government had missed the key man: their boss, Group Executive Arthur Vinson. Their story was a clear-cut account, with few of the ambiguities the Justice Department had come to expect from GE witnesses. (Indeed, a story of such circumspection making the rounds concerned a GE employee who told his boss that he intended to go to Canada on vacation. Said the boss: "I am told you will have a good time.") Vinson, the four said, had authorized them to rejoin a price-fixing conspiracy in the third quarter of 1958. Antitrust was fascinated.

The story, as Clarence Burke told it, began with a 1958 visit by Vinson to the Philadelphia works. Burens had been under heavy fire from other apparatus general managers, who said his cut-rate switchgear prices were bringing complaints from their customers, who considered they should be getting similar discounts on other GE equipment. Now, according to Burke, Vinson himself was taking up the cudgels to get a reluctant Burens to raise switchgear prices by reactivating the cartel.

Burke's best recollection was that the Vinson order occurred between the end of July and September 13, 1958. In independent testimony, Burens set it in August or September; Stehlik, between mid-August and October; Hentschel, the latter part of August. The dates fit in nicely with another story, this one from Ray Smith, of a top-level Boston meeting in June where Westinghouse and GE had allegedly decided to bury the hatchet and get together again on prices.

As a result of this information, Vinson was indicted. Clarence Burke's name was dropped from the new switchgear indictment in consideration of his testimony against Vinson, although he continued to be charged for conspiracy in circuit breakers. Then a few weeks later the government chestily filed a Voluntary Bill of Particulars, which included Cordiner, Paxton, and the board of directors among those charged with the illegal switchgear actions. GE lawyers realized that if Vinson went down, their whole corporate defense—that there had been no authorization—would collapse. Now that the government had particularized the time, place, and individuals, all Vinson had to do was prove he'd never been in Philadelphia during July, August, and September of 1958.

The Vinson case had a vital bearing on how GE would plead on its own indictments, but the issue was also important to the other corporate defendants. The one thing nobody wanted was a trial where the dirty linen of the conspiracies would be washed in public. If one company, or even an employee of one company, chose to stand trial, everyone else might just as well too, for all the juicy details would surely come out. But the problem of settling the case without trial was complicated by the fact that the companies involved were of different sizes and degrees of guilt.

GE and Westinghouse, however, were both convinced that rapid settlement was essential. GE's own hopes of a successful not-guilty plea had been trampled under the parade of grand-jury witnesses. Moreover, Bicks and company still had the grand juries going full blast; any delay in settling might dump a half-dozen additional indictments on top of the 20 already handed up.

On October 31, the lawyers of almost all the affected companies crowded into a Justice Department conference room and from nine in the morning till seven that night worked at hammering out a package of guilty and nolo pleas. On 13 "minor" cases, where only corporations had been indicted, Bicks was willing to accept nolos, but he insisted on guilty pleas in the seven major cases. And he wanted pleas on all 20 indictments at the same time. One thing stood in the way of the package deal: GE's insistence on trial or dismissal of the Vinson indictment in switchgear, a major case.

Early the next month Vinson himself made a move that for cool nerve commanded the respect of even Justice Department attorneys. He offered to let the government see the evidence supporting his alibi. Thus the curtain rose on one of the strangest incidents of the whole affair.

EIGHT FATEFUL DAYS

There were only eight days in July, August, and September, Vinson's attorneys said, that Burens, Burke, Hentschel, and Stehlik were all at the plant between the hours of eleven and one. For those eight days, they continued, his expense accounts showed no Philadelphia trip, and Vinson was a man who put the smallest items on that account. There was no entry in the company-plane log showing a Philadelphia flight for Vinson, nor any such entry in the executive-limousine log. On one of the eight days the head of a fund-raising committee at Michigan State had a toll slip on a telephone call to Vinson in New York at close to noon. On another, a Manhattan banking transaction had been stamped at a late morning hour. And so it went.

Bicks was impressed. The next day the expense-account records of the four (Burens, Burke, Hentschel, and Stehlik) were examined and Bicks made a disquieting discovery. There was no item showing a group luncheon with Vinson. This led Bicks to wonder whether the whole Vinson charge might not be a self-serving fabrication to support a plea of corporate coercion. He summoned the four to Washington, and they volunteered to go through lie-detector tests. All four passed. Still, corroborative evidence, not lie-detector tests, was needed to demolish the Vinson alibi. The government assigned a score of agents to that job.

As the weeks ticked off, FBI men poked Vinson's picture at Philadelphia cab drivers to see if anyone remembered driving him to the switchgear plant, examined notebooks for erasures, interviewed scores of individuals. Nothing. Bicks decided to drop the charges.

So the curtain rang down on the Vinson case, and then went up on the last act of the drama. With Vinson's involvement no longer at issue, GE pleaded "guilty" to all the major indictments against it, and with the government's consent, nolo contendere to the 13 lesser ones. The other major companies followed suit. The way thus cleared, judgment was swift. On February 6, executives from every major manufacturer in the entire electrical-equipment industry sat in a crowded courtroom and heard Judge Ganey declare: "What is really at stake here is the survival of the kind of economy under which this country has grown great, the free-enterprise system." Seven executives went off to a Pennsylvania prison; 23 others, given suspended jail sentences, were put on probation for five years; and 29 companies received a total of nearly $2 million in fines, ranging from $437,500 for GE down to $7,500 each for Carrier Corp. and Porcelain Insulator Corp.

So ended the incredible affair—a story of cynicism, arrogance, and irresponsibility. Plainly there was an egregious management failure. But there was also a failure to connect ordinary morals and business morals; the men involved apparently figured there was a difference.

◆

AFTERMATH

Most of the men who pleaded guilty in Judge Ganey's court (to say nothing of the scores given immunity for testifying before the grand juries) went back to work, holding down key sales and marketing jobs. Only GE cleaned house; out went Ginn, Burens, Burke, Hentschel, and Stehlik, plus ten others. Moreoever, well aware that any repetition of these conspiracies would lay them open to political pressure for dismemberment, Allis-Chalmers, GE, and Westinghouse all set up preventive measures.

In retrospect, the great electrical conspiracy had two effects. First, its discovery and punishment reversed what had been a trend toward the establishment of trusts and cartels over major industries not unlike those that dominated the U.S. economy in the early 20th century. Humiliated and chastened, business largely returned to the idea of competition, not collusion, as the central organizing principle of the economy. Second, it marked a milestone in the emergence of the "compliance culture," a phrase that needs no explanation to any 21st century executive.

7

SOCGEN'S $7.5 BILLION HOLE

---

by PETER GUMBEL

April 16, 2008

Starting in the 1990s, the French bank Société Générale built up a sophisticated in-house trading operation that specialized in derivatives and other complex financial instruments. That operation brought in profits and international accolades for the bank, and it made the bank's irascible CEO, Daniel Bouton, one of the most powerful men in France. Then, in January 2008, Bouton's world suddenly collapsed. Here is how Jérôme Kerviel, a 31-year-old rogue trader, humbled one of France's most distinguished companies—and became a folk hero.

In the early afternoon of Sunday, January 20, Daniel Bouton, the chairman and chief executive of the huge French bank Société Générale, was in his 35th-floor office preparing for a board meeting that evening when one of his lieutenants, Jean-Pierre Mustier, came to break some calamitous news. Mustier, Société Générale's head of investment banking, had already alerted him about a 31-year-old junior trader in the stock arbitrage department named Jérôme Kerviel who had been caught making big unhedged bets on European stock futures.

But it was only now, after auditors had spent two days and nights furiously digging through computer records and Mustier himself had questioned Kerviel, that the bank knew just how big those bets were. Kerviel's open position was a gigantic $75 billion, or almost twice the bank's equity. Société Générale, which Bouton had spent the past 15 years building into one of the most respected and profitable banks in Europe, was suddenly at risk of imploding.

With his 15-member board set to convene in just hours, Bouton, 58, made a stunning decision: He opted, FORTUNE has learned, to tell his full board absolutely nothing about the unfolding scandal.

It was a startling move for an executive who is a French authority on corporate governance and who wrote an official report in 2002 on board transparency and accountability. But it was the first step in a swiftly executed plan that ended up saving Société Générale. By keeping his board in the dark (he did confidentially brief the head of the audit committee that Sunday night) and then handing the task of unwinding Kerviel's positions to a single trader who wasn't even told how much he had to sell, Bouton ensured that word of the crisis wouldn't leak. If it were to, he worried, Société Générale risked provoking a stampede in the markets and among its customers. "We all had Northern Rock in our heads," says an insider, referring to the British financial institution that was brought to its knees last year by panicky customers queuing up to withdraw their savings.

THREE FRENZIED DAYS

Over a frenzied three-day period Bouton and his tiny team shed Kerviel's entire position and at the same time persuaded two U.S. investment banks to guarantee $8.5 billion in new capital. On Wednesday, January 23, only after he had shored up Société Générale, Bouton called an emergency meeting of the board, where he finally disclosed the immensity of Kerviel's position and the very costly steps he had taken to pull the bank back from the brink. Bouton, who declined to comment for this article, would later tell *Le Monde* that when he first heard about the size of the bank's exposure, he had a vision of an aircraft carrier about to sink.

In some places this salvage effort would have turned Bouton into a local hero. Yes, it was imperious and high-handed, much like Bouton himself, but it kept Société Générale afloat at an especially fragile time for financial institutions. The world will never know what might have happened if Bouton had gone public with the crisis sooner, but the carnage elsewhere suggests it would have been ugly. The British government had to nationalize Northern Rock to prevent it from collapsing, and most recently Bear Stearns was sold to J.P. Morgan Chase at the behest of U.S. regulators.

Société Générale, by contrast, is in relatively good shape. Its net losses from the affair amount to about $7.5 billion. (Controversially, the bank offset a $10 billion trading loss with some earlier gains Kerviel had made.) Despite the extraordinary Kerviel-related loss, plus an additional $2.5 billion write-down of its exposure to the U.S. subprime crisis, the bank nonetheless reported a profit in 2007; its capital ratios now are even stronger than they were before the crisis, and just three weeks after the scandal it completed the acquisition of a big Russian bank, as scheduled.

Yet instead of earning praise, Bouton has become France's favorite villain. President Nicolas Sarkozy has called for Bouton's head, and several peers in the French banking world believe his days are numbered; at the very least they expect him to give up either his chairman or his CEO role. Most painful of all is public opinion, which holds him and the bank largely responsible for the crisis in the first place, and for which Bouton has become a symbol of the arrogance and snobbery of the French elite.

By contrast, Jérôme Kerviel, the rogue operator who openly admitted to breaking bank rules, has assumed the unlikely role of folk hero—the common man who humbled a haughty institution. (Kerviel even called the subprime crisis correctly, making some smart, albeit unauthorized, trades before erroneously betting on a market rebound.)

What's behind this *Freaky Friday*-like switch in roles? The French have long been skeptical about the workings of capitalism and the ability of markets to bring prosperity to more than a tiny few; former President Jacques Chirac once described free-market liberalism as a scourge as big as communism. Bouton also appears to have become a lightning rod for a much greater disenchantment—even anger—with the French political and business establishment. "It's a pleasure to discover that the elite are not as good as all that," says Frédérik-Karel Canoy, a gadfly French lawyer who represents small Société Générale shareholders. "In France people are sick of these types who came top of the class and know everything."

Bouton didn't help his cause when he publicly lambasted Kerviel as a "terrorist" and declared Société Générale an innocent victim of the trader's machinations. The bank's own internal investigation into the matter shows that Kerviel's supervisors missed, ignored, or didn't take seriously 75 alerts about his trading activities over a period of two years, a damning record that gives credence to the young trader's defense for his actions: His bosses were aware of his trades but largely ignored his activities as long as he was making money.

MODERN-DAY ROBIN HOOD?

Kerviel is charged with breach of trust and forgery (he admits he faked e-mails to cover up losses) but isn't accused of pocketing any money. This absence of greed—coupled with his Tom Cruise-like good looks and his small-town roots—are cementing Kerviel's image as a modern-day Robin Hood.

"Do you even know what 1.5 billion euros looks like?" asks Christophe Reille, a public relations consultant who has taken Kerviel on pro bono as a client. Reille, who looks a bit like Mr. Bean, is partly responsible for the unprecedented rehabilitation of Kerviel's image.

Most other rogue types in financial scandals are cast as bad boys, or they simply try to maintain a low profile. They don't end up, like Kerviel, with photographs in the glossy magazine *Paris Match*. Reille is explaining why Kerviel couldn't possibly have been trading without Société Générale's complicity. "That's three million 500-euro notes. That's as tall as the Eiffel Tower. Do you think it's possible to hide that without anyone seeing?"

A VERY AUTHORITARIAN BOSS

Bouton's grandfather was a railway signalman and his father an engineer, so there was nothing preordained about his rise to the top of the French establishment. But he stood out early on by dint of his intellectual prowess. After winning a prestigious national history competition at the age of 17, he went on to the most elite college in the country, the Ecole Nationale d'Administration, which for decades has turned out France's top politicians and civil servants. He likes to excel at everything he does—his golf handicap got as low as four—and he isn't modest about it.

Gérard Longuet, a former Industry Minister who was a classmate at ENA, describes Bouton as "extremely rigorous." But he adds, "You can debate as to whether he's sympathetic by nature. He gives the impression of being pleased with himself." Bouton has been known to upbraid unpunctual journalists and take potshots at other French companies; he famously trashed media company Vivendi, for example, when it was struggling during the dot-com meltdown.

Despite his contentious personality, Bouton moved swiftly up the ranks of the civil service to become director of the national budget. Senator Michel Charasse, who was France's Budget Minister in the late 1980s, says Bouton has a sense of humor beneath his austere façade, but as a boss "he's very authoritarian." They had one big fight, when Charasse thought one of Bouton's deputies had been insolent and told him to fire her. Bouton refused point-blank, and Charasse says he almost fired them both—before he calmed down and retreated. Bouton was too good to lose, he says.

He was hired away to Société Générale in 1991 by then-CEO Marc Viénot, who groomed him to be his successor. Bouton took over as CEO in 1993 and has bulked up Société Générale and dramatically boosted its profitability since. He has also fought fiercely to preserve its independence; in 1999, Société Générale ended up in a three-way takeover battle with two French rivals, BNP and Paribas, but managed to avoid being acquired. Almost a decade later bad blood still lingers between the banks. People who know Bouton well say the experience was a critical one that helped him deal with the Kerviel crisis. "He was incredibly involved right from the beginning, unlike in 1999," says one friend.

Since then, Société Générale's net banking income has more than doubled, and it has delivered among the best returns to shareholders of any international bank. Bouton has done that by hiring the brightest and the best, and by building up a powerful trading and investment-banking operation that accounted for almost half the bank's profits in 2006. Among the pearls—at least before the scandal—was the bank's derivatives-trading operation, staffed by math whizzes from elite French schools. In other words, risk—precisely calibrated and calculated risk—has become one of the main engines that drives Société Générale's bottom line.

A SORT OF CLASS WAR

Jérôme Kerviel didn't slot into this world seamlessly. He, too, came from a modest background—his father was a metalworker, his mother a hairdresser but his finance degrees from universities in Nantes and Lyon didn't have the same academic heft as those of some of his peers from France's top schools. That sometimes rankled.

"I was much less respected than the others because of my university education and my personal and professional career," he told prosecutors. It's a line that has gotten a lot of attention in France, where his case is sometimes spun as a sort of class war: the little guy trying to prove that he was as good as or better than his intellectual superiors. It is also the one point on which Kerviel's team and Société Générale actually agree: Both say it's utterly wrong. "He doesn't have complexes. He was on the way up, not the way down," says Reille, the PR man, pointing to Kerviel's promotion from the trading room's middle office, where he was hired in 2000, to full-fledged trader in 2005. In 2006 he earned $150,000 in salary and bonus, far above the French average.

What was it that drove Kerviel to bet a French bank on the stock market? So far nobody has uncovered a gambling habit or any other clues that might cast light on his motivation. (Kerviel declined to be interviewed.) He certainly has portrayed himself to prosecutors as a diligent, even prescient, worker bee: In testimony to prosecutors, the transcripts of which leaked to the press, Kerviel said he began reading up on subprime troubles in March 2007 and got a strong sense that its risks were being underplayed.

Over the following four months he placed a succession of ever larger bets that stocks would take a hit. His hunch proved correct, and he made an eye-popping $2 billion trading profit for the bank by the end of 2007.

Officially he had no authorization to do any of that; indeed, he hid the $2 billion and declared a profit of only $85 million to the bank. As a junior trader on a desk called Delta One, his job was to conduct arbitrage trades—buying and selling the same securities at the same time on different markets to exploit tiny differences in price and thus earn a small but relatively risk-free profit. Unhedged positions were a no-no.

But from early in his career as a trader, he told prosecutors, he overstepped the rules. He earned $750,000 for the bank with his very first one-way bet, on German insurer Allianz in 2005, and while supervisors told him off—one former manager told prosecutors that Kerviel had been formally reprimanded—he didn't take them seriously. Indeed, that initial success gave him a taste for bigger risk.

One former Société Générale senior derivatives trader says new hires were often informally given a little leeway to see what they would do with it. If they made money, it was a sign they could go on to become successful traders. If not, they were quickly shunted aside. Still, the ex-trader says, "the rule was that you watched these guys carefully and made sure they didn't go too far."

But Kerviel continued unchecked and found elaborate ways to mask what he was doing. He explained in detail to prosecutors how he created a separate account of fictitious trades that mirrored his real profits and losses, making it appear as though his books were almost always balanced. In June 2007, as he waited for his subprime bet to come through, the Société Générale internal investigation shows that his trading account was more than $3 billion in the red. That set off a series of alarms in the bank's risk management system and even triggered alerts externally, on a derivatives exchange. Kerviel always seemed able to wriggle out of trouble, including by faking e-mails that confirmed fictitious positions.

Then it all went horribly wrong. This January, Kerviel decided the markets were heading for a rebound. He bet bigger than ever, buying stock index futures rather than selling them, even as the markets were tanking. For days he played cat and mouse with Société Générale's risk managers before they finally caught him on the evening of January 18. The bets were so large they triggered capital ratio alerts. He faked more e-mails from counterparties confirming transactions, but the compliance officers checked with one of them, Deutsche Bank, which denied any knowledge. The game was up.

RAISING CAPITAL

On the afternoon of January 21, as his trader was dumping Kerviel's positions, Bouton called Donald Moore, Morgan Stanley's European chairman and an investment banker he knew well and had worked with during the 1999 three-way takeover battle. Moore at the time was in Shanghai, where it was the middle of the night, and didn't call back till Tuesday morning. Bouton sounded stressed, Moore says, but very alert. The two men talked through the options and quickly agreed on a rights issue as the best way to raise fresh capital. Moore spoke to Morgan Stanley CEO John Mack and then called Bouton back: Morgan Stanley on its own would be willing to guarantee as much as $10 billion because "there's a huge amount of respect and trust" for Bouton and Société Générale management, Moore says.

Bouton also put in a call to J.P. Morgan, another bank he had worked with closely; in the end, both houses of Morgan jointly guaranteed the rights issue. After a marathon overnight due-diligence session Bouton had his financing, and the bank was safe.

The world soon will know exactly how—and perhaps why—Kerviel took risks that nearly destroyed 144-year-old Société Générale.

Prosecutors expect to conclude their investigation into what happened at the bank by summer's end, and Kerviel should go to trial next year. His popularity may wane as the process drags on—the public is fickle, after all— but his place in history is secure: His name, along with those of Barings rogue Nick Leeson and Kidder Peabody's Joe Jett, will without doubt surface next time a trading scandal erupts.

Less certain is Bouton's legacy. Despite the beating he has taken in the French press, Bouton is as confident as ever. The bank is doing "just fine," he told the French Parliament's finance committee this month. "There has been no loss of confidence with the hundreds of financial operators we work with."

And when the Kerviel affair becomes a case study, what lesson will it teach? The need to have impeccable investor, press, and government relations—not just a superb balance sheet.

◆

AFTERMATH:

Thanks to the big capital increase engineered by Bouton, Société Générale emerged from the Kerviel affair with a strengthened balance sheet, just as banks worldwide came under growing pressure leading up to the October 2008 market crash. The capital injection didn't help the bank's stock, however, and it wasn't enough to save Bouton. Three months after the scandal broke, having defiantly told the French press that he wouldn't step down, Bouton announced in April 2008 that he was relinquishing the CEO post but would stay on as chairman. Mustier, the investment banking chief, also was pushed out of his job, but stayed on at the bank and was later appointed head of the investment management division. Société Générale overhauled its risk-management operations and put in place a raft of new rules and controls aimed at preventing a repetition.

Pending his criminal trial, which is expected to start in late 2009, Kerviel continued to maintain that his bank superiors knew and approved of his transactions. (The charges carry a maximum three-year sentence.) With the worldwide financial squeeze dominating the business press, by late 2008, Kerviel had all but disappeared from the headlines of French newspapers and the dinner party conversations in Paris. Yet the apparent ease with which he bet Société Générale's future foreshadowed the enormous vulnerabilities of banks worldwide that were revealed later in the year: weak oversight, technical complexity, oversized egos, and a culture of making money whatever the cost.

JAC/RAN LAZIC

CHAPTER 1: THE PREDATOR

*Giancarlo Paretti liked to see himself as a movie mogul who lived large;
here he is sitting pretty at his spacious Beverly Hills home in May 1990.
Less than a year later, his checks began to bounce.*

CHAPTER 2: THE BIG KOZLOWSKI

*Smiling for the camera, Tyco CEO Dennis Kozlowski could have
no idea that this video of his wife's birthday party in Sardinia in 2001
would be the centerpiece of his trial two years later.*

FIFTEEN CENTS

October 28, 1929

TIME

The Weekly Newsmagazine

TÄNDSTICK ·KONUNG KREUGER
He made the match.
(See BUSINESS)

Volume XIV

Number 18

CHAPTER 3: THE SWEDISH MATCH KING

Ivar Kreuger appeared on the cover of TIME magazine
in October 1929, the week the stock market crashed.
It was also the week his empire began to crumble.

CHAPTER 4: THE ADELPHIA STORY

*John Rigas stands on Main Street in Coudersport, PA. Rigas was the
uncrowned king of Coudersport—until his cable empire fell apart.*

CHAPTER 5: THE LOOTING OF IOS

Once a cult figure and playboy, Robert Vesco is a sadly diminished figure in this 1996 photo, taken during his trial in Cuba for fraud.

CHAPTER 7: SOCGEN'S $7.5 BILLION HOLE

Jérôme Kerviel bet big on a market rebound—and cost Société Générele $7.5 billion; he is expected to face criminal charges. But in the court of public opinion the son of a metal worker became seen as a French Robin Hood.

CHAPTER 8: JUNGLE FEVER

*A Dayak tribal leader, Pebit, pans for gold in the rivers of
Borneo in 1997. Like many others, Pebit hoped that he would
soon be awash in riches. In fact, there was no gold.*

CHAPTER 11: MCKESSON & ROBBINS: ITS FALL AND RISE

*Donald Coster (aka Philip Musica) looks like a mousy little man
in this 1938 picture. He really was a highly creative con artist
who almost destroyed the country's biggest drug distributor.*

CHAPTER 12: THE WRECKING CREW

*Michael Carlow came to Pittsburgh in 1991, pledging to
save the Clark bar. Instead, he wreaked havoc on the city.*

CHAPTER 13: THE INSIDE STORY OF AN INSIDE TRADER

*In 1991, a chastened and reflective Dennis Levine
was out of prison and back in New York.*

CHAPTER 15: BILLIE SOL ESTES:
THREE-SIDED COUNTRY SLICKER

Texas con man Billie Sol Estes (BOTTOM) *made a fortune by selling the same anhydrous ammonia tanks* (TOP) *over and over.*

(TOP) PAM FRANCIS/GETTY IMAGES; (BOTTOM) BRETT COOMER/GETTY IMAGES

CHAPTER 16: WHY ENRON WENT BUST

*Jeff Skilling (top), a cheerful presence on Enron's trading floor in
1993, was one of the key people in the rise of Enron. But he quit
as CEO in August 2001, and by the end of the year, the company was
bankrupt. CFO Andy Fastow (bottom), along with Skilling,
was convicted on criminal charges related to Enron's collapse.*

PAT SULLIVAN/AP

From humble beginnings as the son of Baptist preacher, Ken Lay made it to the top of corporate America as CEO of Enron. His convictions on 10 criminal counts were vacated when he died in 2006.

TERRY ASHE

CHAPTER 17: THE INSATIABLE KING SCRUSHY

Huddled between his lawyers, Richard Scrushy was center stage on Capitol Hill in 2003, at a hearing on the financial collapse of his company, HealthSouth. It was not the kind of stage favored by Scrushy, who fancied himself a country-music star in the making.

CHAPTER 19: CRASH AND BURN

*The De Loreon's distinctive gull-winged doors, as shown in 1985,
became famous—but the car was a commercial flop.*

BRENDAN MCDERMID/REUTERS/CORBIS

CHAPTER 20: MADOFF DOES MINNEAPOLIS

Bernie Madoff made his reputation as an investor and a philanthropist. But if the allegations against him are proved, he will have a new one—as the biggest swindler in financial history.

8

JUNGLE FEVER

The Bre-X Saga was the greatest gold fiasco ever.

by **RICHARD BEHAR**

June 9, 1997

When I stepped off the plane in Jakarta, I was, like the rest of the world's lemmings, swept up in the Bre-X Minerals euphoria. The Canadian company had found the largest gold deposit of the century, buried deep underground in a dense Indonesian jungle on the island of Borneo. As Bre-X vice chairman John Felderhof later explained to me, a volcano had essentially "collapsed back onto itself" three million years ago, causing a massive buildup of heat and pressure, which created the miraculous treasure. He drew a diagram. It made sense. After all, he was on his eighth beer of the evening; I was on my fourth. What's more, everyone believed him—fellow geologists, engineers, financial analysts, business journalists, the world's largest mining companies, government officials, even a former U.S. president. "Geologically, it's the most brilliant thing I've ever seen in my life," Felderhof sputtered. "It's so big, it's scary. It's f—ing scary!"

Horrifying is a better word. Bre-X was a gold-mining hoax—the largest of any century—until it collapsed onto itself in May 1997. Allegedly thousands of rock samples were "salted" with flakes of gold before they were tested. Today Felderhof is rich and sends his regrets from the Cayman Islands, where he professes his innocence and is applying for permanent residency. His deputy geologist, Mike de Guzman, is not so fortunate, having apparently jumped 800 feet into the jungle from a helicopter once the jig was up. Bre-X CEO David Walsh is holed up at the company's Calgary headquarters, scuffling with camera crews. Class-action lawsuits are flying, while criminal investigators are poring over the company's books.

The numbers are heart-stopping. The market value of Bre-X had topped $4 billion—a growth rate of 100,000% in three years. In May 1997, the company melted into bankruptcy. But not before Walsh, his wife, and Felderhof had mined roughly $50 million from stock sales. And the gold? In the weeks before the fraud was exposed, some 71 million ounces of the yellow metal, worth $25 billion at today's prices, had supposedly been "proven" by Bre-X. Then Felderhof said he was "comfortable" with 200 million ounces—far more than the California gold rush. One Bre-X official told me "400 million."

The numbers tell only part of the story. To grasp the enormity of the scam, you had to be there. You had to see the cosmos that Bre-X had created, like an elaborate Hollywood set with hundreds of actors who could be loaded onto trucks and barges once the tickets had been sold. "You have to understand, this thing is like a 20-foot man," gushed Research Capital mining analyst Chad Williams after returning from an early pilgrimage. "For someone in our business, it's like taking the biggest Elvis fan to Graceland."

I spent two weeks in Indonesia in February to chronicle an epic tale of how a bunch of average Joes stumbled onto the holy grail, only to find powerful and greedy forces conspiring to take it away from them. Felderhof told me only one other publication (*The Northern Miner*) had ever been permitted inside Busang, the exploration camp on the island of Borneo. I felt lucky. I proved even luckier when I returned to New York with an illness that delayed my story for several weeks. We held our fire again after Freeport-McMoRan Copper & Gold, Bre-X's new partner, said it was conducting its own drilling tests—the first time in nearly four years anyone independent had checked beneath the surface.

CORPORATE WAR ZONE

The story is familiar now. For nearly a year, until Freeport was awarded the contract, the Indonesian government had delayed giving Bre-X control over Busang. Mining giants were lobbying for the post, none harder than Peter Munk, CEO of Toronto's Barrick Gold, the world's second-largest gold producer. Munk hired Kroll Associates, the world's biggest detective agency, to dig up dirt on Bre-X in anticipation of a hostile takeover bid. He enlisted former U.S. President H.W. George Bush to lobby Suharto, the Indonesian ruler. He retained the services of a daughter of Suharto to get an edge. (Bre-X offered $40 million to a son.)

When I arrived in early February, Jakarta had become a corporate war zone centered on five-star fortresses. Bre-X was at the Shangri-La (the "Bre-X Shangri-La"). From his window Walsh could see the enemy—the "Barrick Hyatt." Just up the road, at the Regent Hotel, a Houston lawyer was assembling spies to help him figure out whom to sue on behalf of Bre-X shareholders. It was impossible to figure out what was going on. "This place is like Casablanca," complained Doug MacIntosh, Bre-X's investment banker at J.P. Morgan. "The story changes every day."

In Jakarta, I talked with Walsh, Felderhof, and other Bre-X officials dozens of times. We met separately. We met together at lunches and dinners. Not once did a yellow flag go up during those talks. Were they all just playing their parts in an elaborate scheme? If so, they were playing those parts quite well.

Even now, I have trouble believing that Walsh participated in the scam. He was a miserable soul when we were introduced in his Jakarta suite, just hours after he'd had it swept for electronic bugs. Chain-smoking, he was depressed and distracted, often staring out his window at the litter and sewage that flowed continuously down a muddy canal. "We all find it hard to believe that we're responsible for the largest gold discovery probably in the history of the world," he said without much feeling. Indeed, Walsh looked more like some poor schlemiel who had just won the lottery and couldn't locate the ticket.

Walsh told me his story: A former stockbroker, he launched Bre-X in 1989. He hunted for gold in Quebec and joined a diamond rush in the Northwest Territories. His luck was so abysmal that he opened his 1991 annual report with the line "Yes, we are still in business." After filing for personal bankruptcy, he decided he needed "a proven gold finder." Enter Felderhof, whose claim to fame was the co-discovery of one of the world's biggest silver and gold mines in Papua New Guinea in 1968. It took Walsh two weeks to track down Felderhof, whom he hadn't seen in ten years. Using his last $10,000, Walsh flew to Indonesia, where Felderhof talked him into buying the rights to part of the Busang property in 1993.

Looking back, maybe I should have been suspicious when I met the Dutch-born Felderhof. He had a shifty mug, a gruff manner, and a hideous laugh trapped in the back of his throat ("Kkh! Kkh! Kkh!...Kkh! Kkh! Kkh!"). Still, his talent for storytelling made him more enjoyable than Walsh. Here was a pirate without the eye patch—a hard-drinking, swashbuckling explorer who had prowled the world's jungles, dodging flash floods and poisonous snakes. He wore his 14 bouts with malaria like medals on his chest. He said he was so poor that in 1992 he had to steal a Christmas tree for his family. Never again. He pulled out a photo of Ingrid, his second wife. "She just bought me a Lamborghini for Christmas," he said. "It's two seats strapped to a f—ing engine. I think she's trying to kill me. Kkh! Kkh! Kkh!"

Shortly after we met, Felderhof took me to dinner with de Guzman, his longtime pal whom he'd invited to join the Bre-X team. The Filipino geologist beamed like a jewel when Felderhof explained that he couldn't have discovered the gold without his deputy's "pioneering theories." De Guzman boasted that his IQ ranged from 150 to 170, which came in handy when he hiked 32 kilometers through dense jungle "with the camp on my back, eating noodles every meal for a week," and hunting for signs of mineralization. The first two drill holes were failures. "In December 1993, John said, 'Close the property,' " recalled de Guzman, "and then we made the hit."

As I continued my work, things got tense. Walsh complained about a break-in at his Calgary office; two weeks earlier his wife had found a spy rifling through the garbage at their Bahamas estate. He claims he sent a memo advising employees to "shred sensitive materials." The company's top financial officer, Rolando Francisco, was also caught up in the hysteria. He would talk in his hotel room only after cranking up the volume on the TV. Over at the Hyatt, Barrick spokesman Luc Lavoie was waxing philosophical: "If this was the biggest oil discovery, so what? More oil. But gold is different... It brings up more emotions. It clouds the minds of people." It clearly fogged the mind of his client. I later learned that Barrick, last November, couldn't find gold in many Bre-X samples. "This can't be a scam!" Munk screamed at his deputies. "Do some more tests! Figure it out! I know it's there, okay? You confirm it's there."

I looked forward to seeing the gold. After four days in Jakarta, Felderhof joined me on the flight to Balikpapan, the only place in Borneo with a runway big enough to handle the plane. During the trip he explained that Bre-X had spent more than $1 million on a social-development program for the tribe of Christian Dayaks that comprised the bulk of the 400 workers. "I've always been interested in developing people," he said. From Balikpapan, it was an exhilarating two-hour jaunt in a helicopter to Busang. The dense, swampy jungle stretched as far as the eye could see. Felderhof leaned over and said that a chopper once made an emergency landing in the area. "When the pilot was found, four days later, his body was covered with leeches," yelled Felderhof, over the roar of the engine. "Kkh! Kkh! Kkh!" Little did I know that, six weeks later, Felderhof's sidekick, de Guzman, would apparently throw himself out of the same chopper we were sitting in. It would take four days to find the body, which had been partly devoured by wild pigs and other creatures.

Once on the ground, you would never know that this wasn't the real deal. What a production! If Busang was a Hollywood set, the 2,000 Dayaks were the extras. Bre-X had electrified their village, built a new church, opened a kindergarten, and organized sewing classes for the local women. A swath of jungle had been cleared for an airport. Bre-X planned to open a fishery and a poultry-farming venture to enable the tribe to sell products to the mine.

I shared a cigar with a young villager who had just received a scholarship from Bre-X to study engineering. I met Pebit, the barefoot Dayak leader, as he was helping construct new homes for the workers— a tribal Levittown, courtesy of Bre-X. Through a translator, Pebit boasted that it was his decision to sacrifice a pig to God that "allowed the gold to be pulled from the ground." Then there was the army of young geologists working the site. At the exploration camp, I drank Bintang (a local beer) deep into the night with ten of these workers, many of whom were fresh out of geology school in Canada, Indonesia, or the Philippines. As we listened to wild monkeys screech like sirens in the darkness, the young men talked about the rigors of life in the bush. They complained about the grueling work schedule (eight weeks on, two weeks off) and the lack of sex. But they believed they were making history. They were the geological equivalent of batboys for the World Champion Yankees. They didn't know that they were pawns in a crooked game that was fixed from the get-go. After two days, my tour was over. I saw no gold. But then again, I didn't know what real gold was supposed to look like buried in those long, tubular core samples.

After a few more days in Jakarta, I returned to the U.S. on February 17, 1997. Bre-X soon unraveled. Even then, many believers chose to stay blind. In March, after de Guzman's death, Barrick's Peter Munk told FORTUNE, "I don't believe that those guys salted the mine ... you couldn't have fooled that many analysts for that long." When Freeport said its drilling showed "insignificant" gold, Bre-X's flacks at Hill &

Knowlton suggested that Freeport was behind a scheme to lower the stock price. The last time I heard from Walsh, March 20, he left me a phone message confirming some arcane historical facts in my story—a day after de Guzman's death and a week after Freeport called Walsh with the news that they were coming up dry at Busang. This is a crook? Or the Mr. Magoo of mining?

Looking back, some things seemed suspicious. Like the "accidental" fire at Busang that destroyed a building containing de Guzman's papers and visible gold samples. I was also disappointed to see no gold at the century's biggest gold deposit. A geologist, Steve Hughes, took me through the bush to a creek. We panned. We found nothing. "That's strange," said Hughes. "You'd think we'd find something." The next day I needled Felderhof, telling him I had bad news for Bre-X. "No gold, huh?" he snapped back. "Kkh! Kkh! Kkh!" There was another peculiar moment. In one of my last meetings in Jakarta with Felderhof, de Guzman walked in. I rose and slapped him on the back, congratulating him on Freeport's emerging as Bre-X's new partner. He should have been thrilled. Instead, he was stone cold. Grim. Icy.

No matter who pulled off the hoax, Bre-X has left a mother lode of victims—from individual investors to the Dayaks. But even the pros got burned in this tale of greed. Recently I caught up with Doug MacIntosh of J.P. Morgan, the Bre-X banker. We'd shared several meals in Jakarta, where he jabbered for hours about how the gold mine would be the most lucrative in the world. Doug is a mining engineer with 30 years of experience. I was curious how it felt to be suckered. "I have been surprised at every turn of this thing," he said, noting how fortunate I was that we had held the presses. "I hope that we're as lucky as you have been." Not a chance, mate.

◆

AFTERMATH

In June 1998, David Walsh died at the age of 52 in the Bahamas of an apparent brain aneurysm.

In the years since Bre-X proved to be anything but a gold mine, no one from the company has been held legally accountable for the estimated $3 billion lost by thousands of shareholders. In July 1999, a U.S. District Court judge dismissed a suit by shareholders against J.P. Morgan, which had been Bre-X's financial advisor, and Lehman Brothers, which had recommended Bre-X's stock, ruling there was no evidence of deception. A Canadian class-action suit filed by Bre-X shareholders is still in the "examination for discovery" stage. And the Royal Canadian Mounted Police never found enough evidence to bring criminal charges against any Bre-X executives.

In 1999, however, the Ontario Securities Commission did manage to charge one man for insider trading and misleading investors: John Felderhof. The central question of the trial was whether Felderhof was aware that the Bre-X mineral samples had been tampered with. But the trial became a "procedural nightmare," in the words of the OSC's lead lawyer, Jay Naster. After eight years, Felderhof was found not guilty.

The collapse of Bre-X spooked so many investors that the Ontario Securities Commission created a special mining task force in July 1997. Its recommendations turned into a set of rules called National Instrument 43-101. This requires public Canadian companies with mineral projects to hire a minerals expert to corroborate any information released about the project.

9

DIAGNOSING FOR DOLLARS

An inside look at mass medical screening for silicosis.

by **ROGER PARLOFF**

June 13, 2005

Severe silicosis is a ghastly disease. Caused by prolonged inhalation of tiny sand particles, it slowly scars and contracts the lungs until the victim suffocates. Severe asbestosis, which is caused by inhaling minute, spearlike asbestos fibers, is just as bad. It has nearly identical symptoms, and it can lead to lung cancer or mesothelioma, the dreaded, inevitably fatal cancer of the lung lining.

Perhaps the only consolation in having one of these diseases is that you almost certainly won't get the other. The massive, protracted dust exposure required to come down with either makes it extremely rare for a worker to get both. And despite their outward similarities, the two diseases are readily distinguishable on X-rays. A panel of four eminent occupational-disease experts agreed on these points in February testimony before a Senate committee.

How, then, to account for this: Of 8,629 people diagnosed with silicosis now suing in federal court in Corpus Christi, 5,174—or 60%— are "asbestos retreads," i.e., people who have previously filed claims for asbestos-related disease.

That anomaly turns out to be just one of many in the Corpus Christi case that sorely challenge medical explanation. At a hearing in February 2005, U.S. District Judge Janis Graham Jack characterized the evidence before her as raising "great red flags of fraud."

The larger importance of those proceedings, however, is what they suggest about a possible fraud of vastly greater dimensions. It's one that may have been afflicting asbestos litigation for almost 20 years, resulting in billions of dollars of payments to claimants who weren't sick and to the attorneys who represented them. Asbestos litigation has bankrupted more than 60 companies and is expected to eventually cost defendants and their insurers more than $200 billion, of which $70 billion has already been paid.

The chief link between the silicosis crackup in Corpus Christi and asbestos litigation is the doctors who diagnose both diseases. Of the 8,179 alleged silicotics in the Corpus Christi case for whom diagnostic information has been disclosed, a single doctor played a role in diagnosing 6,350 (78%). The busy radiologist is Ray Harron, who has, not coincidentally, also had a hand in diagnosing 52,600 asbestos claims, according to the Manville Trust—the payer of liabilities of the old Johns-Manville Corp. That's slightly more than 10% of all the claims the trust has ever received for which it has records of the diagnosing doctor.

But Harron is only the most prolific of a prolific breed. They are known as "screening" doctors, because they work with entrepreneurial screening companies that plaintiffs' attorneys pay to find silicotics and asbestotics among people who do not yet realize that they are sick.

Just five screening doctors account for almost 25% of all the asbestos claims ever filed with the Manville Trust, while the top 25 account for 46%. Not surprisingly, Harron and three other prominent asbestos-screening doctors read most of the plaintiffs' X-rays in the silicosis case. The doctors include James Ballard (with more than 11,000 asbestos claims presented to the Manville Trust), George Martindale (3,200 Manville claims), and Walter Allen Oaks (1,700). Ballard and

Martindale did not return phone messages. Harron didn't return calls or answer a faxed letter. Oaks said, "Nobody's ever asked me to do anything improper, and I haven't done anything improper."

One would think that defendants would have grown suspicious of these champion diagnosers before now—and they have. Since 1986 there have been at least five elaborate efforts to measure the accuracy of litigation-related asbestosis diagnoses. The most optimistic concluded that about 66% were unfounded, while the others found 80% to 97% to be bogus.

So where are the prosecutors? It's not that simple. The claims-generation system has always been protected from challenge by a concept known as inter-reader variability. The best-credentialed radiologists will disagree on X-ray interpretations 20% to 30% of the time, with even wider discrepancies among outliers. When such broad variance is the norm, it's very difficult to prove fraud. It would be only natural for plaintiffs' lawyers to gravitate toward doctors who read at the high end of the disease-diagnosing spectrum. Maybe that's all that's been going on, the argument goes.

Yet even this statistical rampart may now be crumbling. It suffered a severe blow last August when a peer-reviewed article was published in *Academic Radiology*. At the request of defense lawyers, Joseph Gitlin, a radiology professor at the Johns Hopkins School of Medicine, had six outside experts reevaluate 378 X-rays that had originally been read as consistent with asbestosis by doctors working for plaintiffs' lawyers. All six—who weren't told the purpose of the study or its sponsors—agreed that 322 of the films (85%) showed no such thing. Gitlin calculated that the plaintiffs' doctors were 2,227 times more likely to see compensable asbestosis than were the outside readers.

Between the Gitlin study and the preposterously improbable statistics emanating from the silicosis consolidation, the wheels finally appear to be coming off a very rickety cart.

THE ORIGINAL SIN

The starting point of any story about asbestos litigation must be the corporate wrongdoing that spawned it. In the mid-1930s the president of Raybestos Manhattan and the general counsel of Johns-Manville Corp. plotted to suppress research showing just how dangerous asbestos dust could be. As a consequence, millions of workers were exposed before scientists caught up with what was happening in the 1960s, and regulators began imposing protective measures in the 1970s. Thousands are still dying today as a result, including about 2,500 a year from mesothelioma and, by some estimates, 7,500 annually from other asbestos-linked cancers.

But while the number of asbestos-related cancer claims over the years has generally tracked medical predictions, nonmalignant claims—the vast majority of them alleging borderline asbestosis with modest or no impairment—have swamped expectations. Cancer diagnoses are usually unambiguous and often rendered by treating physicians, but diagnoses of mild asbestosis are subjective and almost always made by screening doctors.

Here's the real outrage: The droves of nonmalignant claimants have vied with the cancer patients for the limited dollars available from defendants who are bankrupt or on the verge of it. In 1999, for instance, 77% of the Manville Trust's payouts went to nonmalignants, even though the judge supervising the trust estimated that 66% to 90% of them were unimpaired. That led the trust to institute reforms that took effect in October 2003. Because of those rules changes, claims against the trust plummeted from almost 101,000 in 2003 to just 14,600 in 2004. In 2004 also, cancer victims collectively received more of the trust's payouts than nonmalignants for the first time since 1998. Accordingly, if nonmalignant claims have been generated fraudulently, corporate treasuries have not been the only victims.

By the late 1990s, certain asbestos plaintiffs' law firms began diversifying their portfolios, seeking to convert the sleepy, if reliable, boutique practice of silicosis litigation into a mass tort. The retooling appears to have intensified in 2001, when Congress began considering legislation that might greatly diminish the value of unimpaired, nonmalignant asbestos claims. In the process of retargeting their machine, the claims generators appear to have gravely miscalculated. First, they ran into two defense lawyers with a taste for detective work and spreadsheets. Then they plowed into the plump, quick-witted, frizzy-haired Judge Jack. That one-two punch is having dire repercussions not just for the once budding silica litigation but for the asbestos litigation it had hubristically been modeled on.

SILICOSIS SPIKE

Declaiming in a now extinct, aristocratic accent that most of us have heard spoken only by Margaret Dumont in Marx Brothers movies, a stern woman is advising sandblasters, foundry workers, and quarrymen on how to avert a potentially fatal occupational disease. The woman is then-Secretary of Labor Frances Perkins, and she is speaking in the 1938 newsreel, "Stop Silicosis." John Ulizio, the CEO of U.S. Silica, plays the newsreel to illustrate that the dangers of silica, unlike asbestos, have been well known since the 1930s.

Crystalline silica (silicon dioxide) is quartz. It is the primary ingredient in sand and the second-most-common mineral in the earth's crust after feldspar. Though sand is harmless when coarse—at beaches or in children's sandboxes—it becomes dangerous when industrial processes reduce it to respirable dust.

The one in the best position to protect workers from those dangers—often the only one who really can—is the worker's employer. But under worker's compensation rules, the employer usually can't be sued. So when workers do get silicosis, they typically sue the sand suppliers, like U.S. Silica; the respirator and safety-equipment manufacturers, like 3M and Textron; and the sand-blasting equipment manufacturers, like Ingersoll-Rand. They sue mainly under failure-to-warn and design-defect theories.

In the 1970s and 1980s, while asbestos filings were growing

geometrically, federal courts snuffed out two early attempts to bring analogous silicosis cases against sand suppliers, finding that the workers' direct employers—typically foundries—were at least as expert about the dangers of silica as the defendants who allegedly failed to warn. But plaintiffs refined their theories, added some new ones—an allegation, for instance, that 3M sold respirators that did not perform as claimed—and started filing their cases in more receptive state courts. By the late 1990s silica litigation was gaining traction in Texas.

The other limitation that initially kept silica litigation in check was the intrinsically more modest scope of the problem. Because the dangers of silica were well known, because fewer occupations were at risk than with asbestos, because regulators were tightening controls, and because the relevant industries were in decline, silicosis mortality rates dropped 93% from 1968 to 2002, according to the Centers for Disease Control. Except for three blips readily attributable to events at three specific foundries, U.S. Silica was sued by fewer than 60 plaintiffs per year from 1975 through 1996. But filings did begin rising in 1997, and then suddenly, since January 1, 2002, some 30,000 alleged silicotics have sued.

Ulizio is a blunt, rumpled former litigator who prefers the title "president" to "CEO," considering the latter too highfalutin' for someone who runs a bunch of sand mines. He's cynical about the lawsuits. "It's not about people getting sick," he says. "It's about a legal business model."

Few of Ulizio's views are shared by Mike Martin, a Houston lawyer who has been bringing cases for seriously injured silicotics since 1985. But Martin, too, is suspicious. "The problem I see," he says, "is with legitimate silicosis victims who are getting drowned out in a pool of questionable claims." Martin thinks that some plaintiffs' laywers "started taking the square peg of asbestos litigation and trying to force it into the round hole of silica litigation." And the key means of doing so, he maintains, was the adoption of the screening operations.

Between January 1, 2002, and August 31, 2004—the last day before a tort reform measure took effect in that state—20,466 people diagnosed with silicosis sued in the then-famously pro-plaintiff Mississippi state courts. The number was suspicious on its face. Mississippi is not rich in foundries or quarries. It ranks 38th in the nation in silicosis mortality rates, according to the National Institute for Occupational Safety and Health (NIOSH), having recorded an average of about 1.3 silicosis deaths a year over the previous decade.

Fred Krutz and Daniel Mulholland, of Foreman Perry Watkins Krutz & Tardy in Jackson, Miss., represent more than 30 defendants in those cases. In 2003 they "removed" to federal court cases involving nearly 10,000 plaintiffs—a procedure available to defendants who believe there are bases for federal jurisdiction. A federal judicial panel consolidated those cases before Judge Jack for pretrial proceedings. The group is known as the federal MDL case, for "multidistrict litigation."

In April 2004 the plaintiffs' lead counsel presented the defendants with a letter demanding $1 billion to settle the cases. He suggested that the price was a bargain, because "litigating the Silica MDL will collectively cost the defendants more than $1,500,000,000" in pretrial expenses alone.

When the offer was rejected, the discovery process went forward. But by then that process had taken a fateful turn against the plaintiffs. In February 2004, Judge Jack had granted an unusually detailed level of scrutiny concerning the screening doctors. Such discovery is not common, but Judge Jack ruled that if a screening doctor's diagnosis was the basis for filing the suit, then information about it should be discoverable. "That was a real big deal," says Mulholland.

Indeed it was. In April the plaintiffs began turning over the details of their silicosis diagnoses. That information included the plaintiffs' Social Security numbers, which enabled Mulholland and Krutz to track down the plaintiffs' earlier asbestosis diagnoses from the Manville Trust. That's how they learned that 60% were asbestos retreads.

An animated, stocky, personable man who used to teach computer programming, Mulholland had the documents loaded into a data-management program. Using his litigative GameBoy, Mulholland unearthed many of the most damning facts in the case, including a phenomenon concerning the asbestos retreads, which he dubbed the "crossing of the Rubicon." The Rubicon here is December 31, 2000—the approximate date when the N&M testing service, a key screener in these cases, began looking for silicosis instead of asbestosis. Of the 3,730 putative dual-disease sufferers who had been examined before that date, 3,691 (99%) had been told that their X-rays showed only feathery-shaped shadows consistent with asbestosis but not with silicosis. Yet when those plaintiffs were examined again after December 31, 2000, 3,715 (99.6%) had X-rays supposedly showing rounded, silicosis-style shadows too.

For those workers who were examined for the first time after December 31, 2000, on the other hand, screening doctors now regularly saw both types of shadows from the get-go. In 331 such cases, for instance, screener Ray Harron issued separate asbestosis and silicosis diagnoses based on one reading of one X-ray, with neither report referring to the other. Mulholland calls these "the Harron twofers."

In late October the depositions began—as did the fireworks. The first doctor deposed was George Martindale, who had diagnosed 3,617 people in the MDL. But when questioned, Martindale recanted them all, saying he'd thought he was just offering a second opinion about X-rays that had already been read as positive by Harron.

The next two doctors deposed also recanted. Each said that the diagnostic language in their reports had been added by the screening company's typists without their knowledge. The recantations got Judge Jack's attention. A Clinton appointee, Jack was once a registered nurse and is married to a cardiologist. She is given to dry understatement, delivered in the Texan lilt she acquired growing up in Fort Worth. "I'm very distressed about this Martindale business," she told the lawyers in December. "That's such a fraudulent problem. It is. I mean, you can't label it too many different ways." She ordered the remaining diagnosers and screeners to be deposed in her presence at a hearing in February 2005. There, the rest of the pieces of the jigsaw puzzle began to get filled in. The grand jury will have to fill in the rest.

LAWYERS CHANGING GEARS

In a sense, the narrative of the silicosis MDL begins around June 1996, when a screening company called N&M sprang up in Pascagoula, Miss. N&M provided about 4,000 diagnosed silicotics to one law firm in the MDL case, while shooting X-rays or doing lung-function tests on another 2,500 plaintiffs for other firms.

N&M is run by Molly Netherland and C. Heath Mason, veterans of the so-called Pitts Group, a prodigiously busy cluster of screening operations that had shut their doors in 1996 after being sued for civil racketeering by Owens Corning, a frequent target of asbestos litigation. Owens Corning alleged that the Pitts group was systematically falsifying pulmonary-function tests. When deposed, the owners and two lab technicians invoked their Fifth Amendment privileges against self-incrimination. (The case settled in 1999 with the defendants paying almost $3 million.)

Just weeks after the Pitts Group shut down, Mason, who had managed screenings for it, and Netherland, the wife of a chiropractor, who had run its X-ray operation, launched N&M. Neither had any medical training, so in early 1997 they contracted with Harron to read X-rays for them. For six years, the company thrived.

In 2001, when Congress began debating asbestos reform bills, asbestos screening dried up, Mason testified, and lawyers had him turn to silica testing for the first time. Asked at a July 2003 deposition how the asbestos bills affected his business, Mason said, "It gets lawyers to have to change gears on what they think is going to work."

In January 2002, Mason got a call from Campbell Cherry Harrison Davis Dove, a plaintiffs' firm based in Waco, Texas, and Jackson, Miss., he testified. (Campbell Cherry lawyers did not return repeated calls.) Campbell Cherry had used N&M before for its asbestos work. Now it wanted Mason to canvas its "existing inventory" of asbestos clients to see if any had also been exposed to silica.

"What you run into," Mason explained at the hearing, "is you have a ton of people who call—I mean, multitudes of thousands of people want to be screened for silica." So N&M had "four girls" take their calls—clerical workers—and determine, according to Mason, if their exposures seemed sufficient to have the disease. If so, they'd get an appointment to be screened.

His clerical staff evidently became astoundingly skillful at this task. On February 15, 2002, for instance, N&M screened 111 workers in Columbus, Miss., and found that all 111 had silicosis. On other days it saw 85% to 95% positives. "I prided myself in not testing negative," Mason testified, "because ... we tried harder and harder to weed out the negatives" over the phone. That made good business sense, too, since Campbell Cherry was paying him $750 for each positive diagnosis but nothing for the negatives.

Having clerical workers prepare a one-page medical and occupational history isn't how doctors typically proceed. Many regard the taking of an extensive history as crucial in diagnosing occupational disease. That's because the shadows consistent with asbestosis or silicosis might also be consistent with scarring caused by other dusts (coal, beryllium, cotton), fungal diseases, lupus, rheumatoid arthritis, congestive heart disease, metastatic cancers, certain drugs, old cases of tuberculosis or fractured ribs, or according to some doctors, even smoking, obesity, or old age.

Be that as it may, N&M and many other screeners in the MDL case were extremely successful in finding silicosis—even among those whose earlier X-ray readings had reported only the feathery shadows characteristic of asbestosis. One screening doctor in the case, Ballard—who acknowledged making $500,000 a year in 2000 and 2001 from reading X-rays for litigation—did suggest an innocent explanation for this "crossing of the Rubicon" phenomenon, however. When looking for asbestosis, Ballard explained, he might have focused on the lower lobes of the lungs, where asbestos scarring usually occurs. There, he might have seen mainly feathery shadows. But when looking for silicosis, he continued, he may have focused on the upper lobes, where you typically see silicosis scarring; there, perhaps, the rounded shadows were more prominent.

So maybe that's what happened—3,691 times.

HARRON TAKES THE STAND

Ray Harron, now 73, took the witness stand on Februrary 16. He is an experienced witness, having given "about 50" depositions in his career. That career stretches back to 1961, when he set up a radiology practice in Bridgeport, W.Va., in the Appalachian foothills about 80 miles south of Pittsburgh. Because of the mining, chemical plants, and glass factories in the region, he saw a good deal of lung disease caused by coal, silica, and asbestos. He has estimated that he's read 800,000 X-rays.

Since 1995, Harron's exclusive source of earned income has been reading X-rays as a consultant, mainly for plaintiffs' attorneys or screening firms. He does the readings at his office in Harron Square—a two-building office park he owns on the main strip through Bridgeport—at his home nearby, or at another home in La Marque, Texas, on the Gulf Coast. He also participates in screenings in hotel conference rooms in Mississippi, Texas, California, and other states. On those occasions, he's paid $125 per diagnosis, sometimes with a $10,000-per-day minimum.

Harron has been hard to pin down in depositions, because he claims to keep no records. He also claims to have no idea how much money he makes, having entrusted his finances to an accountant. Judging from transcripts and videotapes of those depositions, Harron is smart, confident, even arrogant in those settings. "I'm a film reader, not a publisher," he tells a defense lawyer who asks if he's ever written articles in his field.

Whenever a defense lawyer politely refers to the people he examines as "patients," Harron abruptly cuts him off. "They're not patients," he'll say, flatly. It's an important point. If they were patients he'd be required to keep records, and he'd also be on the hook for malpractice.

Harron is adamant that he calls films just as he sees them. "It's an insulting question," he responds to a lawyer who asks him if he is paid the same whether the diagnosis is positive or negative. "You're asking me basically if I'm prostituting myself, and I don't."

It was a less combative Harron who took the stand before Judge Jack. Questioned by Mulholland, he was forced to admit that he paid almost no attention to occupational histories when he diagnosed workers. "The only things that are of any importance to me," he had said in an earlier deposition, which he reaffirmed at the hearing, "are that the guy claims that he was exposed to asbestos or silica or whatever, and signs that he was exposed to it."

Next, Mulholland delved into the unseemly mechanics of assembly-line diagnosis. When Harron diagnosed silicosis, he admitted, he didn't actually write a report to that effect—or even dictate one. Instead, he filled out a standard X-ray classification form—writing symbols like "1/0" and checking boxes marked with letters like "t" and "p," which indicate the size, shape, and frequency of the shadows but don't necessarily translate into "silicosis." In a sense, the actual diagnosis was made by his typists, who gleaned it from the symbols and the patient's history. The typist then wrote up a narrative report using templates, stamped Harron's name on it, and sent it back to N&M without Harron's ever reading it. "Oh, this is not good," was Judge Jack's only comment.

Mulholland then showed Harron one of the 331 "Harron twofers," where he had issued separate reports for one worker based on one reading of one X-ray, one diagnosing asbestosis and the other silicosis. Harron said the reports were written months apart and he must have been presented with differing work histories each time.

Then Mulholland showed Harron instances in which he had read someone's X-ray as showing only asbestosis-shaped shadows back in the 1990s, but then read it as showing only silicosis-shaped shadows in

2001 or 2002. Had the irreversible asbestosis healed itself by the time of the second reading?

"So people are making pilgrimages to this man now," commented Judge Jack, to courtroom laughter.

Harron said the discrepancy might be due to "intra-reader variability," or to the films' having been shot differently each time, which can result in highlighting different lobes of the lung and therefore different scars.

"If you're accusing me of fabricating these things, I think that's a serious charge," Harron added.

"I think that's what he's doing," Judge Jack observed. Harron then asked to see a lawyer, and Judge Jack halted the examination to let him to do so. Though Harron returned the next day represented by counsel, neither side chose to question him further.

THE SCREENING DILEMMA

Judge Jack is expected to rule in the silicosis consolidation by mid-June. The defense lawyers have asked her to sanction several of the plaintiffs' firms, and at a hearing in March she indicated she'd love to. "I can sanction all the plaintiffs' lawyers to go to those doctors for the rest of their lives," she joked. But Jack also admitted she wasn't sure she had the power to sanction anybody, because she is likely to rule that in the final analysis, she lacks federal jurisdiction over nearly all the cases. Still, she promised an "extremely detailed" order describing what went on before her in an obvious effort to alert the state judges to whom the cases will return.

It may be too late for the revelations of the silicosis consolidation to remedy all the past abuses in asbestos litigation. So many horses left that barn so long ago, and the specter of inter-reader variability will still vex attempts to prove intentional wrongdoing. But the lessons of the silicosis consolidation extend beyond the asbestos scandals. A March 2005 cover story in *The American Lawyer* reports how the multibillion-dollar settlement of the fen-phen diet pill litigation in 2000 has been undermined by a deluge of low-level claimants identified by attorney-sponsored "echo mills"—i.e., echocardiogram screenings. A recent audit of more than 900 claims by a panel of outside cardiologists found that almost 70% should never have been paid.

Apologists for attorney-sponsored screenings say they benefit workers who can't afford to pay for their own medical examinations. But phony medicine is not a good substitute for real medicine, even for poor people.

The problems posed by attorney-sponsored screening are tricky. Since conscientiously performed surveillance screening is a good thing, it would be hard to fashion legislation that would ban only what should be banned. Enhanced transparency and vigilance seem to offer a safer solution, but in mass torts the need for streamlined claims processing always seems to trump time-consuming efforts to audit, with fraud coming out the winner.

Yet some action is required. Today, on the subways in Manhattan, ads from a group of Texas law firms tell New Yorkers how to get screened for something called welder's disease. Which might be fine and good. But it should also spur corporate defendants, insurers, judges, and possibly legislators to update that wise old saying: Fool me once, shame on you. Fool me 52,600 times, shame on me.

◆

AFTERMATH

Judge Jack ruled in the consolidated silicosis case in June 2005, several weeks after this story appeared in FORTUNE. "These diagnoses were driven by neither health nor justice: They were manufactured for money," Jack wrote in a scorching decision that remanded the cases to the state courts. "It is clear that the lawyers, doctors, and screening companies were all willing participants." In the fall of 2005, the Manville Trust and three others that handle asbestos claims barred nine doctors and four screening firms mentioned in Judge Jack's decision from submitting reports. Among them: Ray Harron, George Martindale, and James Ballard, as well as the N&M testing service.

Judge Jack's ruling also set a new standard for scrutiny in mass tort litigation, effectively reducing the number of silica cases in several states. More than half of the 10,000 suits she remanded to Mississippi were subsequently dismissed. Tougher judicial criteria, as well as state bills tightening medical standards, have led to slimmer silica dockets in Florida, Pennsylvania, Ohio, and Texas as well.

Federal tort reform has proved difficult to negotiate, even though estimates of the costs of such litigation go as high as 2% of GDP. But as the silica saga illustrates, there is considerable activity at lower levels of government. State by state, the tort landscape is changing—to the relief of business, and the great displeasure of much of the trial bar.

10

HOW IBM STUNG HITACHI

From Poughkeepsie to San Jose to Tokyo—a tale of corporate espionage, and how it was discovered.

---

by DAVID B. TINNIN

March 7, 1983

When the FBI arrested two Hitachi employees in the act of buying IBM trade secrets in California in June 1982, the curtain went up on an extraordinary spectacle of corporate warfare. For months, two of the world's mightiest, most respected, and most technologically advanced corporations had been stalking one another—Hitachi seeking to obtain secrets of its dominant competitor, IBM seeking to teach Hitachi a stinging, humiliating lesson. In February 1983, as Hitachi and two employees pleaded guilty in a federal court, the case ended on a hushed and anticlimactic note that gave no hint of the intricate saga that had preceded it—in which IBM helped the FBI catch Hitachi in a superbly executed sting.

During the sting operation, the FBI used hidden cameras and listening devices to obtain 35 hours of videotape and 65 hours of audiotape. The tapes recorded numerous episodes in which Hitachi employees conspired to purchase IBM equipment and documents.

After the arrests, one of Hitachi's foremost objectives was to avoid a trial in which this embarrassing material would be displayed.. Hitachi offered to plead no contest, as long as its employees escaped trial and punishment. The Justice Department countered: Plead guilty and nobody goes to jail. Hitachi agreed. An open admission of wrongdoing was not easy for Hitachi, but ah, those tapes.

In the courtroom in San Francisco the scenario was so well arranged that suspense and drama were absent. Hitachi pleaded guilty to the one-count indictment of conspiring to transport stolen IBM property from the U.S. to Japan. That same day, Judge Spencer Williams imposed the maximum corporate penalty under the statute: a $10,000 fine. Hitachi senior planner Kenji Hayashi, who had been a major actor in the espionage drama, was fined $10,000 and placed on five years' probation. Isao Ohnishi, a Hitachi software expert, drew a $4,000 fine and two years' probation.

Even though the case did not come to trial, the pretrial hearings included a substantial record of evidence and arguments, from both sides. After examining that material and doing some investigating of its own, FORTUNE knit together the story of how IBM stung Hitachi.

PRINTED IN RED

A minor player touched off the chain of events from which all the rest of the drama unfolded. He was Raymond Cadet, 45, a Haitian-born computer scientist, who resigned from IBM's computer labs in Poughkeepsie, N.Y., in November 1980. The parting was amicable. During the routine exit interviews, according to IBM, Cadet signed a pledge that he was taking no confidential material with him. But in reality, says the Justice Department, Cadet took with him ten of the 27 volumes that made up the so-called Adirondack workbooks. Adirondack was IBM's code name for its top-secret program to build a new generation of computers, the 308X. The first model of that series, the 3081, was shipped in October 1981. The workbooks, which were three-ring binders, contained 40 to 200 pages. The first page of each volume carried a warning that the contents were proprietary material, not to be divulged except to fellow IBM employees on a need-to-know basis. Printed in red diagonally across each page were the words DO NOT REPRODUCE.

After he left IBM, Cadet went to work for a computer firm near Washington. Then, on June 1, 1981, Barry Saffaie recruited him for a job in Silicon Valley. Saffaie was a manager at a California company called National Advanced Systems, or NAS for short, a subsidiary of National Semiconductor. NAS marketed Hitachi products in the U.S. and manufactured computer products of its own as well.

The reason Saffaie wanted Cadet is clear enough: NAS closely tracks IBM, and Cadet's relatively current knowledge made him valuable. There is no evidence that Saffaie even knew about the workbooks. Once Cadet joined NAS, though, Saffaie soon got hold of all ten volumes, and many photocopies were run off.

During the summer of 1981, Barry Saffaie shuttled across the Pacific to brief Hitachi on computer developments in the U.S. In August, according to the Justice Department, he delivered copies of the ten workbooks to Hitachi computer specialists. At first, it seems, they did not realize what they were getting. Meanwhile, in San Jose, Hitachi was being offered a study of the 3081 by another source: Palyn Associates, a small consulting firm. Like NAS, Palyn keeps an eye on IBM. Palyn's president, Maxwell O. Paley, spent 21 years at IBM and rose to chief of the Advanced Computing Systems laboratory before leaving the company in 1970. Palyn's brochure boasts that the top executives possess "80 years' cumulative IBM experience."

Paley founded Palyn Associates in 1972, and almost from the start Hitachi was a major client. Hitachi was always on the lookout for information about IBM. The Japanese firm is one of the so-called IBM-compatible manufacturers, which build computers so they can operate with the same software and peripheral equipment as IBM computers.

A company in the business of making IBM-compatible computers has to keep pace with IBM. One way that competitors do so is by "reverse engineering." They purchase an early model, take it apart, and design something with comparable capabilities. But that can allow IBM months of market dominance. It's much more advantageous, obviously, to acquire IBM designs far in advance of the new computer's shipment date. That was what made Paley and his fellow IBM veterans valuable to Hitachi. Using their own knowledge of IBM's techniques and design directions, Palyn Associates had compiled a study of the 3081, and the firm offered it to its regular contact man at Hitachi. He was Kenji Hayashi, a senior engineer in the computer project planning department. Hayashi took an index of the Palyn study back to Tokyo.

At that time, Hayashi knew nothing of Saffaie's delivery of the workbooks; he had never seen the man. But after he learned about the new material in Hitachi's possession, Hayashi sent Palyn Associates a telex, saying that his company was not interested in the Palyn study because "we have already got Adirondack workbook that is similar to your covering [evidently meaning index]. But we have only Vol. 1, 3, 4, 8, 9, 10, 11, 12, 15, 22. If you have another Vol., let me know. We consider again ... Please keep confidential. Regards." As an IBM veteran, Max Paley immediately recognized the message for what it was: dynamite waiting to explode.

In Silicon Valley, where trade secrets are easily spirited from firm to firm in the heads or briefcases of job-hopping engineers, confidential information often ends up in the wrong place. Such problems are frequently settled by a phone call from one company president to another and the return of the filched material. Some Silicon Valley veterans fault Paley for not having turned first to Hitachi. Instead, after intense and agonized discussions with his top associates, Paley went to IBM. "Bob," Paley told his close friend Bob Evans, vice president for engineering, programming and technology, "I think one of my Japanese clients has gotten your crown jewels."

Only a few top executives—no more than eight—were informed of the threat. The man in immediate command was assistant general counsel Donato Evangelista, a tall and robust cigar-chomper who oversees the highly sensitive areas of trade secrets and security. First off, Evangelista wanted to verify whether the Adirondack volumes in Hitachi's possession were genuine. For that mission he relied upon an agent whose performances in past emergencies inspired utmost confidence—Richard A. Callahan. A tall, white-haired, distinguished-looking man in his early 50s, Callahan is IBM's top troubleshooter for security matters.

A Marine captain during the Korean war, Callahan had an outstanding career in federal law enforcement before joining IBM as a full-time employee in 1973. He met with Paley in San Jose and offered him a retainer if he would cooperate with IBM in determining whether Hitachi really possessed those "crown jewels." Paley agreed to take on the assignment. Acting on Callahan's instructions, Max Paley telexed a reply to Hitachi's query on the Adirondack workbooks. Wrote Paley: "I made a contact and was told information you requested is under rather strict security control but can be obtained." He proposed a meeting in Japan in early October. On the flight to Tokyo, Paley and a colleague, Robert Domenico, were accompanied by Callahan.

On October 2, Paley and Domenico met with Hayashi in a room at the Imperial Hotel (Callahan kept out of sight). Well prepared, Hayashi handed over a five-page handwritten set of questions about the operating systems of the new 3081. Then Paley produced attractive bait, prepared by Callahan: a handwritten index of the entire 27-volume set of workbooks. Paley told Hayashi that Palyn Associates did not engage in acquiring confidential material, but that he might be able to find someone who did. According to Paley's affidavit, he asked to see the workbooks in Hitachi's possession so he could identify the genuine article after he returned to the U.S.

At a second meeting four days later, Hayashi handed over copies of three workbooks, volumes 8, 11, and 22, each still bearing the words "IBM CONFIDENTIAL." Hayashi, who said Hitachi wanted four of the volumes "very badly," returned the index Paley had given him. Alongside the listing for each volume, he had placed a letter: A for the highest priority, B for the second, and C for a new copy of the books already in Hitachi's possession if an updated version had been issued. Hayashi had one special request: an early peek at IBM's most advanced disk-drive memory mechanism before volume shipments to customers began. Paley said he would see what he could do. On leaving the meeting, Paley turned over the workbooks and other material to Callahan, who recognized at once that they were genuine.

Basically, IBM had two choices. It could start a civil suit that would seek to prohibit Hitachi from making use of the stolen data and ask for punitive damages. Or it could turn its findings over to the Justice Department and, in effect, start a criminal case. For IBM, the selection of the second, tougher course came naturally.

As a matter of corporate conviction, IBM has no mercy on anyone who steals its trade secrets—or tries to. IBM was aware that the FBI had an undercover investigation under way in Silicon Valley. It was called Pengem, an acronym standing for Penetration of the Gray Electronics Market. One of the operation's objectives was to check the rapidly expanding flow of finished chips and sophisticated chip-production equipment to the Soviet Union and its allies. As a front for Pengem, the bureau rented an office in Santa Clara and established a realistic imitation of a consulting firm, called Glenmar Associates, staffed by FBI agents.

IBM had been involved with Pengem as far back as March 1981. The company's representative was none other than Richard Callahan. IBM pledged to train no fewer than two and no more than seven FBI agents in how to operate in the industry, and to establish cover for two agents by providing credentials and identification badges.

When Callahan told the FBI of IBM's findings about Hitachi's misdeeds, Pengem's focus shifted from the Russians to the Japanese. The FBI agents in the San Jose office, however, thought the Hitachi case would require no more than two weeks or so to clear up, and they could then return to their original mission. Hence, they wanted to avoid letting Paley, a well-known figure in Silicon Valley, discover the true nature of Glenmar Associates and thus blow their cover.

To sidetrack Paley, Callahan arranged a handover operation. Under instructions from Callahan, Paley telephoned Hayashi, then staying at the New York Hilton, with the message that a meeting directly with the source of IBM information could be arranged in early November in Las Vegas. Hayashi agreed. The FBI took care of the rest, installing listening devices in a room at the Las Vegas Hilton. There Paley introduced both Callahan and another FBI agent, Alan Garretson (under assumed identities, of course), as sources who could help Hitachi get its wish list of IBM equipment and documents. In accordance with Justice Department guidelines on undercover operations, Garretson told Hayashi that the material would have to be illegally taken and that the person involved could be "put in jail for stealing." Hayashi failed to recognize the warning signal.

After the Las Vegas meetings, Callahan (not Garretson) conducted the first follow-up conversation with the Japanese. On the line was a Hitachi memory-systems expert named Jun Naruse, who had been assigned to view IBM's new memory device. Naruse was worried. If there was any kind of trouble, he noted, "it's real trouble for Hitachi."

Three days later, Garretson met Naruse at 5 a.m. in the lobby of a hotel in Hartford, Conn. They drove to a parking lot near a Pratt & Whitney Aircraft plant. In the parking lot, a Pratt & Whitney employee, whom the FBI had recruited, gave Garretson and Naruse identification badges that enabled them to gain admission to a high-security area in which one of the new memory devices was installed. In return, Garretson handed over an envelope apparently stuffed with money. "How much did you have to pay?" asked Naruse. "Plenty," whispered Garretson.

The three entered the plant uneventfully. As they reached the door of the room containing the memory device, they found it locked. While Garretson and Naruse hid in a closet, the Pratt & Whitney employee fetched a guard, who opened the door. Once inside, Naruse was ecstatic. Both men carried cameras and began taking pictures. After each had shot many pictures, Naruse asked to be photographed hugging the device. Back in the Hartford hotel, Naruse gave Garretson $3,000 in $100 bills.

Then, on November 18 in Santa Clara, he delivered an additional $7,000 in return for maintenance manuals for the memory device.

As a good hug should, the Hartford embrace produced heightened enthusiasm within Hitachi. Through various channels, more and more requests for secret IBM data and equipment began reaching Glenmar Associates. In a separate letter to Garretson, Hayashi set out an expanded shopping list. He placed a code and price tag alongside each item Hitachi desired. D-14, for example, indicated the magnetic head and platters used to read and write data on the disk drive; for that Hitachi was willing to pay $10,000.

That letter crossed one from Callahan, in his undercover role. Callahan wrote to Hayashi that some IBM people were getting nervous about continuing to supply information: "They are only willing to risk the consequences if the money rewards are great enough."

Hayashi quickly replied that "from the point of us, cost should depend on how we can use it," noting that timing was crucial. To make the point more graphic, Hayashi drew a chart that showed a sharply slanting line declining over a four-year period from a presumably high value to zero. He concluded by holding out the lure of a contract if Glenmar could obtain the complex microcode used to enhance the performance of one of IBM's older computers. "Our top management will understand your potential if you locate it by the end of January," Hayashi wrote.

Glenmar did better than that. On January 7, 1982, Garretson phoned Hayashi in Tokyo to report that he could deliver the microcode for $12,000. On January 18, at a meeting with Hayashi and Hitachi software expert Isao Ohnishi, Garretson was told that a secure money channel had now been established. Hitachi would send funds to Nissei Electronics Ltd., a Hitachi affiliate, which in turn would transfer the money to NCL Data Inc., where the president, Tom Yoshida, would make the payments in bank transfers to Glenmar's account.

From then on, transactions occurred with almost dizzying rapidity. At most deliveries, a Hitachi expert was present to check the goods and often to make on-the-spot requests for an additional manual or part.

Camaraderie was also developing. Viewers of the tapes say that much of the time was taken up by friendly banter about baseball and where the men were going to have dinner together.

All the while, the FBI was seeking to lure higher-ranking Hitachi executives within range of its clandestine cameras. The opening came in March when Hayashi said that the company was very interested in hiring as consultants IBM executives who were about to retire. Garretson insisted that the IBM executives in question were at such high levels they required personal assurances about security from a Hitachi executive of equal rank. The ploy worked. On April 23, Callahan and Garretson met in San Francisco with Kisaburo Nakazawa, general manager of Hitachi's Kanagawa Works, which produces the company's mainframe computers. According to an FBI affidavit, Nakazawa said he was aware of everything Garretson's company had provided and that it had been helpful. He also said he was aware of the risks involved.

As the Japanese shopping list grew ever longer, IBM executives privy to the plot began to worry that they had been giving away too much. IBM told the FBI it could not allow another batch of material to leave the U.S.

From that point the sting rolled toward the climax. Hitachi was offered a package deal that would give the company just about everything it wanted for $700,000. After some haggling, the two sides settled on $535,000.

At precisely 9 a.m. on June 22, a brown Volkswagen van belonging to Tom Yoshida braked to a stop in front of the Glenmar offices. Hayashi and Ohnishi climbed out. Yoshida remained at the wheel.

As he entered the room in which the IBM booty was stacked on a table, Hayashi could hardly contain his delight. Triumphantly, he seized one of the cartons and ripped off the sticky IBM label. With a flourish, he pasted the famed IBM logo on his notebook, souvenir of a job well done.

At that moment, two other men stepped into the room. "It is all over," one of the said. "We are FBI agents."

◆

AFTERMATH

Hitachi was initially humiliated by the arrests, hunkering down and going so far as to suspend advertising. But the Japanese press coverage was anything but hostile, portraying the company as a victim of a dirty trick. Because of the Japanese public's perception that it was not guilty of anything, Hitachi finally felt able to do what otherwise would have been almost impossible for a Japanese company to do: plead guilty.

In all, 13 employees at Hitachi were charged with stealing trade secrets. Two pleaded guilty and were put on probation. Indictments were dropped against another two, and the rest were never extradited from Japan. The only American charged, Tom Yoshida, pleaded no contest in the spring of 1983; he was fined $7,500 and placed on two years of probation. IBM's civil suit against Hitachi never went to trial. Instead, the two parties came to a confidential settlement.

The U.S. public was predictably ticked at Hitachi's shenanigans, agreeing with Paley that what it came down to was that the Japanese "weren't fighting fair." Neither country could understand the other's position—a situation that became a leitmotif of the 1980s, when bashing Japan became something of an American national pastime, and ridiculing America something of a Japanese one. No other incident captures the mutual incomprehensibility of this period in business history as well as the tale of the Hitachi sting.

Still, by the mid-90s, IBM and Hitachi had patched things up and were exchanging patents. Hitachi bought processor modules from IBM to use in their own computers, and they collaborated to attach Hitachi devices to IBM hardware.

In 2003, Hitachi acquired IBM's hard-drive business for $2 billion. It lost money consistently. In late 2007, Hitachi announced it was getting out of the PC business.

III

SCAMS

11

MCKESSON AND ROBBINS:
ITS FALL AND RISE

---

by BILL FURTH, LARRY LESSING AND HELEN VIND

March 1940

Even the most storied family firm can fall prey to a con. In 1938, drug industry behemoth McKesson and Robbins nearly crumpled when its president, who had purchased the company a decade earlier, was accused of embezzlement, then revealed to be a felon living under an assumed name. F. Donald Coster, born Philip Musica, took advantage of auditing standards so crude that they were not really standards at all. He knew this because as a bootlegger in the 1920s, he saw firsthand that auditors would readily certify whatever assets or amounts were provided to them. That insight provided the basis for his next, and biggest, swindle. Here is how a small-timer whose previous frauds had been scamming the human hair and poultry markets hit the big time—briefly.

On December 10, 1938, William J. Wardall, a bushy-browed, even-tempered ex-investment banker, was sitting amid a torrent of telephone calls at the desk of the president of McKesson and Robbins overlooking 44th Street, New York. Two days before, he had suddenly been appointed trustee of the company, which had been thrown into the courts upon suspicion that something was wrong. Six days later the president at whose desk Wardall was sitting, F. Donald Coster, was going to shoot himself through the head, although Mr. Wardall didn't know that. Wardall knew nothing about F. Donald Coster and he knew next to nothing about the drug business, in which McKesson and Robbins was the biggest single corporation. All he knew was that he had put a man in charge of the company's books, had all the locks changed, shifted the bank accounts to his own name and set afoot an investigation.. Then Charles J. Lynn, of Eli Lilly and Company, walked in.

"I know how busy you are," Lynn began, "but I want to ask you one question: Are you going to continue this business?"

Wardall said he hoped so, and that he was doing his best to that end.

"That's all I wanted to know," said Lynn. "Because McKesson is necessary to the function of distributing drugs in this country."

Wardall did not know about the drug industry, but he did know something about creditors and he had never heard one talk like that before. It gave him heart.

Wardall has continued the business. He has, in fact, just seen it through what seems to have been the most profitable year in its history. "Maybe Barnum was right," he reflects, "any advertising is good advertising."

But it is not as simple as that, as Wardall is the first to add. Even had the buying public recoiled from every product that bore the McKesson label—and there are 238 drug products and 42 brands of liquor so labeled—it would have affected only about 8% of McKesson's total sales. McKesson and Robbins is five or six businesses in one, really. It is a drug manufacturer. It is a wholesale distributor of wines and liquors, the largest in the U.S. But, above all, it is a wholesale distributor, or jobber, of other manufacturers' drugs. This division, which grossed $102.7 million last year, is probably ten times as big as any other drug distributor in the country. The McKesson warehouses and salesmen handle no less than 48,000 different items, chiefly pharmaceuticals, biological, and other remedies, but also including $1 million worth of alarm clocks, $1 million worth of Coca-Cola syrup, and smaller quantities of fountain pens, ear syringes, stationery, combs, dolls, and everything else a drugstore carries except ice cream and milk. It was this jobbing business Lynn was thinking of.

And that is the business that has survived the death of Coster with scarcely a ripple. The whole story is an odd one; a tribute, perhaps, to the vitality that resides in a corporation and cannot be extinguished even by its creator. For Coster was the creator of McKesson and Robbins, even though the business is 107 years old. Let us begin at the beginning.

It begins in 1833, the year John McKesson opened a drugstore in Manhattan's Maiden Lane. In 1840 John took as a partner one Daniel Robbins, who had two sons, Herbert and Charles. Importing famous German pharmacists whom Charles had met at Heidelberg, they began to make quinine pills with a unique gelatin coating, which still sell well in the humid climate of India. They also developed a large jobbing business.

Robbins and old McKesson had passed away by 1891, but their kin carried on. A stint at McKesson's was almost a prerequisite to a pharmaceutical career. Just before the World War, John McKesson Jr. and his wife were traveling in Europe, where they ran across a large, personable man with a booming voice named Saunders Norvell. He was retired from a career in hardware; meeting McKesson revived his interest in business. Upon his return in 1914, he bought a partnership in McKesson and Robbins. The firm was shortly incorporated, with McKesson Jr. as president and Norvell as chairman of the board.

In 1924, the firm split up. The McKessons took a chemical manufacturing subsidiary called the New York Quinine and Chemical Works. Norvell and Robbins took the pharmaceutical manufacturing business and the name. Under their management, McKesson and Robbins continued to make and sell Calox, Albolene, milk of magnesia, quinine pills, and the like, around $5 million worth a year. The jobbing business was junked. And in November 1926, Norvell and Robbins sold McKesson outright for $1 million to a younger and more ambitious man named F. D. Coster.

THE MUSICA WAY

Coster's early career deserves a few words, too. He was born in New York City in 1884, the son of a barber from Naples, Italy, named Antonio Musica, and was christened Philip. Philip was the oldest of four brothers, and the smartest. When Antonio started a little importing business—cheese, olive oil, and the like—Philip went down to the docks and bribed the customs weigher to certify that the Musica cheeses weighed less than they did. The Musicas prospered. In 1909 the federal government arrested them. On the witness stand, Philip took all the blame and was sent to Elmira Reformatory in New York with a one-year sentence and a $5,000 fine. But the Musicas were no petty thieves to be kicked around. President Taft himself was besieged by requests for leniency both from the Italian Ambassador and from prominent New York Republicans, including the attorney general. After five months in jail, Philip went free.

Back home, Philip soon induced his father to form the United States Hair Company to export hair for high-end coiffeurs. Again the Musicas prospered. Philip lived at the Knickerbocker Hotel and wore high heels and spats and was a friend of Caruso's.

One day Philip appeared at the Bank of the Manhattan Company in search of a loan. The bank promised him $25,000 but sent investigators to check on the security—bills of lading for hair. Instead of $25,000 worth of long, valuable hair, they found an assortment of worthless ends and short sizes, known to the trade as trash. When detectives reached the Musica home, they found the valuable hair under a trap door in the stables, but they found no Musicas. They caught the family in New Orleans, on board the S.S. *Heredia* just as it was about to cast off. Philip tried to bar the stateroom door. Sister Lucy Grace tried to throw $18,600 in bills into the water. Old Antonio, crying, "I am disgraced," tried to shoot himself on the way to the police station. At the trial Philip once more took all the blame and this time spent three years in the Tombs prison in New York. Released early for his cooperation in unraveling the crime, he stuck pretty close to the District Attorney's office. In 1916, as William Johnson, he was employed as a stool pigeon, specializing in German spy investigations. He also moved around in the poultry racket, and in 1920 was indicted for subornation of perjury in a murder case. But Philip Musica never spent another day in jail. With Prohibition, crime became respectable, and Philip became respectable, too.

After several false starts as a bootlegger, he and his associates secured a permit to withdraw 5,000 gallons of government alcohol every month. The portion of this that did not go into hair tonic or other blinds brought a typical bootlegging profit. It was a sweet business; but Costa had a physical fear of one of his crew, Joe Brandino. Costa—or Coster, as he now became—sent an old friend of his down to Washington to tip off the Volstead Act men. The company lost its permit and was dissolved.

Coster started again, with Girard and Company, which made pharmaceuticals in a two-story rented factory in Mount Vernon, N.Y., at one point forging a signature in order to cash in a $1,900 life insurance policy. But he never had to stoop that low again. Not a petty forger at heart, he thereafter stuck to his true vocation, which was that of a confidence man. And since he was to pyramid his stake into a $43 million corporation by 1928, this is a good place to watch his moves closely.

Girard and Company, having secured an alcohol permit, began making eau de quinine, hair tonic, a polish called Woodtone, and other drugs. When the Volstead men called, Coster charmed some and bribed others, and anyway Girard did not divert any alcohol directly to the bootleg trade. One of its biggest customers was a selling agency called W. W. Smith and Company, which consisted of a small office, a filing cabinet, a stenographer, and a man who called himself George

Vernard. He was really Arthur Musica, Coster's brother. Another brother, George, kept the books of Girard and Company under the name of George Dietrich. In December 1924, Price, Waterhouse and Company received a letter on Girard and Company stationery signed by P. Horace Girard, asking the company to take on the account. It did so starting in 1925.

When an auditor looks into your books, his interest is in figures and documents only. Take the verification of assets. For the cash item, he writes your bank to see how much cash you have, and reconciles that with your own deposit records and canceled checks. For accounts receivable, he takes a sample group and checks the documents on each. He does not—or did not in the 1920s—get confirmation from your customers, especially without your permission. For inventories, he finds out how the goods on hand were counted and valued, but he does not count them himself.

Thus when Price, Waterhouse and Company certified that Girard and Company's assets on December 31, 1924, were $295,000, it did not mean that it knew or cared who W. W. Smith and Company was, only that it appeared to have paid its bills on time. Nor did it know or care that an inventory item called Dandrofuge, was probably alcohol for the bootleg trade. So long as the papers were in order, Price, Waterhouse and Company had no reason to be suspicious, even as inventories and receivables grew rapidly.

On sales of $252,000, Girard and Company showed $33,300 profit for the 1924 nine-month period, a tidy profit that drew the attention of Julian Thompson, a salesman for the New York investment house of Bond and Goodwin. Alert for new business, Thompson called on Coster in Mount Vernon. He saw the firm was too small for public financing but he admired the neat Price, Waterhouse and Company audit and the strong current ratio. After investigating some of the trade references (though not W. W. Smith), Thompson wrote a 17 page memorandum about the firm. Thompson, who died of influenza in 1939, was to be Coster's nemesis as well as his first sponsor.

About the time of Thompson's visit, Coster moved Girard and Company to an abandoned gas-mask factory near Bridgeport, Conn. Horace B. Merwin, of the Bridgeport Trust Company, was quick to solicit the newcomer's banking business. Girard and Company needed $100,000 of short-term money and Merwin accordingly looked over the plant. He looked over the Price, Waterhouse and Company statement, he read a friendly letter from the Mount Vernon bank, and he read Thompson's 17-page memorandum. Above all he talked to Coster, who may have seemed a trifle eccentric, but was obviously an able man. He and two colleagues bought 275 shares of the company and the bank was happy to give Girard and Company a bank loan of $80,000.

When Price, Waterhouse audited the books again as of December 1925, receivables were up to $170,500, with W. W. Smith still prominent ($22,750) among them. Sales had more than quadrupled to $1.1 million; the bank loan had been paid off, and the three bank stockholders were in line for a generous dividend. The following year Coster wanted $300,000 more, and suggested an issue of preferred stock. The bankers thereupon hired an independent accountant to audit Girard and Company's books; but like Price, Waterhouse before him, he merely added and verified pieces of paper and did not write to the receivables. Thus reassured, the Bridgeport bankers went ahead. Most of the money went straight into inventories, which more than doubled to $606,000 in three months. At the end of November 1926, Girard and Company's assets were $1.3 million. In 11 months sales were $1.1 million; profits were $250,200.

How much of this profitable little company's business was legitimate? It is impossible to say. At any rate, the swift rise in inventories and receivables occasioned no eyebrow lifting. In retrospect, Girard and Company was undoubtedly a sort of laboratory in which Coster perfected the technique of his later, larger frauds.

In the fall of 1926, Coster told his bankers that he could buy McKesson and Robbins; Merwin and his friends sold $1.65 million of stock in a new company, McKesson and Robbins of Connecticut. The new company took over both Girard and the old McKesson, whose machinery and stock were moved bodily to the Girard plant in Bridgeport.

A GREAT BUSINESS HEAD

From here on the story of McKesson and Robbins, and of Coster, divides into two separate streams—one clear, rocky, and honest, the other still, crooked, and deep. Let us follow the honest stream first. By 1927 Coster had a $4.1 million manufacturing company in Bridgeport with a 94-year-old reputation, three Yankee bankers on his board of directors, and a $1 million Canadian subsidiary. Profits for 1927 were almost $600,000 when Thompson said to Coster, in effect: You are big enough now for the Street.

Two things favored the swift expansion of the new McKesson and Robbins. One was the voracity of the stock market. The other was a somewhat special situation in the drug trade. The old McKesson company, remember, had gone out of the jobbing business. There were, in fact, no nationwide drug jobbers. The retail chains were growing fast throughout the 1920s, but they specialized in high-traffic locations in big cities, and scarcely touched the smaller towns. The 56,400 independents, who accounted for sales of around $1 billion per year, were buying most of their supplies from some 300 small local independent jobbers, many of them family run.

It was clear to Coster that a nationwide chain of these regional jobbers could be a very powerful distributing medium. And being a merger idea, it was more than welcome in the Street. A new company, McKesson and Robbins of Maryland, was formed in 1928 to acquire both McKesson and Robbins of Connecticut and the assets of the jobbers that Coster invited in. (Jobbers were given cash and stock in the new company.)

By 1929, McKesson and Robbins of Maryland included 49 of the biggest and soundest wholesale jobbing houses in the country. It also owed the banks $16.75 million. This debt was refinanced in 1930 by an issue of 20-year debentures. McKesson was now the colossus of the drug industry. It showed profits of $4.1 million on sales of $140.6 million in 1929. For the wholesalers and their old provincial families, the experience was delirious. For a banker like Merwin, who testified that he had invested about $6,000 in Girard and Company in 1925 and found it worth $250,000 three years later, it was exciting, too.

But at the first hint of depression, the infant colossus grew cranky. The board had 30-odd directors and 200 officers, but Coster, who owned about 10% of the common stock outstanding, favored highly centralized control and wanted to run the whole show. The wholesalers, however, wanted to run their own territories, and resisted his plans to buy retail stories and turn McKesson into a channel of fast-moving items. Eventually, though an independent investigation in 1933 questioned Coster's leadership, they came to uneasy terms. The wholesalers got Coster to agree to keep his hands off their local jobbing operations; Coster got undisputed control of the Bridgeport company.

Sales mounted yearly, soaring to $174.6 million in 1937. Profits rose more slowly, but McKesson was pointing up again. Coster could consider himself the head of a seasoned concern, a role he relished

Large and pudgy, Coster was by turn effervescent, puzzling, and mean to the men who worked with him. He was a tyrant and a hard man to see, which some mistook for efficiency. When irritated, he would seize the long hairs at the back of his head and pull them over his bald spot. He worked 16 hours a day, drank a lot of milk (stomach ulcers), and smoked too many cigars. Coster has sufficient publicity to submit a biography to *Who's Who,* two-thirds of which was fictitious; he even listed several clubs to which he did not belong.

Like Ivar Kreuger, it was a depression that caught him. In the spring of 1937 the directors voted to slash inventories, which had risen in one year by $10 million. It was decided that $4 million should be cut in four months—$2 million from the liquor division, a million from the wholesale drug warehouses, and a million from Bridgeport. The wholesalers went to work with a will; so did the liquor men. Yet the

Bridgeport figures continued to climb. These covered not just the factory; in them were lumped some little-known trading operations called General Sales, or Bulk Department. It was Thompson, the treasurer, who first noticed that although the crude-drug operations showed the best profit figures of all the divisions, the profits were always plowed back into new purchases, and no cash ever came out. He began to tax Coster about it; when was he going to make his share of the $4 million cut? Thompson's questions drew elusive replies. So in February 1938, he began a little private investigation. Ten months later Coster was dead.

AND A HEAD FOR FIGURES

Let us now turn back to 1926, and follow the dark, silent stream of Coster's strictly criminal activities. In 12 years as president of McKesson and Robbins, Coster with his confederates stole about $2,.9 million of the company's cash. They stole $1.023 million in 1929 alone. But the theft was not the most serious of his crimes, nor is it at all clear that cash was his chief object. Except for the yacht and good cigars, Coster had no extravagant tastes. When he died, he had three one-dollar bills in his pocket, and his estate was reported to be only $36,000. So what were his motives? Let us first see what he did.

There is no reason to suppose that he stopped bootlegging. But after 1926 he turned his chief energies to trading in crude drugs.

McKesson's crude-drug division was in two parts. The domestic part was—and is—legitimately operated by Hermann, who buys bulk chemicals and sells them to American manufacturers, laundries, laboratories, and druggists. The other part was speculation in world markets and was Coster's personal affair. His crude-drug figures were always lumped with Hermann's.

If Coster ever actually bought and sold crude drugs, he did not do it long. From 1927 on, his end of the division was wholly fictitious. In brief, it consisted of pretending to buy crude drugs from dummy sources, paying for them with good McKesson money, pretending to sell them to genuine foreign dealers, and then paying McKesson back its own money—some of it, rather—through other dummies. On McKesson's books, these transactions merely meant that cash went down, inventories and receivables up. Large amounts of cash could thus be kept in suspension in the dummies' bank accounts, from which it was an easy trip to Coster's brokerage account or to the pockets of his tribe.

The Bridgeport setup was under the strict control of George Dietrich, (aka George Musica), who signed all the checks. Well liked and well connected, he stuck very close to his job. His office was right next to Coster's. He and Coster never took vacations at the same time, and when he had his tonsils out at nine o'clock one morning, he was back at his desk by one, in time for the afternoon mail. George Dietrich saw all the mail before it was distributed.

The taking of inventory was in charge of Robert Dietrich, the youngest Musica. As for the dummy corporations, they were led by our old friend W. W. Smith, which was still George Vernard and a secretary over in Brooklyn, just as in the Girard bootlegging days. There was another W. W. Smith office in Stamford. One of the secretaries, $20-per-week Rose Otting, had seven typewriters. Rose was an accurate typist who moved confidently from typewriter to typewriter, depending on which of McKesson's phony suppliers was sending Dietrich a bill. It all seemed legitimate to Rose. "I thought they were holding companies or something," she said.

The total payments by McKesson and Robbins for fictitious crude drugs came to $22 million between 1927 and 1932. About $20 million of these payments was returned to McKesson, the rest was siphoned off. Coster's biggest cash killing was in 1929, when he stole $634,000 in the first 72 hours of the October stock-market crash.

After 1932 the method of handling the phony transactions was changed. Diversions of actual cash dropped to much smaller amounts and became much harder to detect; but the crude-drug department on paper was enormously expanded. From a bald steal, it became a bookkeeping symphony; instead of a livelihood, an end in itself. What Coster did was to set up a dummy banking firm, Manning and Company, as fiscal agent for all the department's purchases and sales. When Pierson, Miller, or other dummy suppliers made a "sale" to McKesson, the bill was forwarded to Manning and Company, and Manning also pretended to receive checks from the customers. Every month Manning's statement arrived at Bridgeport, a neat marshaling of debits, credits, and balance. At the same time Coster drew up a contract with W. W. Smith, making it agent for all crude-drug sales. Smith guaranteed all accounts and received an annual fee of $18,000 plus three-quarters of 1% commission. From 1932 until just before the end these commissions and fees paid monthly by McKesson's check were the only cash diverted to Vernard.

This new system enabled Coster to increase his crude-drug figures with a minimum use of cash. Coming when it did, the changeover may have been his way of saving McKesson from bankruptcy. The simple inflation of book assets made things seem better than they were. But the comparatively rapid growth of the crude-drug division was concealed from most of the directors by lumping the figures not only with those of legitimate crude-drug sales but also with those of the Bridgeport manufacturing plant. Actually, fake crude-drug inventories and receivables represented nearly a quarter of the company's assets by 1938. There were only two non-Musicas who had regular access to the breakdown. One was John McGloon, the controller, who is now under indictment. The other was Price, Waterhouse and Company.

From this distance, Coster's befuddling of Price, Waterhouse is perhaps the most interesting aspect of his career. When the first word of suspicion about the crude-drug accounts reached its ears, a Price, Waterhouse man remarked, "Why, that's the best-run department in the business!"

For Price, Waterhouse's sake, George Dietrich supplied it with forged Dun and Bradstreet reports on W. W. Smith, showing it to be worth $6 million or $7 million. He also supplied duplicate bills of lading from Bridgeport and a detailed inventory of drugs in five or six different warehouses, the list being replete with pharmaceutical blunders. Vanilla beans, for example, were counted in 200-pound sacks, as though they were lima beans, although they are shipped in tins. Warehouses would sometimes be credited with greater quantities of procaine or iodoform than the entire domestic supply. In addition to documents, Manning, Smith, and the suppliers maintained real mailing addresses in Montreal and Liverpool.

But if accountants seem easy to fool, consider the directors. Especially the three—Merwin, Phillips, and Seeley—who were also directors of McKesson's Canadian subsidiary. The Canadian company's stated purpose was to make and sell McKesson products in the British Empire, but it never made so much as a liver pill. Save for owning a tiny Calox-making subsidiary in England, it did not do a dollar's worth of business in 11 years. Yet it showed earnings of $100,000 or more yearly and paid dividends of at least $89,000 a year. The transactions on its books (which were kept in Bridgeport) consisted entirely of crude-drug sales, all fictitious.

And then Thompson started his private inquiry. He was struck by the failure of the crude-drug inventories to decrease and the fact that Coster had stalled him. Then he discovered that these stocks carried no insurance. Coster told him W. W. Smith took care of that. Thompson decided to check. From Dun and Bradstreet, he learned that the report on W. W. Smith was forged. (Price, Waterhouse had got it from George Dietrich.) By autumn he had gotten around to checking the Montreal address, which proved a shell, and, later, to going over to Brooklyn to call on George Vernard. Thompson and Vernard had quite a talk. "He started to fence with me," said Thompson later; for a while they were reduced to talking about the New Deal. Vernard was a Dewey man.

Thompson had enough to demand a showdown. He had enough because his signature was required on $3 million of new debentures that McKesson was about to sell to Equitable Life. He had enough to set a deadline for Coster to deliver proof of the physical existence of $10 million worth of assets in the crude-drug division. The deadline was December 5, and on that day Coster, who had been playing sick, instigated an equity receivership in the Connecticut courts.

For more than a week the story did not make the front page of a single New York paper except *The Wall Street Journal.* During that week the New York directors were granted a reorganization. The securities were suspended from trading. The Securities and Exchange Commission called in the Department of Justice. The New York attorney general also started an investigation. On December 14, Coster was arrested and fingerprinted. He was identified as Musica in time for the morning papers of December 16 and shot himself before his bathroom mirror that morning, leaving a tortured, semiliterate and incoherent note. There was no work done at the McKesson plant in Bridgeport that day.

◆

AFTERMATH

Though spectacular in scope, the scandal did not destroy the company. After shepherding McKesson through a reorganization, William Wardall turned over the responsibilities and assets to the new company in 1941, which continued as an independent entity until 1967, when it merged with a San Francisco-based conglomerate, Foremost Dairies. As drug distribution became the biggest part of the business, the company dropped the Foremost name and reemerged as McKesson in 1983. Today, it is the nation's largest drug wholesaler, ranked 18th on the 2008 FORTUNE 500 list with $94 billion in revenues.

The McKesson and Robbins debacle brought the first conviction for filing a false financial statement under the Securities Act of 1934, the legislation that created the Securities and Exchange Commission. McKesson controller McGloon, who was acquitted of 12 other charges ranging from mail fraud to conspiracy, received a sentence of a year and a day, as well as a fine of $5,000, in May 1940. His was the only conviction. Two McKesson directors, including banker Horace Merwin, were acquitted by the same jury. Six of Coster/ Musica's associates pleaded guilty after the indictment, including his brother George Dietrich/Musica, who served as chief government witness at trial. Eighteen McKesson directors, sued for negligence by Wardall, settled in October 1940, agreeing to surrender their preferred and common stock.

Though the case brought few convictions, McKesson's "bookkeeping symphony" had far-reaching implications for the development of auditing standards. The concept of audit committees—non-officer directors who select external auditors—first came up in the New York Stock Exchange's reaction to the McKesson and Robbins swindle. Additional recommendations came out of the SEC's investigation. In a 500-page report, released in December 1940, the agency criticized Price, Waterhouse for failing to independently confirm company assets but admitted that the auditors followed standard practice. Proposed changes included independent selection of external auditors by outside directors, a shareholder vote approving the nominated accounting firm, and greater oversight of audits by the board of directors.

Shamed by the weaknesses revealed by the McKesson imbroglio, the American Institute of Accountants instituted several reforms, including requiring physical corroboration of inventory and accounts receivable. In early 1941, the SEC formally amended accounting rules, requiring more data from auditors as well as reports of financial restatements.

12

THE WRECKING CREW

*Michael Carlow and his dad started out demolishing old
factories—then grew rich destroying companies.*

---

by LEE SMITH

July 10, 1995

What a sentimental guy Michael Carlow seemed to be, going to
Pittsburgh to rescue a candy bar. The Clark bar is a small part
of childhood for a lot of Americans and a significant part of the adult-
hood of the people of Pittsburgh, where for the past 109 years the
candy has been made. But D. L. Clark Company was in trouble in
1991, so Carlow offered to save it. Love of the city moved him, as well
as compassion for the workers whose jobs were in danger. And, of
course, he saw an opportunity for legitimate profit. Or so he said.

That tiny treasure of a candy bar was a little wedge that Carlow used
to open his way into the city. Michael Carlow, 44, is a sort of serial
swindler, it appears, who from Buffalo to Tacoma and places in between has seduced bankers and business executives, coal miners and
county commissioners, lawyers and journalists as easily as if they were
dewy-eyed innocents who wanted desperately to believe in princes.

With the help of his dad, Carlow bought beloved, troubled manufacturing companies with promises to keep the machines humming. But a trail of court actions and lawsuits suggests that he and his father, Frank Carlow, 74, cheated suppliers, workers, and taxpayers, among others. And they apparently used those acquisitions as multiple platforms to write checks in one of the richest and boldest kiting schemes ever uncovered.

Just how much money is missing could take months or years to calculate. The Carlows' biggest caper seems to have been what might be called the Great Pittsburgh Con, of which Clark was a part. So was Iron City Beer, a favorite quaff of steelmakers, or those who like to think of themselves as steelmakers. The city's mighty PNC Bank accuses the Carlows of making the bank a victim of a huge kiting scheme. Compared with the typical kite of a few hundred thousand dollars, this one was more like a space station. The Carlows, says PNC, siphoned a staggering $31.3 million out of the bank before they were caught.

The kite and the Carlows might still be flying high but for an ironic twist that snipped the string and brought everything crashing to earth. In a sequence that sounds as though it had been written for a screwball comedy, the Carlows overdrew their accounts so often and in such huge amounts that the bank charged them $500,000 in overdraft fees. The Carlows apparently paid off those with more bad checks, which the bank blithely booked as revenue. Someone may have even received a bonus based on that imaginary revenue. In late January, PNC management finally understood the deception. "We have been the victims of a major fraud," PNC Chairman Thomas H. O'Brien announced on February 6.

How the Carlows managed to run their alleged scams as long as they did is a sobering tale of the perils of self-delusion, phantom reputations, carelessness, and naivete. The story reveals the American business spirit at its most admirable: a willingness to help a spunky outsider who has the guts and passion to attempt rescues that make insiders tremble. And it also displays the business spirit at its less noble. Prior to PNC, some victims who discovered the Carlows' alleged swindles were inclined to cut a deal with them: Pay us back, and we won't seek to have you prosecuted. The victims didn't seem much concerned about how the Carlows would make restitution. PNC, to its great credit, demonstrated scrupulous ethics by turning the Carlows in and finishing their game.

The Carlow story began in Uniontown, Pa., a dreary and busted place in played-out coal country 50 miles south of Pittsburgh. The area was settled by Scotch-Irish and German farmers in the 18th century; from the late 19th century on, successive waves of Hungarians and Italians came to earn a hard but good wage deep in the mines. As automation displaced workers and speeded depletion of the mines, the region sank into an economic mire. The population has dropped from 200,000 to 140,000 over the past 40 years, while poverty, unemployment, and crime rates have risen to among the highest in the state.

Despite a handful of cheerful shops and busy enterprises, Uniontown looks close to abandonment. Broken-looking men and women amble along Main Street past a personal finance agency, a department store occupied by ghostly mannequins but few customers, and the Fantasy Travel Agency. Fantasy's headline tour is a $138 bus trip to Atlantic City to play the slots, an offering that sums it up. Uniontown dreams small.

Clearly, Uniontown is not a place that could contain the Carlows' ambitions. Frank Carlow's early biography is sketchy, and lawyers for both men said their clients declined to be interviewed by FORTUNE. After service with the U.S. Army during World War II and a couple of years in engineering school at the University of West Virginia, Frank returned home to Uniontown. The Carlows are of Italian descent, and in those days Italians were not admitted to the Uniontown Country Club or into such gentrified commerce as banking.

Frank, who has a stocky build and steel-gray hair, and is not especially social by nature, lived at the fringe of the business community. He opened an electrical appliance store, which went out of business. Starting over, he created in 1953 the Standard Machine and Equipment

Company, which was to become the holding company for many Carlow enterprises. Standard Machine's original business was demolishing failed factories and selling off the machinery and other reusable parts.

Even when he became rich, Frank chose to remain an outsider while still living in Uniontown. Robert E. Eberly, a major shareholder in a large local bank, Integra, says that Frank generally declines to contribute to charities. A few years ago, however, Eberly persuaded him to donate a job, the destruction of an old building on Main Street to make way for apartments for the elderly. When the work was finished, Frank was uncharacteristically expansive. "I'll tear down any building in town, free of charge," he told Eberly. Demolition was the core competence of the Carlow business empire. But it was under Frank's son, Michael, that the potential for taking things apart was fully realized. Frank's wife, Marie, is a simple and devout woman by all accounts. (Her name, nonetheless, is on a trust that creditors believe shelters millions of dollars.) One of the Carlows' three daughters became a nun. Michael, the only son, attended mass almost daily into his teens, a former classmate remembers. But football was Michael's passion. Like a lot of kids, Michael wanted to follow the trail out of western Pennsylvania blazed by Joe Namath, the most glamorous quarterback of the 1960's. Michael never came close, but he did make it as far as quarterback of Uniontown High, and led the team to a winning season. "He had a good arm," says John Fortugna, who played behind him as fullback and is now Uniontown's head football coach. "But he wasn't quick footed." Not at that stage of his career.

What distinguished Michael was his feistiness, his grit, his determination. After high school, Michael left Uniontown and returned only occasionally, mostly to strut. He went to Dean Junior College in Massachusetts, where he played a little more football. Michael then transferred to Boston College, where he forgot about football and worked hard to overcome the dyslexia that had made him a poor student. In 1975 he earned a degree in accounting and went into business with his father. Frank continued to live in Uniontown, but the son moved on.

Within a few years the younger Carlow became the leading partner in Standard Machine, or at least the more visible one. Over the next 20 years the Carlows bought up troubled coal mines and cement companies, failing candy factories and furniture makers, an endangered glassmaker and a brewery. It was Michael who led the way into town after town and explained the takeover to the locals. Although Frank may have been as important to the team, he let Michael have the stage and stayed so far in the background that it's hard to find a photograph of him. The Carlow empire became a bewildering bundle of unrelated, mostly crippled enterprises, more than 40 of them at one time or another in Pennsylvania, Ohio, West Virginia, New York, Connecticut, Alaska, and Washington state. Michael promoted himself as a "turnaround artist" and created a phantom reputation that was rarely challenged. But it seems that the Carlows generally turned companies upside down to shake what they could out of them. For example, in 1984 they gained control of B.C. Industries, a concrete maker in Tiltonsville, Ohio, that was under financial stress. In May a federal jury concluded that they had misappropriated B.C.'s assets and defrauded its creditors. The court ordered the Carlows to pay the victims $5.7 million.

The Carlows generally financed a new acquisition by putting a few dollars down and promising to pay over time. Then they ignored the bills—for taxes, insurance, supplies, whatever. "Michael told me once that he doesn't pay unless he's forced to," says Louis Dudek, an official of an electrical workers' union that represented employees at a company owned by the Carlows. "I guess that's his coat of arms." After an Ohio appellate court upheld a verdict against the Carlows for strip-mining and blasting in a residential neighborhood near Canton, lawyers for the plaintiffs pursued 17 Carlow companies in half a dozen lawsuits around the country before collecting. A court in Fayette County, Pa., ruled in April 1992 that the Carlows owed FMC Corporation $330,000 for cranes they had bought in the 1970s; the company is still chasing them for the money. FMC has lots of company. In the

Fayette County court alone, 55 creditors are seeking millions in unpaid bills.

What were the Carlows after? Clearly they wanted to be rich, and that they achieved. Frank was able to build an $800,000 house in Uniontown a few blocks from the Eberlys'—and more expensive. He also has a condominium in Key Biscayne, Fla. Michael has an eight-bedroom house in Upper St. Clair, a Pittsburgh suburb, where his four children sometimes visit (he's divorced); a ski lodge near Vail, Colo. and a home in Boston. But Michael seemed to yearn for more. An acquaintance of Michael's, Jacque Joseph, a former aide to one of the state's congressmen, says, "My impression was that Michael wanted to be Donald Trump...the Donald of Pennsylvania."

The Carlows would prey on geriatric companies with glorious pasts and grim futures. Professionals in the industry—coal, candy, or whatever—often had little or no interest in buying such moribund companies. Still, boosters were eager to keep them alive, partly for sentimental reasons but largely because they provided good-paying manufacturing jobs.

So Michael Carlow would drop out of the sky in a corporate jet and promise to save the endangered enterprise. Imaginative and resourceful, Michael found hidden opportunities—for the Carlows—in crumbling companies. Take the case of Kittinger Company, a furniture maker in Buffalo. Since 1865, Kittinger had been making elegant desks, chairs, and other pieces, a few of which are in the White House. But competitors in cheaper labor markets have squeezed Kittinger hard in recent years. The privately owned company changed hands a few times in the 1980s as earnings shrank and employment dropped from 250 to about 150. In 1990, Carlow bought Kittinger for an undisclosed price.

Among Kittinger's assets were $9 million worth of parts with which to make reproductions of 18th-century furniture from the collection of the Colonial Williamsburg Foundation. The trouble was that Kittinger no longer had the license to produce the reproductions. The foundation had passed it to someone else. Carlow made and sold the furniture anyhow, changing the design a little to try to escape copyright protection. The foundation has won a $575,000 judgment against Kittinger.

By not paying fringe benefits to which workers were entitled, Carlow saved a lot of money. He always gave employees their hourly wages, but apparently he often cheated on accounts they weren't likely to tap for a while. In the case of Kittinger's factory hands, union officials claim he didn't send payments to the state for workers' compensation, or FICA taxes to the U.S. Treasury. (The workers are out of jobs now, but as long as they can prove they were employed at Kittinger, they can collect their Social Security benefits.) Pennsylvania coal miners who worked for the Carlows discovered after doctors and hospitals dunned them that their health plan wasn't funded. Their union estimates the unpaid medical bills amount to more than $1.6 million.

Finally, the Carlows appear to have used Kittinger and dozens of other companies as a network for what may have been their most profitable business—huge and elaborate check-kiting scams. A kite exploits the float in the banking system, the day or so lag between the time you deposit a check in your bank and the time the check clears the bank it was written on. A very primitive kite might work something like this: Three con men open accounts of, say, $50,000 in three banks, with real money but in the names of dummy companies. Con man A writes B a check for $100,000. B's bank lets him draw on those funds before the check has cleared, so B pockets $50,000 and writes a check to C for $50,000. C then sends A a check for $50,000; A gives B $50,000, and on and on in a variation of musical chairs. If the swindlers write fast enough and get their timing right, they can keep the cycle going for a while before the banks realize that one of them is short $50,000.

Kiting accounts for a significant share of the $800 million or so banks figure they lose each year to bad checks. So banks have computer software that detects suspicious patterns even when kites are elaborately camouflaged. One simple rule of thumb still works pretty well: 90% of worthless checks are numbered lower than 200. A swindler opens a new account, makes a score, and skips town.

Michael Carlow's genius, his accusers say, was that he used real companies, not dummies, and he stayed in town long enough for bankers to feel comfortable. How many kites the Carlows flew may never be known. Banks are supposed to report all frauds of more than a few thousand dollars to the local U.S. attorney's office. In practice, the feds are so overloaded with investigating drugs, violent crime, and now terrorism that simple bank fraud has to run into the hundreds of thousands before they pay attention. Banks, moreover, are not eager to advertise that they have been taken, even when the money runs into the millions. Some would rather settle with the thieves.

The Puget Sound Bank in Tacoma suspected in 1988 that the Carlows had swindled the bank for $5.7 million. "It was a typical kite situation," says Bill Philip, the bank's former chief executive, while declining to go into further detail. The bank agreed not to ask for prosecution if the Carlows would repay them. Does Puget Sound have any regrets about not insisting on prosecution in light of the Carlows' subsequent business dealings? Philip pauses before answering. "The money was very important to us, as you can understand," he says. "We were a small bank. Our total earnings at the time were only $15 million to $20 million a year."

Don Vandenheuvel, Puget Sound's former chief financial officer, defends the way the bank and its attorneys cut a deal with the Carlows and thus protected its shareholders. "When you discover a kite, it is important to be the first one to discover it," says Vandenheuvel. "Because the bank that does gets all the money, and the others don't get anything."

So when Michael Carlow arrived in Pittsburgh in 1991 there were no criminal charges besmirching his reputation, although anyone who did a little checking could have found a heap of civil actions. Carlow's first acquisition was Clark, the candymaker—and a classic Carlow target.

The company was in trouble. The Clark bar commanded some shelf space as far away as New York and Chicago. But Clark didn't produce the candy in the volumes comparable with those of national brands like Nestle's Butterfinger, so Clark didn't have much clout with suppliers and distributors. Moreover, Clark's labor costs, $17.50 or so an hour on average, were higher than those of competitors who made at least some of their candy in cheaper labor markets.

Still, the folks of Pittsburgh didn't want to lose a connection to the past. Their great-grandfathers had snacked on those bars in the steel mills; Clark's big blue and red neon sign was a familiar landmark along the Allegheny River. And if Clark sank, about 100 manufacturing jobs would go under as well. So Carlow bravely offered to save the company. "He was impatient, insisting that things had to be done in a hurry," says Frank Brooks Robinson, president of Regional Industrial Development Corporation, which leased Carlow the plant in which to make the candy. Carlow gave the impression that unless the locals accommodated him in a hurry, he would walk.

Leaf North America, the Illinois company that sold Clark to Carlow, had few illusions about either the property or the buyer. The company knew of the Carlows' reputation for being slow payers. "Before Michael came to us, he had some strange business dealings," says James Hanlon, former president of Leaf. But Carlow offered Leaf the best deal it could get. The purchase price was not disclosed; Clark's assets currently are valued around $3 million. Carlow put a little money down, and Leaf insisted that he pay the installments not quarterly or monthly, but weekly, $50,000 a week, the sort of relationship a boarding house establishes with a tenant who looks as though he might leave in the night.

Pittsburgh, however, took Carlow at his word. "This is a trusting city, more Midwestern than Eastern," says Richard P. Simmons, chairman of Allegheny Ludlum, the specialty-steel manufacturer. Through the early 1990's the Carlows' Pittsburgh domain expanded rapidly. They bought a local brewery, the 134-year-old Pittsburgh Brewing, maker of

Iron City Beer, which, although a sentimental favorite in the city, was losing market share regionally. Production peaked at 850,000 barrels a year in 1985 and had dropped to 670,000 in 1992, the year the Carlows bought it. PNC Bank loaned the Carlows $10 million in operating capital for the brewery, after they offered certificates of deposit as well as stock of Pittsburgh Brewing, Clark Candy, and another Carlow company as collateral. PNC's enthusiasm was understandable. If Michael Carlow was for real, he was just the kind of customer the bank wanted. The economies of western Pennsylvania and eastern Ohio, PNC's heartland, have not been robust. The Pittsburgh area alone lost 160,000 manufacturing jobs in the last decade. So entrepreneurs willing to bring their own money into the city, as Carlow seemed to be, and willing to borrow more were highly prized.

Candy and beer ventures were risky, but at least they stood some chance of success. More puzzling was the Carlows' attempt to revive a wholesale bakery that had failed twice before, a hopeless mission in the eyes of many Pittsburgh citizens. Neglected in the news accounts was that the cash Carlow put into his ventures was money he owed other people.

Anyhow, it would have been gratuitous for Simmons or other members of the Duquesne Club, the grand and ancient watering hole of the corporate establishment on Sixth Avenue, to raise questions about the newcomer. (Carlow is not a member.) What were the grandees trying to do? Break the spirits of working men and women dependent on Carlow for jobs? Carlow, moreover, might have been able to make even a twice-abandoned bakery a success. "Sometimes an outsider can see value where an insider can't," observes Simmons.

Carlow's reckless acquisitions bought him celebrity and good will. To Pittsburgh he was a savior who was scraping the rust off the city's old factories and making them run again. *Pittsburgh* magazine made a flattering profile of Carlow its June 1993 cover story. Like others who met him, the writer was captivated by Carlow's energy, his daring, his desire to save the city. The article extolled Carlow as a "post-modern mogul" and a "messianic hero."

Questions about his character were brushed aside. Carlow suggested to the writer that some people distrusted him because of his Italian ancestry, saying, "Bigotry, in all its forms, never fails to amaze and surprise me. It's a terrible thing." So the reader was left with the strong impression that Carlow's detractors were nothing but bigots. The more famous the "messianic hero" became, the more difficult it was to doubt him.

High in the Frick Building, a stately granite tower that rubs parapets with Mellon Bank and USX and other Pittsburgh pillars, Carlow rented a $13,000-a-month suite for the offices of Pittsburgh Food and Beverage, the holding company for Clark, another candy company, Pittsburgh Brewing and a manufacturer of decorative glass (the bakery flopped in 1994). Persian rugs on the floor, pastoral landscapes on the walls, and—the nicest touch of all—a mahogany reproduction of one of George Washington's writing desks gave the reception room a reassuring look of stability and hushed elegance.

But in the rooms beyond that quiet antechamber, apparently, a massive kiting machine was grinding away furiously. The Carlows opened close to 30 accounts under the names of the Pittsburgh Food and Beverage companies as well as other Carlow properties, including a couple of cement makers and Kittinger furniture of Buffalo. It isn't clear whether anyone at the bank was aware that all belonged to the Carlows.

PNC maintains in a civil action filed in U.S. District Court for Western Pennsylvania that Michael and Frank Carlow and a longtime business associate, Larry Ousky, dashed off thousands of checks from late 1993 to January 1995. The dimensions of the scam were truly impressive. "Daily deposits of millions of dollars of checks were required to maintain the scheme and continue the fraud, and checks in constantly increasing amounts (mostly signed by Michael Carlow personally) were deposited on each and every business day," PNC maintains. The float the Carlows created was immense—half a billion dollars' worth of unsettled checks circulating at the same time through various accounts. To appreciate their boldness, consider that the legitimate revenues of the four PF&B operating companies were a mere $76 million in 1994. Most of that half a billion stayed within PNC. To take a hypothetical example: If Pittsburgh Brewing sent a check to Clark on Tuesday to cover a shortage and Clark sent Pittsburgh Brewing a check in the same amount on Friday, nothing happened.

But $31.3 million did leave the bank. A lot of it went to keep former creditors at bay, including about $1.2 million to repay part of a Small Business Administration-backed loan the Carlows had defaulted on in 1982, $746,000 to American Express for travel and entertainment expenses, $463,000 for leasing an airplane, and on and on.

Keeping track of thousands of checks that have to cover one another and hiding the extraordinary shuffle is a complicated task and is in some respects a tribute to the Carlows' intellectual and managerial skills. The bank unwittingly made it easier for them, however. Each morning at the start of business the Carlows could turn on a computer and call up the balances on their PNC cash disbursement accounts. They had until the end of the day to deposit a whirlwind of checks that would bring the accounts into balance and make everything seem OK until the following morning. The Carlows happily paid overdraft fees with another flurry of worthless checks.

What PNC will not talk about is how the scam went undetected for as long as it did. The avalanche of overdrafts in the Carlow accounts generated $500,000 or so in fees. Again, that would have been a stupendous expense, if real, for the Carlow companies. According to PNC, the bank's control systems, including those that are supposed to discover kites, were working properly. But it wasn't until January 1995, more than a year after the accounts were opened, that PNC executives became suspicious (for reasons they won't talk about), examined parts of the 1994 results very carefully—and were horrified.

Bank executives and lawyers confronted Michael Carlow in the first week of February. "Carlow admitted that he was 'totally wrong' and PNC was owed 'a lot of money,' " PNC maintains in its suit. But despite his confession, Carlow was as self-confident as ever, according to one account. He had been through this before. "Carlow sat down with the bankers and said, 'I'll write you a check,' " says one familiar with the showdown. "He offered them $3 million a year for ten years and gave them a list of a dozen organizations he was paying off in this way." The bankers were stunned at first, caught off guard by Carlow's parry. But by the next day they had recovered and knew what they had to do. "PNC said, 'No, the buck stops here,' " the source reports. The bankers showed Carlow a complaint they were prepared to file in federal court to put Pittsburgh Food and Beverage in receivership. To avoid that humiliation, Carlow quit as PF&B chairman. The bank then called the U.S. attorney's office.

In the aftermath one bank employee has been dismissed. The bank declines to discuss the matter. "But there's plenty more blame to go around," says a colleague. Kittinger furniture has closed. Clark shut down as well for a time, but has a new owner who is ready to start making candy again. Pittsburgh Brewing kept making beer all through the crisis, but production has dropped further, to 470,000 barrels per year. PNC and the other creditors are eager to sell the company. Various other Carlow enterprises are either out of business or operating in a state of elevated anxiety.

"Michael was Icarus, flying too close to the sun," says William Brandt, the trustee the bank hired to run PF&B after it persuaded Carlow to quit. But lest that mythic allusion romanticize Carlow, Brandt adds: "The difference between Carlow and a holdup artist with a gun is that a holdup artist could never hope to get away with so much money."

There are two kinds of con artists. One type ensnares victims by greed, the hope of making money in a deal despite improbable economics or questionable ethics. The victims at least come away wiser. The more vicious con artist traps his victims through their generosity. The suckers come away more cynical, less willing to give the next gent without a pedigree a shot. Michael Carlow, it appears, was that kind of con man.

◆

AFTERMATH

Michael Carlow pleaded guilty in 1996 to charges ranging from bank fraud to filing false federal income tax returns. He served six years in federal prison before being released in 2002. Frank Carlow followed his son to prison after pleading guilty in 1997 to 13 counts of fraud and tax evasion. He died in 2000, shortly after his release from prison, at age 77.

At a bankruptcy auction in 1995, local businessmen bought the Clark bar and Iron City Beer. Though the purchasers wanted to keep the Pittsburgh icons going, the companies continued to struggle, and each went bankrupt again. In 2007, Connecticut-based private equity group Unified Growth Partners bought Pittsburgh Brewing and operates it as Iron City Brewing. The Clark bar survives, but without its Pittsburgh connection. In 1999, the New England Confectionary Company, the country's oldest candy-maker, bought the company and moved production to Massachusetts.

13

THE INSIDE STORY OF
AN INSIDE TRADER

---

by DENNIS B. LEVINE

May 21, 1990

Remember "greed is good," the slogan of the self-described "masters of the universe"? Scandal, of course, was hiding just under the surface of that ethos, and Dennis Levine was there at the beginning—and also the beginning of the end. Here, Levine tells his own story, a personal odyssey of an American dream turned nightmare.

Waking early in my Park Avenue apartment on May 12, 1986, I read the morning papers, checked on the European securities markets, and ate breakfast with my wife, Laurie, then six weeks pregnant, and my son, Adam, who was 4. By 8 a.m. I was in downtown Manhattan, meeting with my staff at Drexel Burnham Lambert. At 33, I was a leading merger specialist and a partner in one of the most powerful investment banks on Wall Street. Among the many appointments on my calendar that day were meetings with two CEOs, including Revlon's Ronald Perelman, to discuss multibillion-dollar takeovers. I was a happy man.

In mid-afternoon two strangers, one tall and one short, came look-ing for me at Drexel. They didn't identify themselves, but the recep-tionist said they weren't dressed like clients. For ten months, I knew, the Securities and Exchange Commission had been investigating the Bahamian subsidiary of Bank Leu, the Swiss bank that had executed insider stock trades for me since 1980. That very morning I had spoken on the phone with one of the bank's employees, who reassured me that everything was under control. Still, I knew something was wrong, and I fled.

While the authorities searched for me, I drove around New York in my BMW, making anxious calls on the car phone to my wife, my father, my boss. Before leaving the car, I hired a legal team headed by superstar lawyer Arthur Liman, who went on to serve as chief Sen-ate counsel in the Iran-Contra investigation and is now representing Michael Milken. By the time I had hired Liman, my darkest secret was being broadcast by TV stations across the country. Early in the eve-ning, I drove alone to the U.S. Attorney's office in lower Manhattan, expecting only to be served with a subpoena. The federal officers read me my rights instead.

At the nearby Metropolitan Correctional Center, they locked me up with a bunch of drug dealers in a cell whose odor I won't soon for-get. It was like an out-of-body experience. As I ate cornflakes at the prison cafeteria the next morning, I watched the story of my arrest on a TV wake-up show. My carefully orchestrated career, years of plan-ning and sacrifice, thousands of hours of work that had lifted me from Bayside, Queens, to the pinnacle of Wall Street—all reduced to noth-ing. Just like that.

I have had four years to reflect on the events leading up to my ar-rest. Part of that time—15 months and two days—I spent in Lewisburg federal prison camp in Pennsylvania. Getting your comeuppance is painful, and I have tried to take it on the chin. Unfortunately, my fam-ily also had to endure the trauma of humiliation, disgrace, and loss of privacy—and they did nothing to deserve it. I will regret my mistakes forever. I blame only myself for my actions and accept full responsibility for what I have done. No one led me down the garden path.

I've gained an abiding respect for the fairness of our system of justice: For the hard work and creativity I brought to my investment-banking career, I was well rewarded. When I broke the law, I was punished. The system works.

People always ask, Why would somebody who's making over $1 million a year start trading on inside information? That's the wrong question. Here's what I thought at the time, misguided as I was: When I started trading on nonpublic information in 1978, I wasn't making a million. I was a 25-year-old trainee at Citibank with a $19,000 annual salary. I was wet behind the ears, impatient, burning with ambition. In those days people didn't think about insider trading the way they do now: You'd call it "a hot stock tip." The first U.S. criminal prosecution for insider trading wasn't until around that time, and it was not highly publicized.

In the early years I regarded the practice as just a way to make some fast money. Of course I soon realized what I was doing was wrong, but I rationalized it as harmless. I told myself that the frequent run-ups in target-company stock prices before merger announcements proved others were doing it too. Eventually insider trading became an addiction for me. It was just so easy. In seven years I built $39,750 into $11.5 million, and all it took was a 20-second phone call to my offshore bank a couple of times a month—maybe 200 calls total. My account was growing at 125% a year, compounded.

I was confident that the elaborate veils of secrecy I had created—plus overseas bank-privacy laws—would protect me. And Wall Street was crazy in those days. These were the 1980s, remember, the decade of excess, greed, and materialism. I became a go-go guy, consumed by the high-pressure, ultra-competitive world of investment banking. I was helping my clients make tens and even hundreds of millions of dollars. I served as the lead banker on Perelman's nearly $2 billion takeover of Revlon, four months of work that enabled Drexel to earn

$60 million in fees. The daily exposure to such deals, the pursuit of larger and larger transactions, and the numbing effect of 60 to 100-hour workweeks helped erode my values and distort my judgment. In this unbelievable world of billions and billions of dollars, the millions I made by trading on nonpublic information seemed almost insignificant.

AT THE ROOT of my compulsive trading was an inability to set limits. Perhaps it's worth noting that my legitimate success stemmed from the same root. My ambition was so strong it went beyond rationality, and I gradually lost sight of what constitutes ethical behavior. At each new level of success I set higher goals, imprisoning myself in a cycle from which I saw no escape. When I became a senior vice president, I wanted to be a managing director, and when I became a managing director, I wanted to be a client. If I was making $100,000 a year, I thought, I can make $200,000. And if I made $1 million, I can make $3 million. And so it went. By the time I made partner at Drexel, I was out of control.

My parents always encouraged me to play straight. I come from a strong, old- fashioned family; I was the youngest of three boys. My mother, Selma, was shortchanged by life: She died of a stroke at 53, when I was 23. I'm still very close to my brothers, Larry and Robert, and my father, Philip. Until he retired in 1983, my father worked long hours running his own home-remodeling business. He taught me to work hard, believe in myself, and persevere. Off and on, from my early teens, he hired me to canvass door to door for new customers. Those cold calls were hard, but they showed me how to sell.

As a kid I always worked. I would be shoveling snow or delivering newspapers. My folks gave me piano lessons from the time I was 7, and during my early teens I started making money as a musician, playing keyboards at parties and dances. I wasn't a particularly dedicated student in those days, but I had a lot of friends. I began studying the stock market when I was 13, reading books and investing part of my earnings—a few hundred dollars at first—in over-the-counter securities. In eighth grade I became a regular reader of *The Wall Street Journal.* I enrolled at City University of New York's Bernard M. Baruch College in Manhattan with the aim of preparing for a career in finance; at a wedding my junior year, I met my wife, Laurie. Upon graduation I entered Baruch's MBA program, going to school at night and working during the day at the corporate counseling department at Citibank, hoping that a stint in commercial banking would provide a springboard to Wall Street.

Laurie and I married, and moved into an apartment in Queens. It was 1977 and mergers and acquisitions was starting to boom. When I began my career, it was rare for people with backgrounds like mine— middle-class, non-Ivy League, without useful social connections—to surmount the barriers surrounding the patrician business of investment banking. But over time those barriers were relaxed. Combined with deregulation, the growth of acquisition activity forced the old-line investment firms into harsh competition, leading them to hire and promote people on merit. Seeing my chance, I began studying the M&A business in my spare time, reading books and following deals in the press. It was at Citibank that I met Robert Wilkis. Bob shared my love of the stock market, and we became close friends. We would meet at the fourth-floor stock-quote terminal, where he monitored his personal portfolio while I tracked the latest M&A deals. As a lending officer in the world corporate group, Bob had routine access to sensitive information about mergers Citibank might finance. Early in 1978 he told me he had identified a major U.S. company—let's call it ChemCorp—as a takeover target. He said he had bought its shares and recommended I do the same. I did: Borrowing on margin, I purchased $4,000 of ChemCorp stock. The merger never materialized and I sold the stock for about what I paid for it. To this day I'm not sure the transaction was illegal; Bob never told me he had inside information about ChemCorp. But it was well over a year before I dared make another such trade. Meanwhile I landed the investment banking job

I had coveted. Smith Barney Harris Upham & Company hired me in 1978 as an associate at $23,000 a year.

THE FIRM SENT ME to Paris for a year. Laurie and I had never been abroad—now we were living in Smith Barney's comfortable apartment on Avenue Foch. I ran into many senior European executives who scoffed at American tax and securities laws. Insider trading was legal in most European countries, and some executives I met seemed to view it as a perk of office.

During that year Bob Wilkis and I kept in touch by telephone, and in the spring of 1979 he visited Paris on business. Bob had also moved into investment banking by then, as an associate in international finance at Blyth Eastman Dillon. We talked at length about trading on the inside information we came across at work.

By nature, investment banking requires that even junior people encounter nonpublic information as they work on prospective deals; both Bob and I learned of transactions long before they were announced. When Bob was in Paris we decided to open accounts at Swiss banks. I borrowed as much as I could from my Ready Credit account and my family, telling them only that I had found some promising investment opportunities. With the $39,750 I raised, I opened a numbered account at Pictet & Cie in Geneva; Bob's was at Credit Suisse. I didn't really begin buying stocks until Smith Barney moved me back to its New York office a few months later. I went to great lengths to avoid creating a paper trail for investigators to follow. Accustomed to confidential arrangements, Pictet's bankers suggested I use the code name Milky Way.

When you call, they said, why don't you just say it's Mr. Way? They sent me no bank statements. I called in my trades from public phones—collect. (The bank extracted a service charge of about $20 per call.) BOB AND I tried to avoid linking our trading activities or creating noticeable patterns. That way, if one of us was found out, the other would be safe. We agreed to pool our information but to avoid any financial relationship.

According to our pact, we would keep our trading secret, never share our stock tips with anyone else, and never trade in the U.S. Bob came up with the code name Alan Darby, which each of us used when calling the other at work. The procedure was simple. In the normal course of business Bob might learn that Blyth—or his next employer, Lazard Freres—was representing one company in a prospective take-over of another.

Let's call the target Flounder Corporation. Bob would phone me at work, identifying himself as Darby if anyone other than I answered. We would set up a meeting, often a quick lunch of pizza or Chinese food. Between bites, he would tell me the inside dope on Flounder. We would also chat about work, family, movies—we were friends, remember—then say goodbye. Before buying any shares, I would do enough research on Flounder to assure myself that its stock was worth buying at current prices even if the takeover never materialized. (Inside information is not always a sure thing: I lost as much as $250,000 on some trades.) If Flounder's fundamentals looked good enough, I would find a moment to step out to a pay phone and call my bank with a buy order. Once the public got wind of the takeover and bid up the stock, I would telephone again with a sell order. It was that simple.

As often as not, of course, I'd provide information and Bob would trade. My initial uneasiness gradually ebbed—there were no inquiries, and all of a sudden the balance in my account was over $125,000. As my trading grew, so did my circle of sources: With Bob's knowledge, I began exchanging information with another junior banker and a law-firm associate. I never told Bob their names; Bob later did the same with a young colleague. Then, during one of my calls, a Pictet banker told me the conservative firm was uncomfortable with my aggressive trading style, which included short-selling securities and trading options. He politely suggested I change tactics or take my business elsewhere. I simply shifted to the Bahamian subsidiary of Bank Leu, Switzerland's oldest. I was developing confidence about my career as well. Along with the other associates in Smith Barney's M&A bullpen,

I read annual reports and labored over financial analysis. The hours were so obscene that my family ribbed me about being a wage slave. But I loved my work.

ONE OF MY ASSIGNMENTS was as breaking-news coordinator. I closely monitored market developments and alerted the firm to opportunities. At first the opportunities I spotted were small. I heard a rumor that a big block of Koehring Company, a producer of excavators and other heavy machinery, might be up for sale, making the company vulnerable to takeover. I told my superiors, and they approached Koehring. Ultimately a bidder did surface, and Koehring hired us to render a fairness opinion for a $250,000 fee. As I rose on Wall Street the fees my ideas generated got bigger, and people kept patting me on the back for being so well plugged in.

Smith Barney promoted me to second vice president, but by 1981 I felt I had learned as much there as I could. I moved to Lehman Brothers Kuhn Loeb, then a private partnership and a major force in dealmaking. Starting as a vice president, in three years I rose to senior vice president. Gradually I was becoming an experienced dealmaker.

A few months later, when Drexel offered me a position as a managing director—the equivalent of partner—I jumped. Drexel was starting to translate its clout in junk-bond financings into M&A deals. The firm had a stable of acquisitive clients, and in case after case I was assigned to get their deals done. Within months I built a string of successes: Carl Icahn's proxy fight against Phillips Petroleum, which forced a restructuring to the benefit of shareholders; Coastal Corporation's unsolicited $2.5 billion acquisition of American Natural Resources; Sir James Goldsmith's hostile takeover of Crown Zellerbach, completed despite a poison pill; and the Revlon deal, the high point of my career. Winning a battle like the one pitting Perelman against Michel Bergerac of Revlon offers excitement far more intoxicating than insider trading.

In 1985 my first bonus at Drexel came to well over $1 million in cash.

My relationship with Ivan Boesky began innocently enough. Having learned to listen to the market's tom-toms as part of my legitimate career, I developed a network of sources that eventually included the man considered America's boldest and most influential stock speculator. He was also an important Drexel client. We met in March 1985 at my first Drexel high-yield bond conference, the famous Predators' Ball. Back in New York, we began talking regularly, mostly about pending deals.

IVAN'S ATTENTIONS were flattering. He invited me to lunch at "21." He would telephone me at home, at work, even when I was on business trips or vacations, seeking information about deals. My home phone would ring well before 6 a.m.; Laurie would answer and hand me the receiver, saying, "It's Ivan," rolling her eyes. With Bob's knowledge, I began giving him tips in exchange for access to the vast store of market information in Ivan's head. I wasn't telling Ivan anything very specific—it was more a matter of suggesting that, say, his investment in XYZ Corporation seemed worth holding on to. I never told him my oblique suggestions were based on nonpublic information, but over time he evidently learned their value.

Then Ivan drastically changed the nature of our relationship by offering to pay for the information I was giving him, based on a percentage of his trading profits. He said something like, "You seem to have very, very good information. You should be compensated for it." Despite my own illicit activities, I was flabbergasted. I couldn't believe he would risk exposing himself so blatantly, by proposing something clearly illegal on its face. I already had a secret life, and it was not something I was anxious to expand. I turned Ivan down and resisted his overtures for weeks. I'm not quite sure why I finally accepted. Stupidity, I guess. And I don't know why Ivan engaged in illegal activities when he had a fortune estimated at over $200 million. In any case, I never received a penny from him, though I was due $2.4 million under our formula when I was arrested.

WHEN MY SCHEME fell apart, it did so quickly. In the summer of 1985, Merrill Lynch received an anonymous letter accusing two of its brokers in Caracas, Venezuela, of insider trading; one was subsequently charged.

Unbeknownst to me, for years several Bank Leu executives had been making trades that mimicked mine, for their own accounts or for others'—apparently, the bank's policies condoned this. Disregarding my instructions to spread my orders among several brokers, they had funneled much of the business through Merrill Lynch. At least one trader there, in Caracas, apparently piggybacked on my trades too. Somebody blew the whistle, perhaps out of jealousy.

Merrill Lynch, it seems, then informed the SEC, and just as my legitimate career was reaching its peak, the government began its ten-month investigation of Bank Leu. Ultimately, Bank Leu handed my head to the SEC in return for immunity from U.S. prosecution, agreeing to testify against me. The day the government came looking for me, I was petrified about Laurie's reaction. Certain that she wouldn't approve and meaning to shield her from any legal consequences, I had never told her about my insider trading. It was a secret big enough to strain any marriage: Some spouses use drugs, others have extramarital affairs, I secretly traded stocks. Laurie had no reason to suspect: We had always lived within my means. We stayed in a cramped one-bedroom apartment for almost three years after Adam was born, though I could have paid for almost any apartment in Manhattan with my offshore trading profits. Though I called my wife from the car phone before I was arrested, I couldn't bring myself to tell her what the problem was. I asked my father and brother to stay with Laurie at the apartment, and they told her. By then my crimes had become public knowledge. I didn't sleep that night in jail. Instead, I spoke with Laurie on the phone, and her initial reaction was disbelief. She was ashamed of me and beyond anger—furious. We had been living this American dream, and now she didn't know how much of it was real.

The pressure on us only increased after I was released on $5 million bail the next day. When I went to my local cash machine to get money, my bank account was empty. The IRS had seized most of my assets to protect its claim to back taxes. Then I learned that a grand jury had been impaneled and the government might use the harsh RICO statutes—designed to fight mobsters—against me. That would have allowed them to seize all my assets, down to the food in the fridge—and the maximum penalty for each RICO violation is 20 years in jail.

Then Bob Wilkis asked to meet with me. To my amazement, he told me that he had tipped others, including a member of his family, and had been executing trades in the U.S. all along. That had created an easily detected trading pattern nearly identical to mine—more than enough to nail me. I knew I was finished, and in the end my attorneys advised me that I had no choice but to settle with the government. I pleaded guilty to four criminal charges related to my insider trading and settled civil charges with the SEC. Turning over cash and other assets, I made full restitution of my $11.5 million in trading profits.

Everyone else involved in the case also entered guilty pleas and cooperated. Ivan Boesky turned himself in, pleading guilty to one criminal count and turning over $100 million. At that point I assumed the investigation was closed, but apparently Ivan's illicit activities extended far beyond his involvement with me. I had no inkling of his secret relationship with Marty Siegel, whose office was right next to mine at Drexel. The revelations of Ivan's paying Siegel off for inside information with suitcases of cash surprised me as much as anyone. So did Drexel's collapse and Michael Milken's settlement with the government. I don't think the firm's ethics were materially different from any other investment bank's.

ON FEBRUARY 20, 1987, I learned that few experiences are more humbling than standing before a federal judge, publicly acknowledging guilt, and being sentenced to jail. Less than four months after Sarah's birth, I began serving my sentence.

Although minimum-security prison camps have no walls, you are constantly reminded of your separation from family and society. I had no privacy, my moves were monitored, and my daily routine was controlled by others. I went from never having enough time to a place where everyone kills time. I mopped floors and mowed grass and spent hours just thinking. At first I could not come to grips with the turbulent changes in my life; I was burning with anger at myself.

Eventually I decided to change my priorities and try to regain control over my life. I had entered prison grossly overweight, at 241 pounds. One outward sign of my new resolve: I lost 67 pounds in prison. I got along all right with the other prisoners, many of them drug offenders with no convictions for violence; nobody bothered me. They loved TV shows like *Wiseguy* and *Miami Vice*—and the inmates always rooted for the crook. The other prisoners called me "Mr. Wall Street" and asked me for market advice. I always said no. Money had little value, but there was a lively barter economy: If you were long cigarettes, you could often buy a plate of linguini with clam sauce, heated in an aluminum pie tin over an electric iron. As one of the few nonsmokers in an institution that rationed cigarettes, I was a wealthy man.

On weekends and holidays, I was allowed visits. I have painful memories of Sarah learning to walk in a prison visiting room, and of Adam pleading with a guard who wouldn't let him bring in a Mickey Mouse coloring book. Toward the end of my sentence I urged them not to come. It hurt to be reminded of what I was missing. Until I got out I didn't understand the ordeal Laurie was going through. She had lost her father to cancer, given birth, and become a single parent, all in a few months. While I was in Lewisburg she kept her feelings to herself, to spare me worry. And we couldn't talk intimately with guards monitoring our visits and recording our calls. When I was released, I was so overjoyed to be free that I didn't realize I was coming home to a woman whose anger had been growing since the day of my arrest. Instead of celebrating my return, Laurie forced me to confront the misery I'd caused her. Now that we've had it out, our marriage is stronger than it was when we were divided by secrets.

I am rebuilding my life. I still feel the consequences of my mistakes and doubtless will forever. But I've been granted a precious second chance. This time around, I'm spending far more time at home with my family than ever before. I love the investment-banking business— it's in my blood—but as part of my settlement I agreed never to work for a securities firm again. I can still advise companies about raising money or doing deals, so I have started my own New York advisory firm, named Adasar Group after my children. My clients are smaller than they used to be, but much to my surprise, most people have treated my reentry into business with fairness and compassion. I also have been addressing students at Columbia, Wharton, New York University, and other schools, hoping to steer them away from the mistakes I made. They are conscious of ethical issues—all the way from misappropriating office supplies to out-and-out felonies like insider trading or illegal dumping of toxic wastes. The enthusiasm of their response encouraged me to write this article. My former life was destroyed because I figured the odds were 1,000 to 1 against my getting caught. It would comfort me if I could help even one person avoid throwing away a lifetime on a foolish gamble like that.

◆

AFTERMATH

Levine was not the only figure to fall from grace when investigators tore into the insider-trading ring. Ivan Boesky was next. In 1986, he turned himself in. As part of his deal with the SEC, Boesky informed on friends and colleagues including Siegel and Milken. He was also fined $100 million, sentenced to three-and-a-half years in prison (he served two), and banned from the securities business. In 1989, Michael Milken was indicted on 98 counts including racketeering, tax evasion, stock parking, repayment of illicit profits, and securities fraud. Milken also agreed to work with investigators. He pleaded guilty to six securities and reporting charges and was sentenced to a decade behind bars, plus $200 million in fines. Milken also disgorged $400 million to pay shareholders who had been hurt by his fraud and banned from the securities industry for life. Milken served two years; since his release, he has worked to rehabilitate his reputation by dedicating time and money to charity.

In response to these and similar scandals, in 1988 Congress passed the Insider Trading and Securities Fraud Enforcement Act (ITSFEA), which increased penalties for those convicted of insider trading and offered rewards to those who turned them in. The Levine case also had an unintended side-effect of consequence: It helped the political rise of then-prosecutor, Rudolph Giuliani. One of Giuliani's innovations was to use the Racketeer Influenced and Corrupt Organizations Act, designed by Congress to bust organized crime, to bring Wall Street to heel. This was and remains a controversial use of RICO. What can be said, though, is that these prosecutions signaled that insider trading and other securities violations would henceforth be treated like serious crimes.

14

WALL STREET'S MOST RUTHLESS FINANCIAL CANNIBAL

More than just a con man, Dennis Helliwell
cold-bloodedly ruined relatives and friends.

---

by **RICHARD BEHAR**

June 8, 1998

H e seems so harmless in his prison khakis, in rural Pennsylvania, so many miles from the financial powerhouses—Marine Midland Bank and Donaldson Lufkin & Jenrette—that gave him his stature. His hair is golden, his body plump, his voice high, his face almost cherubic. Dennis Lindsay Helliwell will soon turn 40, but when his blue eyes grow moist and he says, "Well, you don't think I'm a bad person, do you?" he seems barely 10 years old, the age when he was orphaned. A visitor feels a sudden urge to comfort this man-child, to give him whatever he wants. Like most great con men, Helliwell has that special power, plus a whole lot more, enough to earn him a niche in the history of financial evil. He is the Hannibal Lecter of Wall Street: a monetary cannibal who devoured his own loved ones.

Most Ponzi schemes fall apart after a year or two. The master himself, Charles Ponzi, paid his investors with money from new clients for a mere eight months before he was caught in 1920. But Dennis Helliwell, who was sentenced to federal prison last October, ran his Ponzi for 11 years. He raised nearly $5 million. And he did it by promising some 50 investors lucrative returns from an exclusive fund at Marine Midland Bank that turned out to be his checking accounts.

That feat aside, what most distinguishes Helliwell's scam is how ruthlessly he plundered his closest friends and relatives. He started with his wife Gigi's sister and eventually her husband, whom he persuaded to invest their entire savings, $225,000, in his special fund. Now it's all gone. "I was raped," says the brother-in-law, Michael Heffernan, who runs a small landscaping business in Massachusetts. "That was my kids' college money. Today I don't trust anybody—anybody for anything. That's a bad way to live." For months after the scam he found it difficult to sleep without alcohol or pills.

Later Helliwell bilked Gigi's elderly grandmother of $635,000.

He took Gigi's parents for $140,000, plus their share of the grandmother's estate. The man Helliwell called his best friend, and made godfather to one of his daughters, he bilked of $667,000.

Diane Gardner was sick, elderly, and recently widowed when Helliwell began to pour on the charm. Her husband had always handled the investments, and she knew little about them. Offering to help, Helliwell took $565,000 off her hands.

His uncle John and aunt Mary, both in their 70s, invested $334,000 with him; it was for their three children and the education of their seven grandchildren. "Dennis knew this," says John.

When one of Helliwell's cousins left his wife, she struggled to raise their two young children. She had only $12,500 in savings, which she wanted to hide from her husband. Helliwell said he knew just the place for it.

When his brother died of leukemia, leaving a 7-year-old daughter, Helliwell announced he was setting up a trust fund. That fund does not exist today.

Wife Gigi, once a glamorous regular on Manhattan's black-tie charity circuit, is on food stamps and living with her embittered, elderly parents in Buffalo.

Like Oscar Wilde's Dorian Gray, Helliwell's baby face betrays no sign of the carnage he has left behind. Why did he do it? "I truly don't think that greed was my motive," he says, over and over. "It was more trying to please people." Told that many of those people are devastated by all this, he explodes, "So am I! They should try coming into prison if they want to know devastated!" He does say he loves the prison food, and it shows. He talks of remorse but sends no letters begging forgiveness.

Helliwell is serving a four-year sentence, but his judge was so moved by the victims that he ordered the felon to take the rest of his life, if necessary, to pay them back the $3,446,378.40 that he squandered. "No, no, no!" proclaimed the Honorable Eugene Nickerson as a prosecutor rounded off the numbers. "I want every cent. ...I'm going to take every nickel he has if I can!" It's rare for federal judges to order full restitution along with maximum jail sentences, but this was no ordinary case.

FORTUNE conducted dozens of interviews and reviewed numerous documents, including records of government regulators and internal, confidential files of Marine Midland, one of America's largest regional banks. Evidence is strong that Helliwell could easily have been stopped, and enormous suffering averted, years earlier. Key findings:

◆ After Helliwell's arrest, a Marine Midland spokesman said the bank had been unaware of his con. In fact, bank officials spotted and investigated the scam in 1991 but chose not to alert regulators, despite a law requiring them to do so.

◆ The law requires banks to report cash deposits or withdrawals of more than $10,000 to the IRS, but Marine Midland neglected to file reports with regulators on roughly two dozen occasions when Helliwell deposited or withdrew more than that amount in cash from his checking accounts.

◆ Helliwell failed his Wall Street licensing exams eight times but was still permitted by Donaldson Lufkin & Jenrette to work closely with wealthy customers, some of whom he persuaded to invest in his fund and then bilked. Helliwell was finally pushed out of DLJ in 1995 amid a review of the firm's registration practices by the National Association of Securities Dealers (NASD), which led to a fine and a consent decree.

◆ Marine Midland stonewalled the Securities and Exchange Commission during the agency's 1996 investigation of Helliwell, according to a former SEC attorney who was involved in the case. In addition, DLJ gave statements to the SEC regarding Helliwell's departure that conflict with what the firm is now telling FORTUNE.

"Dennis Helliwell did not have to happen," says Sean O'Shea, a former prosecutor in the Justice Department's white-collar crime unit who is filing a case against DLJ on behalf of many of the victims. "This ranks as the number one case I've ever come across in terms of sheer cold-bloodedness."

Like many con men, Dennis Helliwell had a painful beginning. Abandoned by their alcoholic father, Dennis and his brother, Michael, were raised by their struggling mother in Detroit until she died of cancer. Dennis was 10. The boys were taken in by a stern aunt (herself an orphan) and an alcoholic uncle just outside Syracuse, in upstate New York. Michael never adjusted to the Glenny family; he immersed himself in drugs and was booted from the house. But Dennis forged a close bond with his aunt and enjoyed good relations with his four Glenny cousins. He was also popular with his peers, who elected him class president at the high school and head of the student government at Niagara University, a private Catholic school outside Buffalo. "Dennis was the last person in the world I thought would hurt anybody, because he needed to be liked so much," recalls family friend Barbara Nicholson, a 52-year-old psychologist. "I knew he'd never hurt me." Helliwell bilked her of $76,000.

The Glennys were prosperous, but most of their money was held in a trust for Dennis's cousins that had been set up by their grandparents. At one point, he tried to persuade his aunt and uncle to allow him to manage the Glenny trust, but it was tied up in a way that prevented him from gaining control. Instead, he spent years "manipulating" his aunt and uncle out of the family's heirlooms; these are now being auctioned off to pay victims.

Helliwell joined Marine Midland Bank as a 23-year-old loan systems analyst in 1982 and, a year later, met his future wife on a special teller line for employees. Georgia (Gigi) Pooley was a Smith College grad from a prosperous family that had lived in Buffalo for many generations. Her father, Montgomery, had worked as a senior attorney in Marine's trust department and had helped her land the job. At first she was ambivalent about Helliwell, but she liked the fact that a friendship between the Pooley and Glenny families dated back more than 100 years. He wooed Gigi and her family, and made sure they believed he came from money. In fact, Helliwell's spendthrift habits had led him to file for personal bankruptcy in 1984.

Court records show that Helliwell emerged from bankruptcy in early 1985, just as he hatched his Ponzi scheme. The procedure, perfected over time, was essentially this: Helliwell told his investors he had access to a special fund for high-net-worth individuals at Marine called "Trust B" that held notes returning a "guaranteed" 12% to 21% annual interest. The lucrative rate, he said, came from sophisticated trading activities in Hong Kong, where Marine's parent company (HSBC Holdings) was once headquartered. The fund was so popular, he added, that investors could join only when an existing investor left, which was rare. Helliwell provided his victims with statements on bank letterhead, deposit slips documenting their investments, even 1099 tax forms in Marine's name. When investors' "notes" came due, Helliwell would sometimes have to apologize for having "rolled" the money over into a new note without telling them.

Dennis and Gigi were married in an extravagant upstate society wedding in 1986. By then, Helliwell had joined Marine's private-clients group, where he was selling trust products to wealthy customers. He was hardly a model employee. His personnel file, obtained by FORTUNE, shows he was praised for his ability to make new contacts but was criticized heavily for low productivity and a lack of knowledge about the bank, the industry, and the products he was selling. He was refused entry to the bank's management program, in part because of his inability to "think independently." Moreover, sometime around 1987 bank officials discovered he had created stationery that falsely identified him as "director of marketing and sales." Helliwell was reprimanded but allowed to keep his job.

By the late 1980's, Helliwell's Ponzi was in full gear, and the money was rolling in. He celebrated Gigi's 30th birthday in 1988 by renting a yacht and flying in family and friends for a cruise of New York Harbor. The couple also broke into the city's black-tie charity circuit by co-chairing the Red Cross's Humanitarian Award dinner dance at the Waldorf-Astoria in 1989. Fellow charity committee members included George Plimpton, Cyrus Vance, and Laurance Rockefeller. But he was laid off from Marine Midland, where he was making $26,400. No problem, he assured his investors—Trust B was also available to former employees.

Several months later, the bank uncovered evidence that he was a criminal—yet did not alert authorities or do anything else to stop him. Marine officials launched an internal probe in April 1991 after receiving an inquiry about Trust B from a bank in Virginia, where one of Helliwell's investors kept his pension funds. The Marine execs soon discovered that Helliwell had typed out receipts to the investor on Marine letterhead, while the investor had written letters directing his bank to send $95,000 to Helliwell for deposit into a "guaranteed Trust B of Marine Midland Bank" paying more than 18% per year.

Marine officials alerted the bank's legal and investigations units. "We certainly started the ball rolling in the right place," recalls former executive Susan Rau, who supervised the bank's private-clients group at the time. Rau says the investigation lasted at least a few weeks. "It was thorough," she says. "[The investigators] went through all the records that he had kept, that the bank had kept, all his customer files. We certainly had very qualified investigators who were asking all the right questions."

What answers did they find? FORTUNE has obtained Marine's investigative file from 1991. "Suspicion of possible IRS fraud," wrote a senior bank investigator. What else they may have found may never be known: Marine officials reviewed Helliwell's bank statements and grilled him in person, but no notes of the interview seem to exist. Helliwell's former boss, Alan Trench, spoke to the SEC two years ago (he declines to comment today) and conceded, says a former SEC attorney, that the bank knew it had uncovered illegal activity.

The rules governing Marine Midland, then a nationally chartered bank, were clear: Any "known or suspected" criminal violation involving bank transactions had to be reported within 30 days. Marine Midland reported the matter to no one.

Why not? The bank won't say anything about the Helliwell case. Some experts speculate that Marine may have feared civil liability by blowing the whistle. The bank also failed to take other steps that might have been expected—and might have stopped Helliwell. Its review of Helliwell's checking accounts would have turned up scores of Trust B investors whom the bank (or government regulators) could have contacted but didn't. In addition, Marine failed to shut down Helliwell's checking accounts, though it had strong evidence they were being used for illegal purposes. Apparently Marine Midland's only significant response to its 1991 investigation was to get an affidavit from Helliwell clearing the bank.

Marine's investigators apparently now realize the bank should have done more, but a former Marine executive who was involved in the Helliwell probe defends the bank's behavior. "There was no indication that there were large sums of money flowing through his Marine accounts," says the executive, who insists on remaining anonymous.

That statement is false, however. FORTUNE has obtained Helliwell's checking account statements from 1989 to 1995, and they show that in the two years before Marine's probe, nearly $800,000 flowed into his accounts. Of that amount, nearly $600,000 came in checks from investors for Trust B.

For the next five years the Helliwells became fixtures in the charity world, where Dennis cultivated the credibility that would fuel his Ponzi. It was a busy life: One day luring in new victims, the next day co-hosting glamorous charity balls with the Manhattan A list. There was the Polo Luncheon in Greenwich, Conn., honoring film star Isabella Rossellini. There was the evening at Manhattan's Sky Club in 1991 when Dennis and Gigi received the Child's Champion Award, given to those "who exemplify in their daily lives the ideals of the Boy Scouts." They even co-chaired annual dinners for the National Victim Center, a group that raises money for crime victims.

Through it all, the Helliwells were living it up with other people's money. Helliwell's checking account records show a man living way beyond his means: In the year before Marine's probe—for half of which he was unemployed—he spent $60,000 just to cover his American Express bills, his limo driver, his floral arrangements, and his private-club expenses. The couple rented a five-story brownstone and filled it with art, antiques, the finest clothes, and enough jewelry to sink a ship. "Dennis was a compulsive shopper," says a former assistant. Former assistant U.S. attorney Mark P. Ressler notes, "He would take people in a limousine to a Broadway play and then a fancy dinner at a private club and insist on picking up the tab—but he'd be using their money." Far from being ashamed, Helliwell still seems to think his open-handedness ought to count in his favor. "A lot of these people involved in Trust B were frequent visitors at our home, and every luxury was laid out for them," he says from prison.

After some six months of unemployment, Helliwell was hired by Sanford C. Bernstein, one of Wall Street's top money management houses, as a "financial advisor." SEC records show that Helliwell failed to pass his basic brokerage licensing exams on two occasions and left the firm five months after he joined. These exams are required for all Wall Street reps who engage in counseling, advising, or selling securities to customers, and Bernstein's policy is that those who cannot pass the exams have to leave.

Helliwell did not find such a barrier at Donaldson Lufkin & Jenrette, where he was welcomed on the recommendation of a senior VP who was active with him on charity committees. His assignment was to sell portfolio-management services to customers with at least $250,000 to invest. Helliwell lasted three-and-a-half years without ever passing his basic brokerage exam.

Securities laws are fairly clear on what unlicensed employees may and may not do. Unlicensed clerks can service customers in a minimal way, but "anyone who is chatting with a customer about a recommendation and helping guide them into a decision needs to be registered," says Mary Alice Brophy, a top enforcement official of the National Association of Securities Dealers. DLJ insists Helliwell never crossed that line. "He was always paired up with someone who was registered," says company lawyer Timothy Mayopoulos. But that's not at all how Helliwell or his clients recall it. One investor, Katherine Hoffman of Buffalo, who lost $250,000, maintains that when she first contacted DLJ about investment possibilities, she was referred to Helliwell and never dealt with anyone else at the company.

Is DLJ's behavior unusual on Wall Street? Not in underground boiler rooms perhaps, but the NASD's Brophy says she's unaware of any respectable Wall Street house that has unlicensed reps who are reeling in rich people. Or as ex-prosecutor Ressler puts it: "A premier financial institution is not supposed to have unlicensed brokers rendering financial advice."

In fact, during the time Helliwell worked at DLJ, the firm was under pressure from the NASD for employing unlicensed executives and had paid a small fine and quietly signed a consent decree promising to shape up. In February 1995, two weeks before DLJ's deadline to have all its reps licensed, Helliwell—having failed yet again to pass his exam—cleaned out his desk. "Given that he had not passed his examination, there was no longer any useful point in his being at DLJ, and he was encouraged to look elsewhere," says Mayopoulos. But in a routine filing with the NASD and in discussions with the SEC, the company said Helliwell left voluntarily. The distinction was important. "If DLJ's attorneys had told us Helliwell had been encouraged to leave, that would have set off bells," says a former SEC attorney.

One of the many charities Helliwell got involved with was Abbott House, a program for hundreds of abused and disabled children just outside New York City, on whose board he briefly served. He got to know Abbott House's CEO, Denis Barry, who decided to invest his savings, $45,000, in Trust B. When Barry's investment came due in September 1995 and Helliwell "rolled it over" into a new note—and then tried to get him to invest yet more money—Barry says he "sensed a scam" and shared his fears in a phone call with DLJ broker Tim Low. Barry's handwritten notes, taken at the time of the conversation, reveal that the DLJ rep was also becoming nervous about Helliwell. Low spoke about "early warning flags," such as the 18% returns, and the fact that some elderly investors "have 80% of [their] assets" in Helliwell's Trust B. "Low said he felt an obligation to alert some of their DLJ clients that Dennis was encouraging people to withdraw their money from DLJ to invest with him," recalls Barry. But he didn't alert the authorities.

Meanwhile, a growing number of Helliwell's investors were asking for their money. His checks were bouncing left and right, prompting Marine Midland finally to close his two accounts—but a close friend at the bank allegedly helped him open a new one. A second pal, Charles Liggio, a senior VP at Republic National Bank, was calling Helliwell repeatedly to keep his checks from bouncing in an account he kept there.

But the walls were closing in. In mid-January 1996, three of his relatives flew to New York seeking proof from him that Trust B existed.

"We really didn't have an interest in blowing him up," says Gigi's brother, Monty Jr. "We naively thought he must have assets somewhere, and we wanted to try and negotiate something." It was too late. On February 7, the SEC received a detailed letter from a Connecticut investor. The following day, three SEC agents were in Helliwell's Manhattan office, watching him shake for nearly ten minutes while his lawyer gave him advice over the phone. Helliwell's assets were frozen five days later.

For nine months after his arrest, Helliwell fought the charges. Gigi stood by her man. The couple even renewed their wedding vows in August 1996. Several weeks later Helliwell was led sobbing from a courtroom after having been remanded into custody for violating the travel restrictions of his bail deal. He pleaded guilty in November. Gigi and their two daughters moved in with her parents and started receiving welfare checks and food stamps. Gigi filed for divorce within months.

How do you recover from such ruinous betrayal? Not quickly or easily. At least eight victims have sought therapy. Some, like Buffalo dentist Michael Collard, rarely venture beyond the office, which he calls a "controlled environment." Collard was Helliwell's best friend, the one who was godfather to a Helliwell daughter and was conned of $667,000. Collard has since gained about 80 pounds and "just doesn't want to meet new people," says a girlfriend who helps him cope. "If you can't trust your local bank and your best friend, who can you trust?"

Emotionally, Helliwell's in-laws have been hardest hit. Gigi's father, Montgomery Pooley, had built a reputation in Buffalo as a loyal, well-bred gentleman, both as a lawyer and as a champion squash player. Today, at 81, he finds it unbearable to be associated with such a scandal, particularly since he had introduced his son-in-law to many friends in his social circle. "My dad has aged dramatically through this whole thing," says Gigi's brother, Monty Jr. Gigi's mother, Georgia, 69, is working overtime as a nurse.

The question that continues to haunt the family is, How much did Gigi know? She declines to be interviewed. What's known for sure is that she was a signatory on Helliwell's accounts and clearly benefited from the scheme. She called Dennis's cousin Kelly Glenny last year to wish him a happy birthday. "Toward the end of the conversation, she said, 'Well, it was fun while it lasted,' " he recalls. "I was furious when I hung up the phone." Says Gigi's brother, Monty: "I choose to believe that she didn't know. But her inability to recognize what was going on is distressing."

Today Gigi is trying to pick up the pieces, in part by attending college classes to become a teacher. "She didn't just lose her lifestyle; she lost her life," says brother-in-law Michael. "She has her mom and dad, but pretty much everybody in the family wants nothing to do with her. And none of her old friends wants anything to do with her."

As for Dennis, he has kept busy tutoring inmates on the fine points of Christianity, teaching them English, even sharing his prison allowance money with those in need. "I can't say who he was before, but clearly he is now a very compassionate man," maintains Alan Larsen, a volunteer for a nationwide prison ministry group.

What, ultimately, made Dennis do what he did? FORTUNE posed the question to Dr. Steven Berglas of the Harvard Medical School, whose entire clinical practice consists of successful businessmen who self-destructed. "While I've never met or spoken with Helliwell, he manifests the characteristics of certain abused or abandoned people who engage in what I call Pyrrhic Revenge," says Berglas. "They use success to try and compensate for the feeling that they're damaged goods. Ultimately, the success they seek doesn't mollify that feeling, so they use self-destructive tactics as a way to draw in and punish others."

Berglas says that without intensive therapy, people engaged in Pyrrhic Revenge "definitely" strike again. Helliwell calls that prediction "preposterous" and is declining to take advantage of prison counseling. "I'm not one to dwell on problems," he says.

Or scarcely one to acknowledge them. The word "denial" doesn't begin to describe Helliwell's attitude toward his past. Asked how he felt during the pressures, the juggling, the deceptions of running an

11-year Ponzi scheme, his answers are consistent: "I never thought about it." "I don't even want to think about it." "I don't really know." His version of what went wrong? "I really thought I could have worked everything out and paid everyone back, but then the government got involved, and it turned into a colossal nightmare." His attempts to defend himself or describe his own suffering are often ridiculous or pathetic. On the dentist he drilled for $667,000, he reflects, "Collard says I'm a pathological liar. Those statements really hurt. We were good friends." Another time Helliwell explains, "I never took money without giving a receipt."

He is no more engaged with reality when he talks about his future. His cousin Kelly Glenny reports that Helliwell called his foster mother from prison not long ago and told her "when he gets out, he can go back to work doing what he was doing, and everything is going to be fine."

Helliwell is legally barred from Wall Street. Still, when he gets out of prison, he'll be out of prison and looking to make money. "I have every intention of paying these people back," he says. Maybe so—but he's appealing the judge's order requiring him to do it.

Helliwell was released from prison on May 12, 2000.

15

BILLIE SOL ESTES: THE THREE-SIDED COUNTRY SLICKER

The Texas con made his first big score in, of all things, ammonia tanks. Here's how he did it.

by SAMUEL BRYANT

July 1962

Born into a poor farming family on the eve of the Great Depression, Billie Sol Estes became, in the words of an Amarillo newspaper, "the biggest wheeler and dealer in all of West Texas"—and perhaps its most infamous. In 1962, his agribusiness empire collapsed when federal investigators found Estes had bilked a dozen major financial companies out of more than $20 million by peddling mortgages on phantom fertilizer tanks. It also emerged that Estes, who boasted political connections that stretched all the way to the Kennedy White House, had fueled his rags-to-riches rise by deftly exploiting the government's vast array of agricultural subsidies.

In July 1962, as a federal district court declared Estes bankrupt, FORTUNE took a bemused look at this quintessential Texas con.

I n a way, the most obvious point about the Billie Sol Estes case is the one that is hardest to believe: that it is still possible for an outlandish rascal working a bizarre, Ponziesque scheme to take some of the biggest corporations in the U.S. for millions of dollars. People who have talked to Estes himself have come away with the impression that he regards most businessmen as pretty easy marks. A lawyer who spent some time in Estes' splendid home in Pecos recalls that he was startled, in looking about the living room—a barn-sized space, adorned by, among other things, a waterfall and several palm trees coming through the floor—to note a monkey in a cage. He asked what the monkey was all about, and Estes replied, laughing: "You know why I have that monkey there? I want to keep reminding myself how goddamn dumb those finance companies are."

The rough dimensions of the fraud and the principal victims have come to be well known. There are 12 finance companies—Walter E. Heller and Company and C.I.T. Financial Corporation have the biggest involvements—from which he swindled a total of $22 million. This sum is secured by mortgages on the now famous, but mostly nonexistent, anhydrous ammonia tanks, which means that the finance companies will have trouble getting their money out.

There is the Commercial Solvents Corporation, to which Estes owes $5.7 million. This sum is secured principally by liens on Agriculture Department payments to Estes for grain storage, but Commercial Solvents' claim on the payments may be shaky now that Estes is in receivership.

There is Anderson, Clayton and Company, to which Estes will owe $650,000, an amount secured—solidly, it appears—by the cotton now growing on Estes's farmlands. Estes also owes various uncertain sums to farmers and small-business men all over West Texas; he seems to have been slow paying many of his bills. But there is no doubt the bulk of his $38-million-odd indebtedness is to "big business."

How could Estes have got so many businessmen to believe that he was a man on whom millions could be ventured? What kind of businessman was he, in reality? In an effort to get to close quarters with these questions, FORTUNE has analyzed 18,000 entries in Estes's "cash journal," studied other available records, and spoken to a number of men who were close to Estes.

One point that soon becomes clear, in talking to Estes's associates, is that there are several different sides to the man. Frank Cain, a lawyer for Pacific Finance, one of the companies taken in by Estes ($3 million), won his confidence to a considerable extent. Cain observed that Estes has three personalities, and he can slip rapidly and easily from one to another. First, he can be cold-blooded and businesslike, entirely ruthless with anyone over whom he might have an advantage.

Second, Estes can impress people as a deeply religious man, which, in some sense, he certainly is; he can quote Scripture endlessly, and had literally convinced many people that his main reason for being in business was to help establish a Christian way of life. He was an elder and frequent preacher at various local Churches of Christ.

Finally, Estes can be profane, witty, and gregarious. Even as his misfortunes began attracting the attention of the FBI, he persisted in seeing the humor. Estes conceded everything, and appeared to take an uproarious delight in recalling the businessmen he had bilked. Cain's recollection of Estes gabbling away on the finance companies went about like this: "Imagine those sons of bitches. I don't have much respect for them. They'd come down here, send two or three men. They'd first go to the farmer, and the farmer would say, 'I don't have the tanks. I rented them. You go up to Estes Enterprises.' When they'd get here, I'd say, 'Just what tanks do you want to look at?' They would give the serial numbers. I'd say, 'It's going to take some time to find out where they are; they're hauled around from farm to farm, you know.' Then I'd just go back here to this room where the serial numbers were. I'd get the numbers we needed, get them flown to my ammonia dealer in the area, and tell him to put those numbers onto the tanks right away." Estes actually had 1,800 ammonia tanks (he had sold mortgages on some 30,000), and these were strategically placed so that he could always display a few in any one area.

Sometimes the serial numbers could be screwed on; sometimes they had to be spot-welded. Then they would be painted; Estes had a special white-lead paint that was quick-drying. His men could get the serial number to the tank, attach it, spray on the paint, wet it down, and throw a little dust over it to create a weather-beaten effect—all within two or three hours after Estes had first got the alarm. "If we couldn't do it that fast," Estes explained to Cain, "we'd tell them that some of the tanks they wanted to see were in the county farthest away; that would give us some extra time. Then when they got there, we might tell them some other tanks they were looking for were maybe 25 miles from where they'd started out in the first place. Can you imagine those guys, driving all over West Texas? They'd have tanks coming out of their ears! One C.I.T. fellow inspected the same tank three different times, with three different serial numbers on it and identified it as three separate tanks." Estes made it clear that he thought this was a very funny story.

THE CASE OF THE FOUR-GALLON COW

Estes may have come by his contempt for "city boys" naturally. He was born in 1925 on a farm three miles northwest of Clyde, Texas, a dusty little hamlet on the Texas and Pacific Railroad. The second child in a family of six, he worked hard tending sheep, cattle, and pigs, and did his turn in the cotton and wheat fields. He went to the nearby one-room school.

His precocious flair for business was revealed in the now well-known story of the ewe. When he was ten, his parents gave him a beribboned ewe lamb for a Christmas present. When she grew up, Billie Sol sheared her, sold the wool and bought more lambs until he had a flock of sheep. He traded the sheep for hogs and the hogs for cattle and in a few years had a considerable herd of his own.

Not so well known (except in Clyde) is the story of the "four-gallon" cow a 14-year-old Estes sold to a neighboring farmer. The neighbor found the cow didn't produce four gallons a day, and complained to

Billie Sol's father. Whereupon Billie Sol told his father that he hadn't said how long it took the cow to deliver the four gallons.

In Clyde High School, his entrepreneurial talents still flowering, he often contracted to remove prickly pear cacti from ranchland. He would organize a group of his schoolmates, give them pitchforks and get them out in the fields to dig up the cacti. In the summer he contracted for wheat harvests in Kansas. He was sometimes slow at paying his boys off, but apparently they didn't hold this against him; they elected him "king" of the junior class. (The girl he was to marry, Patsy Howe, was queen.)

While he was still in high school he discovered the possibilities in government wheat. What he discovered, specifically, was that the Commodity Credit Corporation would sell wheat for less than the going market price around Clyde, and that any dealer who held his distribution costs down could make a good profit. Billie Sol got a friendly banker to lend him $3,500, and with it he paid for the first carload of wheat.

Then, using the boxcar as both warehouse and store, he sold the wheat to all comers, while his crew—schoolmates he had recruited for the job—shoveled it out into baskets, buckets, or anything that would hold it. The "wheat deal" continued into 1943, by which time Billie Sol had sold 14 carloads.

He didn't get into the armed forces during World War II because he had bad eyesight and one leg shorter than the other. But in 1945 he did manage to get into the Merchant Marine, serving in the Atlantic as a wiper and mess attendant. Despite these menial positions, his voyages were profitable for Billie Sol. He bought hard-to-get supplies in New York and sold them in Europe for U.S. postage stamps, which were then used as an informal substitute for dollars by both Frenchmen and Americans. He returned to Clyde with $700 worth of stamps.

After the war, when many other veterans were cashing in on the educational benefits of the G.I. Bill of Rights, Estes—who has never been to college—was bidding on surplus government housing at abandoned Army and Navy bases. He found that he could buy the houses with small down payments and begin to resell them before he had to complete his payments. Estes's housing deals were worked in a lot of different places—West Texas, New Mexico, California, Washington, Arkansas—and it is likely that his attempts to influence government officials started with these surplus-housing deals.

In a typical instance, Estes would pay $35 apiece for a group of buildings, move them off the base, spend $200 or $300 apiece fixing them up, and then sell them to someone desperate for housing for, say, $3,000 or $4,000 each.

THE NEW MAN IN TOWN

By 1951, the year Billie Sol moved to Pecos with his family—two of his five children had been born by this time—he had accumulated about $28,000. He arrived unostentatiously one day, wearing his country clothes, and wandered around talking to gas-station attendants, waitresses, and truck drivers. He asked for the name of "an honest real-estate broker," got one (a Church of Christ member) who satisfied him, and bought a "section" of land—640 acres. Estes said he proposed to put in some cotton. To house his family he bought a small structure that had been built over an abandoned Army swimming pool (which served as the basement). The house was made of wood from icebox crates, coated with stucco.

This all had an undeniably modest look about it, and Pecos must have gotten quite a jolt when Estes began operating in his own distinctive way. He began by selling prefab buildings. To encourage the expansion of grain-storage facilities, the Agriculture Department was other then offering financing at 2%. Estes apparently noted that there was nothing in the fine print to prevent the department from financing these structures even if they ended up being used for purposes than grain storage. He sold the prefabs as garages, airplane hangars, and housing for Mexican labor, pointing out to the buyers that they could still get the government's 2% money. His profits from this operation are unknown, but within a year or so he was named one of the five leading young Texans by the state Junior Chamber of Commerce. And he was picked by the National Junior Chamber as one of the ten outstanding young men of 1953.

Another of the ten, as it happened, was Governor Frank Clement of Tennessee, who met Estes at the banquet celebrating the occasion. Later, in Nashville, Estes met Judge Clement, the governor's father, who was much taken with the energetic and devout young Texan. For a while, Estes and the Clements were partners in a surplus-housing company, the Delta Homes Investment Company.

The Clements pulled out of that partnership in 1956 but Billie Sol kept on buying and selling the surplus houses. His church connections helped him to raise cash for his venture.

These enterprises were by no means his only business preoccupation during those early years in Pecos. He was expanding rapidly in several different directions, and this fact is confirmed in the successive balance sheets he prepared for his creditors. Even allowing for his habitual tendency to exaggerate his resources, the balance sheets were impressive for a farm boy from Clyde who was still younger than 30. In December 1954, he listed his net worth at $1,471,685.64, chiefly in real estate, farmland and oil.

Still, Billie Sol's affairs were being run chaotically, and he had a reputation in town for not paying even the smallest bills. Both problems were solved, at least partially, in 1956 when an old friend from Clyde, A. B. Foster, came to work as Estes's accountant and business manager. A brilliant man and a CPA, Foster became indispensable to Estes, and was soon the only man in the organization—probably including the boss—who understood the details of the multifarious operations.

The first definite sign that Estes was far overextended came in 1958. He then owned 1,600 shares (worth $5 apiece) of the Pecos Growers Gas Company, of which he had also been one of the founders. The company's biggest customers were farmers, whose irrigation pumps used the gas. The pumps were distributed by still another Estes enterprise, Equipment Service Company.

In August 1958, Equipment Service had a sizable number of mortgages from farmers in the area who had bought the pumps on credit and to raise cash Estes sold a lot of the mortgages to a finance company, Associates Investment. Most of the payments on these mortgages were maintained by the farmers, but early in 1959 some $600,000 worth fell into default. Estes had earlier accepted responsibility for any payments in default, but now he refused. Furthermore, when Associates began to press the point, it made the disconcerting discovery that some of the mortgages were for nonexistent pumps.

Associates decided that it would not take any more of Estes's paper from then on.

AMMONIATED GREEN PASTURES

While he was wrestling with the debts represented by the irrigation pumps, Estes continued to expand. It appears to have been sometime in 1958 that Estes made his decision to expand his ammonia operations. As usual, he expanded furiously by going into debt furiously.

In the period around 1958, anhydrous ammonia sold to farmers in West Texas for something like $120 a ton. The manufacturers, including Commercial Solvents, sold it to the distributors for something like $90 a ton. But beginning in 1958, Estes sold the ammonia at a retail price of $80 a ton—in other words, at a $10 loss. By the end of 1958, Commercial Solvents found that he was slow in his payments and, in fact, owed the company upward of $500,000. Estes was invited to come up to New York for a conference about this situation.

Estes arrived unabashed, with a plan. He explained that he could not pay the $500,000 very readily, but that he would be able to make good if Commercial Solvents would back him in a further expansion of his operations. Specifically, he suggested—and Solvents finally agreed—that the corporation lend him $900,000. About $550,000 of this was to cover the accounts receivable that Solvents was already holding. Another $125,000 was to be used to buy more ammonia. And $225,000 was to be used to purchase a grain-storage elevator in Plainview, Texas. The whole $900,000 was to be repaid over five years, and as security Solvents received a lien on the elevator's future receipts. The agreement also provided that Estes could continue to receive anhydrous ammonia from the company on credit.

Taking advantage of this last feature, Estes moved into the south Plains area and began cutting prices so low ($60 a ton was not unusual) that rival dealers sometimes posed as farmers to buy from him because his retail price was cheaper than their wholesale cost. Soon Estes had a lot fewer competitors. A good many dealers gave up in despair, or sold out to Estes.

A $40 MILLION FANTASY

By late 1959, Estes owed Commercial Solvents for about $3.5 million worth of ammonia. At that point Solvents decided it was time to work out a new agreement. It is easy to understand why the company was concerned. Even though the Plainview elevator had been licensed for government storage, and was being steadily expanded (that year it was able to hold 12 million bushels), the lien on the payments, which ran to 13.5 cents per bushel per year, could not nearly cover the new indebtedness. Accordingly, Solvents asked for, and got, assignments on Estes's accounts receivables and chattel mortgages on his inventory of anhydrous ammonia. And the company began to put some limits on the amount of fertilizer Estes could receive. The company tried to ensure that the cost of making and shipping the ammonia to Estes would be covered by its liens on the grain-storage receipts. Solvents, it is clear from the evidence, did not think Estes was completely trustworthy. His unaudited 1961 net-worth figure, for example, represented that he was worth about $40 million.

An indication that the $40 million figure was indeed something of a fantasy came early in 1962, when Estes broke the sad news to Solvents that he was unable to meet some impending payments on the first mortgage on his grain elevators—by now he had six, five of which were organized in his United Elevators Company. Would Solvents advance him another $400,000 to take care of this embarrassment? Despite its growing misgivings about Estes, Solvents agreed to the deal because it had second liens on Estes's grain elevators. As collateral at this time, it secured first deeds of trust on some land owned by Estes.

In backing Estes, it is now clear, Solvents was not out on as long a limb as some newspaper accounts have suggested. In its four-year relationship with Estes, he had run up a bill for $12,628,000. The company had collected $6,959,000 in grain-run payments, which left Estes owing it $5,669,000.

But the fact is that, even if the $5.7 million proves to be entirely un-collectable, Solvents is in the black in its dealings with Estes. Solvents' total production and shipping costs worked out to about $40 a ton, while Estes was billed for $90 a ton. The $6,959,000 generated by the grain liens more than covered the production costs of all the ammonia Estes got.

Furthermore, Solvents is presumably entitled to write off the entire unpaid balance as a bad debt, and it has a fair chance of coming out of the affair with a strong position in the West Texas fertilizer market. The company is now operating the network Estes built up. (It pays the receiver a royalty.) Whatever its misgivings about Estes, Solvents seems to have known what it was doing.

EMPIRE BUILDER ON A BICYCLE

It is not so clear that Estes himself knew what he was doing; at least, his strategy in these transactions seems to have been a fairly desperate one, entailing steadily heavier losses and an increasingly crushing debt load. Estes doubtless hoped in the end to corner a sizable share of the ammonia and grain-storage businesses in West Texas, and hoped that both might then be profitable. Meanwhile, both were losing money furiously.

And on top of everything else, he was living on a multi-millionaire's scale. By 1960 his home, which he had valued at $14,000 in late 1954, had been expanded by the addition of two wings, a swimming pool, tennis courts, servants' quarters, and a second floor; Estes now listed its worth at $90,000. It was and is the biggest house in Pecos, with a barbecue pit in which three steers can be roasted at once. He had an airplane and two Cadillacs in his driveway. Ironically, his driver's license had been lifted for recklessness, and so he often rode a bicycle to work.

Late in 1961, he owned a dozen or so businesses in Pecos, most of them bought with little or no cash. His Water Well Service Company serviced pumps all over the endless acres of irrigated land in the region. His Pecos Transit Mix Company sold sand and gravel to contractors for miles around. His Equipment Service Company, earlier involved in his dispute with Associates Investment, was still selling irrigation pumps. Perhaps the most bizarre of all Estes's many operations was his Colonial Funeral Home, the most imposing building in Pecos, completed this year at a cost of $250,000. Thus far, all of seven bodies have passed through the funeral home.

One other Estes venture that proved important in his affairs was his newspaper, the *Pecos Daily News*. He founded it in mid-1961, at a time when he was blaming his defeat in a school-board election (a write-in movement beat him) on the *Pecos Independent and Enterprise*. He asked his 400 employees not to buy from stores that advertised in the rival paper.

This proved to be a crucial mistake, for the Independent knew something about Estes. One of its owners, John Dunn, had earlier been collecting evidence about bogus mortgages on ammonia tanks, and in March 1961, he had turned some of it over to the FBI in El Paso. After Oscar Griffin was hired to be managing editor of the paper in July 1961, he did some further checking on the story. It was the *Independent* that broke the story early this year.

It is not quite certain when Estes actually began selling the bogus tank mortgages. But as his ammonia losses and grain-storage debts began piling up in 1959, he was desperately mortgaging all the property he had, including the ammonia tanks. When he ran out of real tanks, he began selling paper on fictitious ones, just as he had done earlier with the fictitious irrigation pumps. That venture had blown up because he had (1) used his own name, and (2) unloaded all the paper on one finance company. This time he did not make those mistakes.

His scheme was wonderfully simple in its basic conception, but complex in its execution. Since he had exhausted all his own credit, Estes now proposed to use the credit of his well-heeled customers, the farmers who bought his ammonia. Obviously, he had to pay for their cooperation, and he saw a way to do that by giving them a share of the money he borrowed. A larger problem was to keep the farmers from realizing that he was borrowing against nonexistent tanks, and that the deal was fraudulent. He solved this problem by arranging that the farmer would never have to see the tank; the farmer would buy it, make a 20% down payment, sign a delivery receipt, and immediately lease it back to Estes.

The farmer would be reimbursed for all his expenses. He would make the down payment to the Superior Manufacturing Company, of Amarillo, which had made the tanks already mortgaged by Estes—in other words, the real ones. Then the farmer would receive a check from Estes for the amount of the down payment. (Superior later turned the farmer's payment over to Estes. This transaction was concealed by having Superior send the check to the Texas Steel Company, a dummy corporation Estes set up with an account in the First National Bank of Pecos.) The farmer would also be reimbursed for his mortgage payments, for these would be precisely covered by Estes's lease payments. Estes would make this odd arrangement seem more plausible to the farmer by explaining that tax reasons made it more desirable for him to lease the tanks rather than own them.

The final step in the deal was reselling the mortgages to the finance companies. This proved to be not too difficult; if they had any doubts that a bona fide sale of an ammonia tank had taken place, Superior could show them photostats of the farmers' down-payment checks and delivery receipts. Estes's own name never appeared on the paper—an omission that was, of course, essential to his success in selling the paper to the finance companies. In general, the finance companies would take mortgages for 80% of the tanks' presumed value, and discount this paper by 6%—i.e., they would lend Superior some 75% of the tanks' stated value. Superior would take 1% of this amount as its payment for going along with the deal, and give the rest to Estes (again, via Texas Steel). Estes would thus get about two-thirds of the stated value, but he had to give the farmer 10% of that. With all these other fingers in the pie, Estes was, in effect, borrowing at a staggering rate of interest; in general, he seems to have collected about $3 for every $4 of debt he incurred. At the time the scheme was revealed, his monthly payments on the debts were running over $500,000; he was keeping up the payments in part with the proceeds from his ammonia sales—and in part by selling more bogus mortgages.

A BAD DAY IN LUBBOCK

On the night of February 23, the Dallas law firm of Irion, Cain, Cocke and Magee took a conference call from a client in Los Angeles, the Pacific Finance Company. Frank Cain and M. R. Irion of the firm spoke on the phone to two officers of Pacific, who wanted to know if those articles in the *Independent* meant that they were holding a lot of worthless paper. They told Cain that the tanks could be identified only by their serial numbers. Cain suggested, "You'd better send out every available man and hit the farmers all at the same time."

Pacific set up headquarters in Amarillo, and assigned 18 investigators to talk to farmers and find the tanks. After about six hours the investigators were reporting back that they could find no tanks with Pacific Finance serial numbers on them and that farmers were getting scarce, too.

By this time Estes had retained Hobert and Bert Nelson of Lubbock as legal counsel. Cain and Irion arranged to meet Estes and the Nelsons in Lubbock on February 28. Before the meeting, Cain stopped off in Amarillo at the Superior plant. He determined that Superior's monthly capacity, on a three-shift basis, was 800 tanks. Yet the tank mortgages filed in Reeves County in January 1962, alone had run to 3,376.

When Cain and Irion arrived at the Nelsons' office in Lubbock, Cain said to Estes, "I want you to know our main interest is in getting paid out. I want to know where the tanks are." Estes smiled and said, "There aren't any tanks." Irion, who has a low boiling point, grew red in the face and exploded at this. "Do you mean to tell me there are no tanks?" he demanded. Estes had a broad smile on his face. "No," he told Irion, "there are no tanks."

Cain then asked how many finance companies were involved altogether. Estes had such a list, which proved to be quite accurate, which showed how much he was paying in monthly installments and how much he still owed. Cain decided to try flattering Estes in an effort to draw him out. He said, "You sure have made a damn fool out of some of the most brilliant financial men in the country. What have you done with the money?" Estes dodged the question.

AT HOME WITH BILLIE SOL

Cain went to Pecos on March 13, checked in at the Brandon Hotel, and spent most of the next three days with Estes. It was a memorable experience for Cain. When he pressed Estes for some suggestions about working out their mutual problem, Estes told him that the grain terminals were to be the major source of the income he needed. Keeping the elevators full of grain would be easy, Estes boasted. "You know, I'm on the Cotton Advisory Committee. We've gotten our people so entrenched in the entire agriculture program that if these so-called conservatives came in it would take them eight years to get control out of our hands."

Cain noted that the grain payments were already tied up by Commercial Solvents, but Estes brushed this objection aside with some large boasts about his influence in the company.

At times Estes really seemed to be trying to help the finance companies. Once he referred to "this cotton allotment program that we have worked up—it's a fortune-making thing. And that's another thing that I can look to for paying you fellows out." Estes was suggesting that his cotton-growing income, which amounted to $489,000 in 1961, was secure from other creditors. He had a total of 5,166 acres in cotton, of which 2,043 acres were his; the rest was land he had sold to and leased back from farmers in order to get their cotton allotments. (In May 1962, after the Estes case broke, the Agriculture Department canceled the leased allotments, ruling that the technique Estes had used for getting them was illegal, and fined him $554,000.)

At several points during Cain's stay in Pecos, Estes put on a display of his contacts with politicians that made Cain's head reel. On the office walls were row after row of photographs of politicians—Ex-President Truman, President Kennedy, Vice President Lyndon Johnson, Senator Yarborough, and many lesser lights—all autographed and inscribed with warm greetings to a staunch supporter of the Democratic party. Estes showed Cain a gold-laminated card denoting his status as a $100,000 sustaining member of the Democratic party. Once Estes called up Democratic National Headquarters, chatted with someone there, then told Cain he had Emery Jacobs of the Department of Agriculture coming down to make a speech in Pecos. Cain didn't know who Jacobs was, and Estes explained, "He's one of the big men in this cotton allotment program." (Jacobs later resigned after there was testimony that Estes may have bought him some clothes.)

Half-convinced that Estes might, after all, find a way to pay his debts, Cain flew to Los Angeles and reported to Pacific Finance's president, Maxwell King. King said that the situation had become "an industry problem," and asked Cain to call a meeting of all the finance company creditors. The two men also discussed Commercial Solvents' relations with Estes, and Cain mentioned that its president, Maynard Wheeler, was visiting Estes at that very moment. King didn't believe it, and so Cain called Estes on the phone and confirmed it. Then he asked Estes if he could fly over right away, explaining, "I'd like to talk to you and

Mr. Wheeler. I need the cooperation of Solvents."

Estes sent a plane to meet Cain at Midland and fly him back to Pecos in time for Sunday breakfast. While Cain was at the house, he later testified (at the Texas court of inquiry), Estes said to him, perhaps mischievously, "They [Solvents] want to put me in business in Brazil."

There were other cryptic references to Estes's going abroad. At one point, Cain testified, he mentioned to Wheeler that Estes was in trouble with the finance companies and Wheeler said, "If Billie gets too involved, we can always use him as a consultant in Switzerland." Estes interrupted to say, "Well, I think Brazil will be better." (Wheeler later denied any suggestion of sending Estes abroad.)

When he got back to Dallas, Cain called each of the finance companies on Estes's list of his creditors, told them they were holding mortgage paper on nonexistent ammonia tanks, and arranged for a creditors' meeting. The meeting took place on March 27 in the boardroom of the Mercantile National Bank in Dallas, with 33 executives and lawyers from the finance companies in attendance. Cain and Irion explained for two-and-a-half hours just how Estes had done them out of at least $22 million. Estes came in the room only briefly, with his lawyer; he seemed, in turn, arrogant, disconsolate, and deflated. On the whole, he did not leave the financiers optimistic about their prospects of getting any money out of him.

By the time Estes left the meeting and returned to Pecos, even he must have known he was in deep trouble. The next day the FBI picked him up on a charge of having transported false mortgages across state borders, and he spent the weekend in the local jail. He took this opportunity to send in his resignation as an elder of the Church of Christ.

By this time Estes's case was a national news story, setting off loud echoes in Washington, D.C., as well as Texas. It is clear now that Estes liked to feel that he "owned" politicians, and that he did a lot of boasting about his acquisitions in this line. It is not so clear how much he was really helped by his political connections. Perhaps some of the treatment he received from the Agriculture Department could be considered as favored. For example, the department accepted a balance sheet that Estes had a CPA send in and that considerably inflated his assets—even though the CPA's accompanying remarks made it clear that no real audit had taken place.

It is also possible that Estes was favored in his grain storage. Some 5,200,000 bushels of grain from Kansas were moved to his Texas elevators last year, versus 141,985 bushels in 1960.

Whatever his past influence with politicians, Estes is plainly having trouble finding anyone on his side these days. At present, he is under nine separate indictments. He has also been asked to testify at an investigation into the mysterious shooting of an Agriculture Department official who was looking into his cotton allotment operations. But with all his problems, Estes still does not seem terribly downhearted. He once said, "I can be happier in jail than most people can be out of it." He will undoubtedly have a chance to prove this statement.

◆

AFTERMATH

How much did Estes take in? FORTUNE came up with a figure of $20.6 million for the period from January 1961 through February 1962; only about $11 million of that could be accounted for.

Colorful con men like Billie Sol Estes don't go away quietly, but few set legal precedents on their way to prison. Estes's star turn came during his state trial in 1962, when the presiding judge allowed live broadcasts from the pre-trial hearings. Though the result was chaos, Estes was eventually convicted. Estes appealed on the basis that the media circus deprived him of a fair trial. In June 1965, the Supreme Court agreed, issuing a 5-4 decision that overturned his conviction and limited televised broadcasts of "notorious" trials. But the court did not rule definitively on the constitutionality of televising trials, and for the next 16 years the Estes opinion served as a legal touchstone. It was not until 1981 that the Supreme Court decided unanimously, in Chandler v. Florida, that televising trials did not infringe on defendants' rights.

Estes was found guilty of mail fraud and conspiracy in federal court in 1963, and sentenced to 15 years. Naturally, he appealed, and made a little money on the side by opening his home to tourists—$5 a carload, $20 for photographs—until the city zoning board shut him down. In 1965, his appeals exhausted, he went to prison, serving six years. But Estes, who once compared his appetite for deal-making to alcoholism, could not stay *out of trouble. In 1978, he was caught peddling non-existent steam cleaners for oil-field machinery. The following year he was sentenced to ten years in prison for concealing assets from the Internal Revenue Service and for conspiring to defraud investors. He ended his last stint in federal prison in December 1983.*

Shortly after his release, Estes, who always bragged about his friendship with Lyndon B. Johnson, began to hint that he helped to cover up the former president's alleged crimes. His attorney wrote a letter to the Department of Justice in 1984, claiming that Estes knew that the former President not only was implicated in the murder of Henry Marshall, the Agriculture Department official who died mysteriously while investigating the Estes cotton allotments in 1961, but also John F. Kennedy and several others. Asked to provide further information, Estes never did; he also refused to speak to DoJ officials. But his charges have been picked up by many conspiracy theorists.

Estes still lives in the Lone Star State. He's had a few more brushes with the law, including a 1989 indictment for stealing trade secrets; the case was later dismissed. And he's never lost his penchant for self-promotion. In 2004, he published his autobiography, Billie Sol Estes: A Texas Legend.

IV

DOWNFALLS

16

WHY ENRON WENT BUST

---

by BETHANY MCLEAN

December 24, 2001

Year after year in the 1990s, business people named Enron one of America's "Most Admired Companies." Journalists were also impressed— including at FORTUNE, which in April 1998 ran an article, "Enron: The Power's Back On," that praised the company's increased transparency and willingness to "acknowledge its problems." Ouch. In March 2001, FORTUNE's Bethany McLean took a harder look at the energy giant, pointing out that the company's financial statements were almost impossible to figure out. In an emperor-has-no-clothes moment, McLean asked: "Is Enron Overpriced?" In retrospect, that article marks a clear turning point in the Enron story. In late 2001, when Enron had degenerated into a byword for corruption, greed, and arrogance, McLean returned to the subject.

"Our business is not a black box. It's very simple to model. People who raise questions are people who have not gone through it in detail. We have explicit answers, but people want to throw rocks at us."

So said Enron's then-CEO, Jeff Skilling, in an interview I had with him last February. At the time, Enron's market capitalization was around $60 billion, just a shade below its all-time high, and its status as a Wall Street darling had not yet begun to crumble. I was working on a story that would ultimately raise questions about Enron's valuation, and I'd called with what I considered fairly standard queries in an effort to understand its nearly incomprehensible financial statements. The response from Enron was anything but standard. Skilling quickly became frustrated, said that the line of inquiry was "unethical," and hung up. A short time later Enron spokesman Mark Palmer called and offered to come to FORTUNE's New York City office with then-CFO Andy Fastow and investor-relations head Mark Koenig. "We want to make sure we've answered your questions completely and accurately," he said.

Now, in the wake of Enron's stunning collapse, it looks as if the company's critics didn't throw enough rocks.

Until recently Enron's attitude, expressed with barely concealed disdain, was that anyone who couldn't understand its business just didn't "get it." Many Wall Street analysts who followed the company were content to go along. Bulls, including David Fleischer of Goldman Sachs, admitted that they had to take the company's word on its numbers—but it wasn't a problem, you see, because Enron delivered what the Street most cared about: smoothly growing earnings. Of course, now that it's clear that those earnings weren't what they appeared, the new cliché is that Enron's business was incredibly complicated—perhaps even too complicated for founder Ken Lay to understand (something Lay has implied since retaking the CEO title from Skilling last summer). Which leads to a basic question: Why were so many people willing to believe in something that so few actually understood?

Of course, since the Enron collapse, there are other basic questions as well—questions for which there are still no adequate answers. Even today, outsiders still don't know what went wrong. Neither do Enron's employees, many of whom expressed shock as their world cratered.

Was Enron's ultimate collapse caused by a crisis of confidence in an otherwise solid company? Or were the sleazy financial dealings that precipitated that crisis—including mysterious off-balance-sheet partnerships run by Enron executives—the company's method of covering up even deeper issues in an effort to keep the stock price rising?

A CULTURE OF ARROGANCE

If you believe the old saying that "those whom the gods would destroy they first make proud," perhaps this saga isn't so surprising. "Arrogant" is the word everyone uses to describe Enron. It was an attitude epitomized by the banner in Enron's lobby: THE WORLD'S LEADING COMPANY. There was the company's powerful belief that older, stodgier competitors had no chance against the sleek, modern Enron juggernaut. "These big companies will topple over from their own weight," Skilling said last year, referring to old-economy behemoths like Exxon Mobil. A few years ago at a conference of utility executives, "Skilling told all the folks he was going to eat their lunch," recalls Southern Company executive Dwight Evans. ("People find that amusing today," adds Evans.)

To be sure, for a long time it seemed as though Enron had much to be arrogant about. The company, which Ken Lay helped create in 1985 from the merger of two gas pipelines, really was a pioneer in trading natural gas and electricity. It really did build new markets for the trading of, say, weather futures. For six years running, it was voted Most Innovative among FORTUNE's Most Admired Companies. Led by Skilling, who had joined the company in 1990 from consulting firm McKinsey (he succeeded Lay as CEO in February 2001), Enron operated under the belief that it could commoditize and monetize anything, from electrons to advertising space. By the end of the decade, Enron, which had once made its money from hard assets like pipelines, generated more than 80% of its earnings from a vaguer business known as "wholesale energy operations and services." From 1998 to 2000, Enron's revenues shot from $31 billion to more than $100 billion, making it the seventh-largest company on the FORTUNE 500. And in early 2000, just as broadband was becoming a buzzword worth billions in market value, Enron announced plans to trade that, too.

But that culture had a negative side beyond the inbred arrogance. Greed was evident, even in the early days. Compensation plans often seemed oriented toward enriching executives rather than generating profits for shareholders. For instance, in Enron's energy services division, which managed the energy needs of large companies like Eli Lilly, executives were compensated based on a market valuation formula that relied on internal estimates. As a result, says one former executive, there was pressure to, in effect, inflate the value of the contracts—even though it had no impact on the actual cash that was generated.

Enron also developed a reputation for ruthlessness, both external and internal. Skilling is usually credited with creating a system of forced rankings for employees, in which those rated in the bottom 20% would leave the company. Thus, employees attempted to crush not just outsiders but each other. Enron traders, says an executive at a rival firm, were afraid to go to the bathroom because the guy sitting next to them might use information off their screen to trade against them. And because delivering bad news had career-wrecking potential, problems got papered over—especially, says one former employee, in the trading operation. "People perpetuated this myth that there were never any mistakes. It was astounding to me."

TRADING SECRETS

"We're not a trading company," said Fastow during that February 2001 visit. "We are not in the business of making money by speculating." He also pointed out that over the past five years, Enron had reported 20 straight quarters of increasing income. "There's not a trading company in the world that has that kind of consistency," he said. "That's the check at the end of the day."

In fact, it's next to impossible to find someone outside Enron who agrees with Fastow's contention. "They were not an energy company that used trading as a part of their strategy, but a company that traded for trading's sake," says Austin Ramzy, research director of Principal Capital Income Investors. Indeed, Enron had a reputation for taking more risk than other companies, especially in longer-term contracts, in which there is far less liquidity. And it's no secret that among non-investment banks, Enron was an active and extremely aggressive player in complex financial instruments such as credit derivatives. Because Enron didn't have as strong a balance sheet as the investment banks that dominate that world, it had to offer better prices to get business. "Funky" is a word that is used to describe its trades.

But there's an obvious explanation for why Enron didn't want to disclose the extent to which it was a trading company. For Enron, it was all about the price of the stock, and trading companies, with their inherently volatile earnings, simply aren't rewarded with rich valuations. The odd mismatch between what Enron's management said and what others say isn't just an academic debate. The question goes to the heart of Enron's valuation, which was based on its ability to generate predictable earnings.

Why didn't that disconnect seem to matter? Because like Enron's management, investors cared only about the stock price, too. And as long as Enron posted the earnings it promised (and talked up big ideas like broadband), the stock price was supposed to keep on rising—as, indeed, it did for a while. Institutions like Janus, Fidelity, and Alliance Capital piled in. Of course, earnings growth isn't the entire explanation for Wall Street's attitude. There were also the enormous investment-banking fees Enron generated. Nor was asking questions easy. Wall Streeters find it hard to admit that they don't understand something. And Skilling was notoriously short with those who didn't immediately concur with the Enron world-view.

WHERE ARE THE PROFITS?

Although it's hard to pinpoint the exact moment the tide began to turn against Enron, it's not hard to find the person who first said that the emperor had no clothes. In early 2001, Jim Chanos, who runs Kynikos Associates, a highly regarded firm that specializes in short-selling, said publicly what now seems obvious: No one could explain how Enron actually made money. Chanos also pointed out that while Enron's business seemed to resemble nothing so much as a hedge fund—"a giant hedge fund sitting on top of a pipeline," in the memorable words of Doug Millett, Kynikos's chief operating officer—it simply didn't make very much money. Enron's operating margin had plunged from around 5% in early 2000 to under 2% by early 2001, and its return on invested capital hovered at 7%—a figure that does not include Enron's off-balance-sheet debt, which, as we now know, was substantial. "I wouldn't put my money in a hedge fund earning a 7% return," scoffed Chanos, who also pointed out that Skilling was aggressively selling shares.

Not only was Enron surprisingly unprofitable, but its cash flow from operations seemed to bear little relationship to reported earnings. Because much of Enron's business was booked on a "mark to market" basis, in which a company estimates the fair value of a contract and runs quarterly fluctuations through the income statement, reported earnings didn't correspond to the actual cash coming in the door. That isn't necessarily bad—as long as the cash shows up at some point. But over time Enron's operations seemed to consume a lot of cash; on-balance-sheet debt climbed from $3.5 billion in 1996 to $13 billion at last report.

Skilling and Fastow had a simple explanation for Enron's low returns. The "distorting factor," in Fastow's words, was Enron's huge investments in international pipelines and plants reaching from India to Brazil. Skilling told analysts that Enron was shedding those underperforming old-line assets as quickly as it could and that the returns in Enron's newer businesses were much, much higher. It's undeniable that Enron did make a number of big, bad bets on overseas projects—in fact, India and Brazil are two good examples. But in truth, no one on the outside (and few people inside Enron) can independently measure how profitable—or more to the point, how consistently profitable—Enron's trading operations really were. A former employee says that Skilling and his circle refused to detail the return on capital that the trading business generated, instead pointing to reported earnings, just as Fastow did. By the late 1990s much of Enron's asset portfolio had been lumped in with its trading operations for reporting purposes. Chanos noted that Enron was selling those assets and booking them as recurring revenue. In addition, Enron took equity stakes in all kinds of companies and included results from those investments in the figures it reported.

Chanos was also the first person to pay attention to the infamous partnerships. In poring over Enron documents, he took note of an odd and opaque mention of transactions that Enron and other "Entities" had done with a "Related Party" that was run by "a senior officer of Enron." Not only was it impossible to understand what that meant, but it also raised a conflict-of-interest issue, given that an Enron senior executive—CFO Fastow, as it turns out—ran the "Related Party" entities. These, we now know, refer to the LJM partnerships.

When it came to the "Related Party" transactions, Enron didn't even pretend to be willing to answer questions. Back in February, Fastow (who at the time didn't admit his involvement) said that the details were "confidential" because Enron "didn't want information to get into the market." Then he explained that the partnerships were used for "unbundling and reassembling" the various components of a contract. "We strip out price risk, we strip out interest rate risk, we strip out all the risks," he said. "What's left may not be something that we want." The obvious question is, Why would anyone else want whatever was left either? But perhaps that didn't matter, because the partnerships were supported with Enron stock—which, you remember, wasn't supposed to decline in value.

SKILLING SENDS A SIGNAL

By mid-August enough questions had been raised about Enron's credibility that the stock had begun falling; it had dropped from $80 at the beginning of the year to the low 40s. And then came what should have been the clearest signal yet of serious problems: Jeff Skilling's shocking announcement that he was leaving the company. Though Skilling never gave a plausible reason for his departure, Enron dismissed any suggestion that his departure was related to possible problems with the company. Now, however, there are those who speculate that Skilling knew the falling stock price would wreak havoc on the partnerships—and cause their exposure. "He saw what was coming, and he didn't have the emotional fortitude to deal with it," says a former employee.

What's astonishing is that even in the face of this dramatic—and largely inexplicable—event, people were still willing to take Enron at its word. Ken Lay, who stepped back into his former role as CEO, retained immense credibility on Wall Street and with Enron's older employees, who gave him a standing ovation at a meeting announcing his return. He said there were no "accounting issues, trading issues, or reserve issues" at Enron, and people believed him. Lay promised to restore Enron's credibility by improving its disclosure practices, which he finally admitted had been less than adequate.

Did Lay have any idea of what he was talking about? Or was he as clueless as Enron's shareholders? Most people believe the latter. But even when Lay clearly did know an important piece of information, he seemed to be more inclined to bury it, Enron-style, than to divulge it. After all, Enron's now infamous October 16 press release—the one that really marked the beginning of the end, in which it announced a $618 million loss but failed to mention that it had written down shareholders' equity by a stunning $1.2 billion—went out under Lay's watch. And Lay failed to mention a critical fact on the subsequent conference call: that Moody's was considering a downgrade of Enron's debt. As recently as October 23, Lay insisted that Enron had access to cash, that the business was "performing very well," and that Fastow was a standup guy who was being unnecessarily smeared. The very next day Enron announced that Fastow would take a leave of absence.

We now know, of course, that Enron's dealings with its various related parties had a huge impact on the earnings it reported. On November 8, an eye-popping document told investors that Enron was restating its earnings for the past four-and-three-quarters years because "three unconsolidated entities should have been consolidated in the financial statements pursuant to generally accepted accounting principles." The restatement reduced earnings by almost $600 million, or about 15%, and contained a warning that Enron could still find "additional or different information."

THE LAST GASP

On the surface, the facts that led to Enron's December 2 bankruptcy filing are quite straightforward. For a few weeks it looked as if Dynegy (which had long prided itself on being the anti-Enron) would bail out its flailing rival by injecting it with an immediate $1.5 billion in cash, secured by an option on Enron's key pipeline, Northern Natural Gas, and then purchasing all of Enron for roughly $10 billion (not including debt). But by November 28 the deal had fallen apart. On that day Standard & Poor's downgraded Enron's debt below investment grade, triggering the immediate repayment of almost $4 billion in off-balance-sheet debt—which Enron couldn't pay.

But even this denouement comes with its own set of plot twists. Both companies are suing each other: Enron claims that Dynegy wrongfully terminated the deal, "consistently took advantage of Enron's precarious state to further its own business goals," and as a result has no right to Enron's Northern Natural pipeline. Dynegy calls Enron's suit "one more example of Enron's failure to take responsibility for its demise." The irony is clear: Enron, that new-economy superstar, is battling to hang on to its very old-economy pipeline.

To hear Dynegy tell it, a central rationale for abandoning the deal was what might be called the mystery of the missing cash. General counsel Ken Randolph says that Dynegy expected Enron to have some $3 billion in cash—but an Enron filing revealed just over $1 billion. "We went back to Enron and we asked, 'Where did the cash go? Where did the cash go?' " says CEO Chuck Watson. "Perhaps their core business was not as strong as they had led us to believe," speculates Randolph.

Enron has not conceded yet. The company's biggest lenders, J.P. Morgan Chase and Citigroup, have extended $1.5 billion of "debtor in possession" financing to Enron, which will enable it to continue to operate for a while. And Enron is still searching for a bank that will back it in restarting its trading business.

In any conversation about Enron, the comparison with Long-Term Capital Management invariably crops up. In some ways, it looks as if the cost of the Enron debacle is far less than that of LTCM. But in other ways the cost is far greater. Enron was a public company with employees and shareholders who counted on management, the board, and the auditors to protect them. That's why one senior Wall Streeter says of the Enron saga, "It disgusts me, and it frightens me." And that's why, regardless of how the litigation plays out, it feels as though a crime has been committed.

◆

AFTERMATH

In the wake of Enron's spectacular collapse, Congress passed the Sarbanes-Oxley Act in 2002. This legislation, which had been gathering dust for years, was perhaps the most comprehensive regulation of the securities industry since the 1930s. Among other things, under SarbOx, company officers are personally responsible for the accuracy of the books. To improve independent accounting practices, SarbOx created a Public Company Accounting Oversight Board that creates and upholds accounting standards. When Enron imploded, it took with it the once venerated accounting firm Arthur Andersen. In 2002, Andersen was convicted in a criminal trial of obstruction of justice for shredding tens of thousands of Enron-related documents. Though the Supreme Court overturned that conviction in 2005, it was only a symbolic win. By that time, Andersen was defunct.

As for the primary players in the case, former chief financial officer Fastow pleaded guilty to two counts of conspiracy in January 2004. He agreed to forfeit $23.8 million and to serve ten years in prison. In September 2006, his prison term was reduced to six years. Fastow was willing to help the prosecution by testifying against Skilling and Lay. Fastow's wife, Lea, was convicted of not reporting income and began serving her one-year sentence in May 2004. She completed her sentence shortly before her husband started his.

In two separate trials, Lay was convicted on a total of ten counts of conspiracy and bank fraud in May 2006; he immediately appealed and six weeks later died of heart attack. He was never sentenced and in October of that year Judge Lake vacated the convictions, noting that a dead defendant cannot appeal his verdict. As a matter of law, once the convictions were vacated it was as though the case never happened.

Skilling was convicted in May 2006 on 19 counts of insider trading, securities fraud, and conspiracy. He was acquitted on nine counts of insider trading. Skilling was sentenced to 24 years and four months in prison, but that sentence was reversed in January 2009 by the Fifth Circuit Court of Appeals. He awaits resentencing.

17

THE INSATIABLE KING SCRUSHY

Richard Scrushy started as a nobody. He became a hotshot CEO.
He tried to be a country star. Then it got interesting.

---

by JOHN HELYAR

July 7, 2003

Shortly after dawn on July 30, 2002, William A. Massey Jr. backed his GMC Yukon out of his driveway in a suburb of Birmingham, Ala., and turned the wrong way down Weatherly Club Drive. Instead of heading for his office in town, he drove to the back of the subdivision, where the paved road turns to dirt. There he got out of the SUV, sat down, put a shotgun in his mouth, and blew his brains out.

The act was horrifying. The man's identity made it shocking. Massey's boss was Richard Scrushy, chairman and CEO of Health-South. Scrushy's interests ranged from medical companies that did most of their business with HealthSouth to a pajama company called Uppseedaisees.. Bill Massey was Scrushy's personal CFO for those private interests, doing the financing, paying the bills, moving around money—and, allegedly, stealing a lot of it.

Massey's life came totally unraveled in just one week, after he was found to be both an embezzler and an adulterer. The 37-year-old CPA had a wife and two kids and looked like an accountant from central casting. Yet he'd somehow taken up with a beautiful brunette named Hope Launius, who worked for Uppseedaisees and was Leslie Scrushy's close friend. Some of the $500,000 he siphoned from Scrushy's accounts was probably spent on lavish dinners and gifts for Launius. Scrushy learned of both transgressions, financial and marital, the week of July 22.

The day after Massey's suicide, Scrushy sold $25 million of his shares in HealthSouth. Taken together with the $74 million of stock he'd sold in May, that meant he'd shed one-third of his holdings in his own company that year. Also on July 31, he reported Massey's alleged theft to local police and confronted Launius. She won't comment on this or any matter. But the consensus account is that Scrushy demanded to know what she knew about his financial affairs. Launius, various sources say, told him that Massey had been nervous about the $74 million sale of HealthSouth stock in May, when Scrushy was making rosy forecasts. It made her think, she told him, that he'd been inflating the stock price, the sources say.

Launius eventually returned to her old job at a Parisian department store's cosmetics counter. It seemed a world away from the magical one that had blown up on her. Then HealthSouth blew up too. On August 27, 2002, it announced that it would suffer a $175 million profit shortfall because of changed Medicare regulations. Its stock plunged 58% in two days, to $5. The papers said federal investigators were looking into Scrushy's stock sales ahead of the bad news. But the person who'd actually handled the sale of three-quarters of those shares was dead. And so, according to law-enforcement sources, Launius picked up the phone and called the FBI and the SEC.

The world Richard Scrushy once ruled has collapsed with stunning swiftness. Only six months elapsed from the start of the SEC's investigation to the filing of its $1.4 billion fraud suit against him in March 2003. (. It took just seven weeks, from March 19 to May 5, for the Justice Department to accumulate 11 guilty pleas from Scrushy aides. All five CFOs in the company's history have admitted to cooking the books.

In a state of tired old mills, he created an exciting growth company. In the bureaucratic universe of health-care management, he fashioned a starry kingdom. Then, over time, it all went quite mad. Vision gave way to delusion, success to excess—and once-loyal followers became informers. Hope Launius put in her calls, CFO Bill Owens put on a wire, and at the U.S. Attorney's office, tipsters had to take a number and get in line. At HealthSouth, the man once called King Richard is now known as Kool-Aid Richard. On Yahoo message boards and in a brief phone call to FORTUNE, Scrushy insists he's a victim. "I've been so mistreated, so lied to, it's just massive," he says, vowing that once his name is cleared, his attorneys will seek damages from those who spread lies. (Scrushy declined to be interviewed for this story, though he responded to some questions through an aide.)

Of all the recent accounting scandals, this one may well be the strangest. That's because it has as much to do with narcissism as it does with greed. Scrushy certainly enjoyed the trappings of corporate gentry—the four mansions, the ten boats, the $135,000 bulletproof BMW, the $7.5 million Sikorsky helicopter, the G-5 jet he sometimes piloted himself. But for him, it wasn't enough to come along at a time when successful CEOs were treated like rock stars. He wanted to be a rock star. Did Dennis Kozlowski ever sing lead vocals for a professional band? Did Bernie Ebbers work the crowd at the Grammys? Did John Rigas do ads for a bar called the Live Bait? Scrushy did all that. In fact, in his later days as CEO, he wasn't in the office much—he was managing a girl group called 3rd Faze, which had once opened for Britney Spears.

ONCE UPON A TIME

The Scrushy story is not just a fable for our time but a mystery to people who knew him growing up in Selma, Ala., a sleepy river town of some 24,000 people, made briefly infamous in the 1960s as one of the pivotal battlegrounds of the civil rights movement. Richard Scrushy was never called a comer there; he wasn't even called Richard. He went by his middle name, Marin, and he was the unremarkable middle child of Gerald Scrushy, a cash register salesman, and Grace, a nurse. The Parrish High yearbooks of the late 1960s bear photos of Marin Scrushy but no evidence that he was in any school activities. He did play in garage bands, but these were as undistinguished as every other facet of his youth.

Scrushy dropped out of high school when he got his girlfriend pregnant and they married. He became a bricklayer to support his accidental family (another baby soon followed) and possessed all the attributes of a trailer-park lifer, except for some that just didn't fit. "You went over to Marin's trailer," his friend Gary West recalls, "he served wine and cheese."

One other quality: He was very smart. One day, according to a story Scrushy has told friends, he was struggling to haul a load of cement up a ladder as a worker at the top berated him and told him to hurry up. He heaved the load before his tormentor, who snarled, "Now go get another one." He did not. He walked off the job and all the way to his parents' house and told his mother he wanted to get his GED and go to college.

She said there was growing demand for respiratory therapists at the hospital, and he agreed to try that field. Scrushy enrolled at Jefferson State Community College in Birmingham, then did a year of clinical training at the University of Alabama at Birmingham (UAB). He graduated in 1974 and turned to teaching respiratory therapy. Starting to sense his possibilities, Scrushy divorced his wife, cut off his ponytail, and started going by "Richard." He jumped from teaching at UAB to running a Birmingham hospital's respiratory therapy unit to starting a new department to teach again at Wallace Community College in Dothan, Ala. His circumstances were still modest, though: At age 26, he was teaching at a two-year vocational school and living in a government-subsidized house with the second Mrs. Scrushy, a local woman named Karen Brooks.

His big break came in 1979, when he was hired by a Houston-based company called Lifemark, a for-profit hospital chain. "These people were all mercenaries," says one person who knows both the industry and Scrushy. "He fit right in, and he had to have been saying to himself, 'Holy cow, I can do this!' " Scrushy made his mark building up a respiratory therapy unit at a hospital where Lifemark had a contract.

After Lifemark was acquired in 1983, Scrushy led four colleagues out the door to start a chain of outpatient clinics based in Birmingham. The co-founders pooled only $50,000—but Scrushy had big plans. Stopping by the house of an old Selma friend, Jimmy Mitchell, one day, he vowed, "I'm either going to make it big or go flat broke." Mitchell could sort of tell by the gold Mercedes Scrushy was driving.

When renowned sports surgeon James Andrews moved his practice to Birmingham in 1986, he planned to affiliate his clinic with a big national health-care company. But when he was told about this local startup company, he met Scrushy and he was sold. "He had boundless energy, and he was a great motivator," recalls Andrews, whose clinic moved onto the first floor of the one hospital HealthSouth operated. "He was working so hard himself, it was almost like you couldn't let him down."

By 1986, when HealthSouth had grown to $20 million in annual revenues and gone public, Scrushy's transformation was underway. It was good to be the king—you could set the past right. Scrushy formed a rock group called Proxy and recruited three of the old Born Losers, the top teen band of his youth, to play in it; two of them also joined HealthSouth. Fielding Pierce, who had gone from ultra-cool high-schooler (and lead singer of the Born Losers) to manager of a Wendy's, must have been a particularly satisfying hire. Scrushy would let vendors know about an upcoming Proxy gig and suggest they help pack the hall. HealthSouth employees knew to be in the crowd too. This was known in the company as "purchased applause."

Scrushy needed applause the way he needed oxygen. But when the lights came up and real life resumed, he was terribly insecure. The kid from Selma was clothes-conscious and proud of his huge Hermes tie collection. At HealthSouth's Monday management meetings, discussion wasn't part of the drill. Officers made two-minute, numbers-packed reports, then braced for Scrushy's decrees and judgments. They might not get that far if he interrupted with his dreaded catchphrase: "That was the stupidest thing I ever heard."

Nothing was too small to incite King Richard's wrath, not even dust specks. Especially dust specks. Every HealthSouth facility was subject to a "pristine audit," a white-glove test conducted by Ernst & Young staffers with 50-point checklists. They may have missed billions in financial fraud, but they were great at finding dust bunnies. Woe to the person whose clinic failed the test or a Scrushy spot check. "It might be one o'clock in the morning, and he'd call at home to say, 'I'm out in your parking lot, and there's a piece of paper,' " says a former HealthSouth manager.

If King Richard was a tyrant, why did his executives stick around? Partly it was because they knew the idea of HealthSouth was so good. Freestanding clinics were more efficient than big hospitals, and a consolidator could get economies of scale. Partly it was because HealthSouth paid so well. Plus, the stock options became quite valuable as the shares rose, at a 31% annual clip from 1987 to 1997. Partly it was the glamor. Bo Jackson, Herschel Walker, Roger Clemens, and other superjocks would visit Dr. Andrews for treatment and leave as HealthSouth spokesmen.

Scrushy himself became a celebrity in Birmingham. He made big donations to Alabama schools, charities, and other causes. It was HealthSouth money that supported most of this philanthropy, but it was Scrushy's name that appeared on buildings, stadiums, and in the case of his community-college alma mater, a whole Richard M. Scrushy Campus.

Not everyone was enthralled by him. Scrushy was rejected for membership in the elite Birmingham Country Club—a reminder that in the eyes of Birmingham's old money, he still wasn't so far removed from the trailer park. When some society types did attend a charity roast for Scrushy, they recoiled at Bo Jackson's tribute: "Richard Scrushy fuckin' gets it done."

Scrushy had two responses to the bluebloods. One was to torture them at a favored enclave, Lake Martin, where he built a 14,000-square-foot mansion dwarfing the other houses and roared around in a cigarette boat. The other was to use HealthSouth's growing fleet of company jets to create, in effect, his own elite club. Politicians like Newt Gingrich and Orrin Hatch were HealthSouth frequent fliers. So were athletes like Troy Aikman. Scrushy okayed the jets' every use and accrued many favors.

He also used the jets a lot for business, because, starting in 1994, he went on an acquisitions binge. That year he doubled HealthSouth's size and catapulted it from the No. 3 company in the rehab-services industry to No. 1. HealthSouth became a $1 billion company.

Scrushy was just getting started. HealthSouth began the year 1995 with no surgical facilities. After four acquisitions totaling $1.3 billion, it was by year-end the country's biggest surgical-center operator. The people actually managing all these acquired businesses were run ragged. HealthSouth's antiquated technology made computer integration alone a nightmare. But Scrushy cared less about what people in the trenches thought than about what people on Wall Street did. His pay was closely tied to the stock price, and HealthSouth's shares rose 60% in 1995 alone. Scrushy was paid $7.4 million that year, more than twice his 1994 pay.

Somewhere along the line he started to believe his health-care-industry stardom was transferable to show biz. After all those years performing with Proxy, he decided to renounce his amateur status, turn to country music, and take some power lunches in Nashville.

Scrushy recruited professional musicians from the likes of the Oak Ridge Boys and Sawyer Brown. He named his new group Dallas County Line (Selma is part of Dallas County, Ala.), and their debut album was accompanied by a video that must be seen to be believed. There's Scrushy, dressed in black from the tip of his boots to the top of his cowboy hat, singing the CD's lead song, "Honk If You Love to Honky Tonk." The camera cuts from him to faces in a crowd that includes Bo

Jackson, wrestler Lex Luger, NASCAR driver Bobby Allison, and, just for good measure, Neil Diamond.

Scrushy showed the video to applause at the HealthSouth annual meeting in 1995, though shareholders might have withheld it had they known how much company money was going into the band. Scrushy flew the band on HealthSouth jets from Nashville to Birmingham twice a week to rehearse. He and his sidemen also flew to Australia on a corporate jet for the Dallas County Line Down Under tour. The trip's business justification was due diligence for an acquisition there. And that explains HealthSouth's hospital in Melbourne, one of only four company facilities outside the U.S. There was a flaw with Dallas County Line, however: As a lead singer, Scrushy was no better than damn good—for a CEO. He finally had to face it: This was one enterprise he couldn't will to success. Dallas County Line broke up.

So did Scrushy's marriage. Fed up with his absences and his quirks, Karen filed for divorce and tore out Scrushy's heart. It was a big blow—he wept openly and often, friends say—and a bad omen for HealthSouth. Karen was the one person who could give Scrushy reality checks—and she no longer wanted the job.

On the surface, life otherwise remained good. In 1997, HealthSouth's stock rose 44%, and Scrushy was America's third-highest-paid CEO, taking home $106 million. Most of that came from cashing in $93 million of stock options. But there were big problems below the surface. Congress passed a Medicare-overhaul bill that year, aimed at cutting payments from that program by $100 billion over a five-year period. HealthSouth stoutly maintained that its earnings wouldn't suffer, even though more than a third of its revenues came from Medicare. The company's stock thus didn't immediately suffer, at a time when Scrushy was exercising stock options.

Indeed, through the first part of 1998 the company's trajectory still seemed straight upward. It reached $4 billion in revenues, made the FORTUNE 500, and met or exceeded analyst earnings expectations for the 48th straight quarter. But in September, HealthSouth issued a warning: It would miss analyst estimates for 1998 and 1999, and its growth rate was markedly slowing. The company's stock plunged 43% in just two days, to $10.50.

This was not only the prequel to the events of 2002, when Scrushy again sold stock ahead of a profit warning, but also, according to the SEC suit, when the serious accounting fraud started. HealthSouth's profits had in fact been hurt by the Medicare cuts, and its acquisition binge was about over. There was simply little left to buy. The beauty of acquisition accounting—perfectly legal—was the room it allowed for all sorts of gimmicks and restatements, masking true operating performance. Now HealthSouth had to get more brazen about how it made its numbers.

It allegedly worked like this: Scrushy met monthly with company finance executives. "If we weren't making the numbers, he'd say, 'Go figure it out,' " said Mike Martin, CFO between 1997 and early 2000, in court testimony. Lower-level bean counters then inflated assets and used other creative accounting to plug the gap. Eleven of the co-conspirators, who called themselves the "family," have entered guilty pleas in connection with the fraud. From 1997 through mid-2002, according to the SEC, HealthSouth overstated its earnings by $2.5 billion. Its fictive profits were 2,500% higher than the true ones.

If Scrushy had been managing HealthSouth as closely as he once did, its true earnings might have been better and its need for fictive ones smaller. But he wasn't. He remarried in 1997 and promptly had two more children with his new wife, Leslie. He accumulated prodigious amounts of toys, including 34 cars. "The corporate culture created the fraud, and the fraud created the corporate culture," says a former HealthSouth executive.

Scrushy was also involved in a growing number of other enterprises. One was MedPartners, a company based on the conceit that HealthSouth's savvy could be applied to the physician practice management business. It was a disaster. Scrushy also had private stakes in companies that did much of their business with HealthSouth, including Source Medical Solutions, a specialty-software company, and MedCenters Direct, an Internet procurement concern. GG Enterprises, a company that sold millions of dollars of office equipment to HealthSouth, was owned by Scrushy's parents, Grace and Gerald.

Scrushy grew increasingly paranoid. At HealthSouth's new headquarters building, completed in 1997, there was a separate entrance and elevator for him and his top lieutenants. At the Monday meetings he was preceded by bodyguards. HealthSouth's current managers say they found that he could listen in on the phone calls of the senior executives on his floor from his secretary's phone; Scrushy denies he did any such surveillance.

Meanwhile, his interests strayed further afield, in particular back to show biz. HealthSouth had since 1996 staged "Go for It" road shows, in which jocks delivered inspirational messages to kids. Schools bused students by the thousands to arenas for it. In 2000 the show's producer made the mistake of suggesting that they add some music. Scrushy's inner impresario went wild. He contracted with an Orlando music producer who'd developed such synthetic teen groups as the Backstreet Boys to put together a girl group. The fellow assembled three perky young women and called them 3rd Faze, and Scrushy took it from there, setting them up with a snazzy choreographer, a sexy wardrobe, and in short order a record deal. Scrushy also transformed the "Go for It" road show into a promotional vehicle for the girl group. Teachers who'd brought their classes for inspirational messages instead found 3rd Faze shaking their booty. Some marched their kids right out.

But Scrushy wasn't through. He wanted to develop a Go for It TV show, also as a 3rd Faze showcase. That's how he came to meet one Jason Hervey, who had played the obnoxious older brother, Wayne, on *The Wonder Years* TV series. Now he was a Hollywood producer. Scrushy engaged him to produce the "Go for It" show. Then Scrushy recruited Hervey to become a HealthSouth executive in charge of marketing and communications. Hervey's main job, really, was to reinforce Scrushy's show business obsession.

In a conference call with analysts on May 2, 2002, Scrushy said he was "very comfortable" with analyst estimates of 39% profit growth that year. On May 14 he sold $74 million of his stock, at $14 a share. Three days later, on May 17, in a development noted only by devoted health-care bureaucrats, Medicare issued a clarification of payment rules for individual vs. group physical therapy. HealthSouth didn't seem to take note of it either, reaffirming its "guidance" for robust profits on July 11 and again on August 7.

Yet on August 27, when the company announced its $175 million shortfall, it suddenly attached major significance to the Medicare changes. That was a scant two weeks after the day corporate America's CEOs had to swear to the purity of their financials under the Sarbanes-Oxley Act. Not surprisingly, HealthSouth's stock tanked.

Scrushy insisted he didn't know of the Medicare issue until well after selling his stock on July 31 and making the "guidance" announcements. A company-commissioned review by the Fulbright & Jaworski law firm backed him up. But in mid-September the SEC notified HealthSouth it was being investigated.

Scrushy took to radio to proclaim his innocence. First it was on HealthSouth's weekly show on a Birmingham station, hitherto loosely related to health issues. It became a Richard Scrushy rant about how untrue and unfair it all was—especially the coverage in *The New York Times* and *The Wall Street Journal.* Then, in November, he started a twice-weekly program on another station, called the Richard & Jason Show. For two hours Scrushy and Hervey would banter, calling each other "Cowboy" and "Gator." They interviewed everyone from country stars to Parisian fashion consultants, talked about their weekend plans, even did commercials for a Florida Panhandle bar they frequented called the Live Bait.

Scrushy conducted his last staff meeting at HealthSouth on March 18. As usual, it was part intimidation— he was cutting off access to Internet chatrooms from the HealthSouth computers—and part pep talk. That evening, after Scrushy had left, agents of the FBI and the SEC took over the executive suite and began gathering evidence.

◆

AFTERMATH

Fired from HealthSouth in March 2003, Scrushy surrendered to the feds that November. The 85 counts in the Justice Department indictment against him included one conspiracy charge, two securities fraud charges, 17 counts of wire fraud, 19 counts of mail fraud, five false statement charges, three charges of false certification or attempted false certification, 19 money-laundering counts, and 14 counts of criminal forfeiture. (Eventually, these would be distilled to 36 charges.) Scrushy was the first CEO to be charged under the CEO/CFO certification provision in the Sarbanes-Oxley Act of 2002, which punishes executives who knowingly file false reports to the SEC.

Though five CFOs and five former vice presidents in the finance and accounting departments testified that Scrushy had planned to defraud the company and hide its true financial circumstances, he was acquitted on all counts in June 2005. Scrushy's lawyers argued that the executives had simply lied; Scrushy never took the stand. The decision was a huge blow to the government, which had won big cases against executives at Adelphia, Tyco, and WorldCom earlier in the year.

That was not, however, the end of the affair. The SEC had also brought a civil suit against Scrushy and HealthSouth charging that the company overstated earnings by at least $1.4 billion. The suit, filed in March 2003, said that Scrushy had masterminded a plan to inflate company revenues and personally profit from the scheme. The suit included two counts of fraud, two counts of reporting violations, and three counts of violating record keeping and internal controls. After the Justice Department lost its case in 2005, the SEC pressed its civil case. Scrushy settled. Neither admitting nor denying the accusations, he agreed in April 2007 to pay more than $81 million in fines. The amount of the payment made at that time was less, since the federal judge ruled that he could count settlements from three other civil cases toward payment.

And still, the legal consequences continued to unroll. In 2006, Scrushy was convicted on nine counts of bribery, conspiracy, mail fraud, and wire fraud. But this case had nothing to do with his earlier troubles at HealthSouth. This time, Scrushy was accused of putting $500,000 into the coffers of a state lottery campaign run by former Alabama Governor Don Siegelman in exchange for a seat on an important hospital regulatory board. This is the case that finally brought Scrushy down. In June 2007, just two months after he settled with the SEC, Scrushy was sentenced in the bribery case to six years and 10 months in prison, as well as 500 hours of community service, a $150,000 fine and $267,000 in restitution to the United Way of Central Alabama.

In an unusual turn of events, Siegelman was convicted on seven of the 33 counts against him in the Scrushy affair: one count of bribery, one count of conspiracy, four counts of mail fraud, and one count of obstruction of justice and was sentenced to seven years and four months. He initially went to prison, but then he filed an appeal bond motion with the 11th Circuit Court of Appeals and was released. He remains free until the court decides whether to overturn or affirm the conviction.

Scrushy, on the other hand, was sent to prison directly after sentencing and without a bail hearing. The 11th Circuit Court of Appeals in Atlanta turned down his bid to remain free pending appeal, arguing that he posed a flight risk. He now resides in a minimum security prison in Beaumont, Texas, and no decision has yet been made about his appeal.

18

THE FALL OF FANNIE MAE

By BETHANY MCLEAN

January 24, 2005

It began with an accounting scandal—billions in overstated earnings that cost CEO Franklin Raines his job in 2004. But the fight over Fannie was always about more than the numbers. It was a nasty political showdown where everyone had his own agenda. And it didn't go away. Three years after this article was published, as the housing and credit markets began to melt down, Fannie took a large share of the blame.

Here is a tough-minded look at how a once-boring, below-the-radar government enterprise founded during the Depression raised its profile—and then became famous for all the wrong reasons. Author Bethany McLean notes that in the early 2000s, people were beginning to ask, "What would happen if anything went wrong—and not just to Fannie and Freddie but to the entire financial system?" As everyone now knows, that was surely the right question—but the answer came far too late, and at far too high a cost.

On a sunny Monday in June 2002, President George W. Bush stood in the St. Paul AME Church in a formerly dilapidated neighborhood on the south side of Atlanta. Sitting in prime seats were Franklin Raines, the CEO of Fannie Mae, and Leland Brendsel, the CEO of Freddie Mac. The President was there to unveil an initiative aimed at helping 5.5 million minority families buy homes before the end of the decade—"Part of being a secure America," he said, "is to encourage home-ownership."

Raines and Brendsel were there because, well, encouraging home-ownership was what their congressionally chartered companies existed to do. By purchasing hundreds of billions of dollars' worth of mortgages held by banks, Fannie and its cousin Freddie made it possible for financial institutions to turn around and make more loans to prospective homeowners. Or at least that's the theory.

Franklin Delano Raines is a prominent Democrat, but that hadn't kept him from currying favor with the new Republican President. For more than 30 years Fannie Mae has straddled two worlds—business and politics—and the company placed enormous emphasis on maintaining good relations with key government officials. In 2001, Raines had written an op-ed in *The Wall Street Journal* lauding Bush's faith-based initiative. He had also reached out to Bush allies in the faith-based community, including Kirbyjon Caldwell, the Houston pastor who gave the benediction at Bush's first inaugural. In October 2002, at the White House Conference on Minority Home Ownership, Raines and Caldwell were both on hand to be praised warmly by Bush for their work.

It hasn't even been three years since that sunny day in Atlanta, but oh, how the world has changed. Both Brendsel and Raines have been deposed in the wake of multibillion-dollar accounting scandals. Brendsel fell in 2003, after government regulators accused Freddie Mac of understating billions in profits in an effort to smooth earnings. More recently the Securities and Exchange Commission ruled that Fannie Mae—the larger and more important of the two companies—had violated accounting rules, overstating profits by an estimated $9 billion since 2001, which represents almost 40% of its total earnings during that period. Raines, who was paid more than $90 million during his six years as CEO—much of it linked to meeting profit targets—made a last-ditch effort to save his job, but to no avail. CFO Tim Howard was also forced out. Fannie's accounting firm of 36 years, KPMG, was fired. Once one of the most politically powerful companies in America—with staunch allies in Congress who did its bidding, a notoriously weak regulator, and a willingness to steamroller its critics—Fannie today is more vulnerable, in both a business and political sense, than it has ever been before. However it emerges from this scandal, it will almost surely never again be the unstoppable force it once was.

The Fannie story is not like other accounting scandals, though. Yes, the company broke the rules to produce a smooth stream of earnings, just as Enron, Tyco, WorldCom, and all the others did. But that's only one of a half-dozen different story lines. The Fannie Mae saga is also about a company that lost sight of its original mission. It's about power politics run amok, and the combustible blend of politics and business. It's about a company whose huge debt terrified top government officials, and whose very existence drew ideological opposition. It's about an orchestrated, behind-the-scenes campaign to rein in a financial powerhouse. It's about a regulator who learned to fight back against a much more formidable foe.

It's about all these things and one more. Fannie Mae thought itself so different, so special, and so powerful that it should never have to answer to anybody. And in this, it turned out to be very wrong.

THE 'BIG FAT GAP'

The Federal National Mortgage Association (Fannie) and the Federal Home Loan Mortgage Corp. (Freddie) are unique institutions. They are publicly held, for-profit corporations that were legislated into existence by Congress and operate with a congressional charter to help lower- and middle-income Americans buy homes. (They are often referred to as government-sponsored enterprises, or GSEs.) Fannie was founded in 1938 as a federal agency and became a for-profit company in 1968. Freddie, started in 1970, offered shares to the public in 1989.

The central idea behind the GSEs was that they would encourage home-ownership by buying mortgages from banks. This was in an era when federal law forbade interstate banking—which meant that most banks were necessarily small. When Fannie or Freddie bought a mortgage, it freed up the bank's limited capital, allowing it to make more loans. The purchase also relieved the bank of both the credit risk and the interest rate risk—that is, of having to worry that people might default, or that interest rates might rise during the life of the loan. Fannie and Freddie are one reason America is one of only two countries where lenders offer 30-year fixed-rate mortgages. (Denmark is the other.)

Their congressional charters give Fannie and Freddie unmatched advantages. For example, the Treasury is permitted to buy $2.25 billion of each company's debt (commonly referred to as Fannie and Freddie's line of credit). Fannie and Freddie are exempt from state and local taxes and have much less stringent capital requirements than banks. Best of all, their cost of capital is only a smidgen higher than long-term Treasuries—and lower than that of even the most creditworthy companies. This last advantage, however, is not due to any regulation. Rather, it is the result of the market's belief that the U.S. government will never let them default.

In fact, there is no such federal guarantee. But the two GSEs play what former assistant Treasury secretary Rick Carnell calls "a double game"—disavowing federal backing in their public boilerplate, while quietly encouraging the notion. In 1998, for instance, Fannie argued in a letter to the Office of the Comptroller of the Currency that its securities were safer than all AAA-rated debt because of the "implied government backing of Fannie Mae."

Fannie and Freddie dominate the mortgage market, but they don't originate home loans. Instead, they make their money in two major ways. One is conservative: They get a fee for guaranteeing the payments on mortgages they buy, which they then resell to investors, usually in the form of mortgage-backed securities. The more aggressive way is to hold on to the mortgages, assume all the inherent risk, and make money on the spread between their low cost of capital and the higher yield of the mortgage portfolio. (Alan Greenspan would later call this "the big, fat gap.") The more mortgages the GSEs buy, the faster their profits can grow. Since 1995, Fannie and Freddie's holdings of residential debt have grown an average of 20% a year, and together they now carry $1.5 trillion in home loans and mortgage securities on their books—more than the top ten commercial banks combined. Thanks in large part to this growth, Fannie has had double-digit profit gains for the last 17 years—and an average return on equity of 25%. But the GSEs' size has people increasingly worried about what might happen if anything went wrong—and not just to Fannie and Freddie but to the entire financial system.

There is one additional concern: derivatives, which institutions rely on to hedge interest rate risk. Over time, Fannie and Freddie became two of Wall Street's top users of derivatives. Of course, derivatives have their own risks—as America discovered in 1998 when hedge fund Long Term Capital Management blew up—and very nearly brought down the U.S. financial system with it. The idea that its activities might pose a danger infuriates Fannie Mae, which describes itself as "a bulwark of our financial system." For some of its critics, though, Fannie's refusal to acknowledge that its portfolio posed any risk would become the scariest thing of all.

THE BEAR IN THE CANOE

Fannie Mae has always been run by power brokers. Its CEO in the 1980s was a savvy and extremely charming man named David Maxwell. He left two legacies. First, he rebuilt the company after its one brush with death in the early 1980s, when interest rates spiked and the payments on its mortgage portfolio didn't cover the cost of its debt.

Fannie survived in part because banks kept lending it money—based on the perception that the government stood behind it.

Maxwell also put in place elements of the political and business machine Fannie would become. But it was his successor, Jim Johnson, who perfected the machine. The smooth, Princeton-educated son of a Minnesota politician ran Fannie for most of the 1990s. He had worked as an advisor to Walter Mondale and was a longtime member of the Washington establishment. Indeed, last year he headed Senator John Kerry's search for a vice-presidential candidate and was rumored to be a top choice for Treasury Secretary in a Kerry administration—along with Franklin Raines.

Like both his predecessor and his successor, Johnson could speak passionately about Fannie Mae's mandate—to help create affordable housing. "The mission," he liked to say, "flows in our veins." But that idealism could be accompanied by a win-at-all-costs attitude, traits that were, and are, reflected in Fannie.

Johnson's essential belief was that Fannie would always be vulnerable to the whims of politicians because so few people really understood what it did. "There's nothing in the home-owner's life called Fannie Mae or Freddie Mac," he would say. He came up with two key strategies he believed would insure that Congress never took away Fannie's special status. He called them "indispensability" and "tangibility." To put it simply, he wanted Congress to see that America couldn't live without Fannie Mae. And he wanted Fannie Mae to be practically synonymous with the idea of home-ownership.

The cornerstones of the Johnson political machine were the Fannie Mae Foundation and the company's Partnership Offices ("POs," in Fannie parlance). The foundation had existed in a small form since 1979, but in 1996, Fannie Mae seeded it with $350 million of its own stock and gave it responsibility for Fannie's advertising. Over the past five years the foundation has given away some $500 million to thousands of organizations ranging from the Congressional Black Caucus to the Cold Climate Housing Research Center in Fairbanks.

Fannie began opening its Partnership Offices in 1994. These are regional offices that Fannie says act as catalysts for housing projects in their communities; but inside Fannie, the POs are also referred to as the "grassroots" of the political operation. The opening of a Partnership Office is always a grand ceremony featuring prominent politicians. And it's often accompanied by an announcement that Fannie's American Communities Fund will make an investment in a high-impact local project. Politicians may not understand the secondary-mortgage market, but they do understand a photo opportunity and the dispensation of pork.

Over time, Fannie built close alliances with homebuilders, Realtors, and trade groups—whom it could call on to pressure lawmakers whenever the need arose. It employs more high-powered lobbyists than just about any organization in Washington. Under Johnson, Fannie Mae also developed a reputation for invincibility tactics. "You did not question Fannie Mae," says former Housing and Urban Development Secretary Andrew Cuomo. "Fannie did as Fannie wanted." Partly that was because Fannie people had an almost religious conviction about the virtues of housing—a sense that they were both right and righteous.

Another reason for this uncompromising attitude was Fannie executives' continuing fear that what politics giveth, politics could take away. There was some truth to this. The Reagan administration, for instance, ideologically opposed to government-subsidized corporations, worked hard to privatize the company. (Fannie beat back the effort.) Fannie execs felt they couldn't afford to lose even one fight, because that would open the floodgates. "You're thinking survival—winning, not compromise," says a former employee. The attitude, says a former Fannie lobbyist, was "Just win, baby."

At the same time Johnson was turning Fannie into a political juggernaut, he was also transforming it into one of the greatest growth vehicles ever. In the years Johnson ran Fannie, its market cap grew from $10.5 billion to more than $70 billion. It posted steady earnings gains, and its executives made fortunes. (The wealth-sharing had begun before Johnson; when Maxwell left, he walked away with a $19.5 million retirement package.)

In the mid-1990s, Franklin Raines told *The Washington Post* that "we are the equivalent of a Federal Reserve system for housing." The same article noted that Fannie's financial moves generated more than $100 million a year in fees for Wall Street firms. By the time Johnson retired in late 1998, Fannie guaranteed a stunning $1 trillion of mortgages and held $376 billion of mortgages and mortgage-backed securities on its own books.

Inevitably, Fannie's growth began to prompt serious questions from a variety of critics. There were ideological foes who believed that GSEs shouldn't have special advantages bestowed by the government. The big national banks wanted more of the mortgage securities market—and wanted to see Fannie shackled. Many housing activists believed the company had become so focused on Wall Street that it had lost sight of its mission. What, they asked, did Fannie's ever-growing portfolio do to lower mortgage rates? Other critics looked at that portfolio and saw huge potential risks—risks that would likely be borne by taxpayers if anything went wrong. Financial consultant and prominent GSE critic Bert Ely is among those who argue that Fannie has created a moral hazard; namely, that if everyone thinks the government will rescue the GSEs, the companies aren't subject to market discipline.

Fannie's knee-jerk response to criticism was to push back hard. It accused anyone who questioned it of being anti-home-ownership. In 1996, when the Congressional Budget Office issued a critical study, a Fannie official sneered that the report was "the work of economic pencil brains who wouldn't recognize something that works for ordinary homebuyers if it hit them in their erasers." And it was quick to remind politicians where their interests lay. Fannie put together a book, personalized for each member of the House Banking Committee, detailing all the good things it did in each district to bolster home-ownership. Even that critical CBO study acknowledged that it would probably be impossible to get rid of the GSEs even if it made economic sense—because Fannie and Freddie had become so inextricably linked to the idea of home-ownership. "Once one agrees to share a canoe with a bear, it is hard to get him out without obtaining his agreement or getting wet," said the report.

THE EARNINGS TRAP

"The future is so bright that I am willing to set as a goal that our EPS will double over the next five years."

So said Franklin Raines at an investor conference he hosted in May 1999, five months after becoming CEO. During his tenure, that promise was at the heart of everything the company did. The board even tied much of management's compensation to earnings goals. And though Fannie met the target—announcing profits of $7.3 billion in 2003—the intense focus on consistent earnings growth did a lot to bring Raines down.

In assuming the top job at Fannie, Frank Raines—everyone calls him Frank—became the first African-American CEO of a FORTUNE 500 company. He was born in Seattle to blue-collar parents; his mother cleaned offices at Boeing, where Raines was appointed to the board in 1995. (He is now on the boards of PepsiCo and Pfizer.) Raines graduated from Harvard and Harvard Law, became a Rhodes Scholar, interned in the Nixon White House, and served in the Carter administration before leaving government to become a partner at Lazard Frères. In 1991, Johnson lured him to Fannie Mae, where he became vice chairman. Five years later Raines was named Bill Clinton's budget director; he returned to Fannie when Johnson retired.

Raines, who would not comment for this article, has what Andrew Lowenthal, a lobbyist whose clients include Freddie Mac, calls "extraordinary presence.... You see him, you meet him, you want to believe him." (Some Fannie lobbyists referred to him as "The Great One.") And like Johnson before him, Raines could talk the talk with great sincerity; former Goldman Sachs analyst Bob Hottensen remembers him often telling a story about how his father had to get a high-priced loan rather than a lower-cost mortgage. "You cannot hurt Fannie Mae without hurting the housing market," Raines liked to say. One of his great assets, people said, was his strong will—but that eventually became a liability. "If a lot of people disagree with you, you have to ask, are they all wrong?" says someone who knows Raines well.

Under Raines, Fannie began to come under increasing criticism—and it responded ever more aggressively. In June 1999, for instance, Fannie's banking competitors banded together to form a group called FM Watch. The company reaction can only be described as over-the-top: It called FM Watch "fat-cat bankers," compared it to the ruthless ex-dictator Slobodan Milosevic, and went around hiring powerful lobbying firms just to keep them from working for FM Watch.

FM Watch, however, wasn't the biggest of Fannie's worries. The real problem was that as Fannie's mortgage portfolio continued to balloon, top government officials became concerned about the potential consequences. In late 1999, then-Treasury Secretary Lawrence Summers made a speech that included this sentence: "Debates about systemic risk should also now include government sponsored enterprises, which are large and growing rapidly." It was an incendiary remark. Then in March, Gary Gensler, Treasury's undersecretary for domestic finance, suggested in a speech that the Treasury should reconsider Fannie and Freddie's $4.5 billion line of credit.

All hell broke loose. Yields on GSE debt rose dramatically, meaning that investors wanted to be compensated for taking more risk. This, of course, reduced the spread Fannie was able to earn on its portfolio—and threatened Fannie's earnings. Fannie called Gensler "irresponsible," "unprofessional," and (of course) anti-housing. Raines wrote that repealing the line of credit would "disrupt the capital markets and inexorably lead to higher mortgage rates for consumers."

The market reaction was so ugly that Fannie and Freddie realized they had to respond. And so, in an October 2000 press conference, Brendsel and Raines announced "six voluntary initiatives" to disclose more information about, for instance, interest rate risk. Both stocks shot up by almost 10% that day. What few knew was that Raines furiously resisted the "voluntary initiatives" and signed on only when it became clear that Freddie was going to proceed.

One of the six voluntary initiatives was that the "duration gap," a measure of sensitivity to interest rates, would be disclosed monthly instead of quarterly. In 2002 accounting sleuths and short-sellers became suspicious of Fannie's smoothly growing earnings. Fannie's duration gap made it clear that the company had been on the wrong side of interest rate bets during a period of rapidly declining rates. Yet that didn't seem to have had any effect on Fannie's earnings. John Barnett, then an analyst at the Center for Financial Research and Analysis, which produces detailed accounting reports for institutional investors, suggested that Fannie Mae was distorting economic reality by putting billions of dollars in derivative losses on its balance sheet instead of on its income statement. Fannie's responses were rarely illuminating. When Republican Senator Chuck Hagel of Nebraska asked for details on Fannie's derivative losses, the company said the information was "confidential and proprietary." Eventually, it provided some additional data.

In fact, the situation was worse than even the harshest critics believed. "We thought their accounting was lousy but legal," said Mark Haefele, who helps run Sonic Capital, a hedge fund that is short Fannie's stock. "It turns out it was just lousy."

The chain of events that eventually brought Frank Raines down starts with Enron. When the Enron scandal exploded, Freddie Mac, which had employed Enron's accounting firm, Arthur Andersen, quickly fired the firm and hired new accountants. In the fear-ridden environment of 2002, the new accountants, PricewaterhouseCoopers, scrubbed Freddie's books. The result of that scrutiny was Freddie's admission, about a year later, that it had understated its profits for years, in an effort to smooth out earnings. The company agreed to a $5 billion restatement and ousted many of its top executives, including Brendsel.

Fannie responded to Freddie's problems with astonishing self-righteousness. Raines held a press conference in which he accused Freddie of causing "collateral damage." The Frequently Asked Questions section of Fannie's website included the following statement: "Fannie Mae's reported financial results follow Generally Accepted Accounting Principles to the letter.... There should be no question about our accounting."

Just days before the Freddie crisis had erupted into public view, the Office of Federal Housing Enterprise Oversight (OFHEO)—the agency that regulates the GSEs—had pronounced Freddie's internal controls "accurate and reliable." This was a colossal misjudgment. Embarrassed by the error, OFHEO's director, a Texas Democrat named Armando Falcon Jr., who had been appointed to his job in 1999, resolved to make sure it didn't happen again. In early 2004, OFHEO hired Deloitte & Touche and began an investigation of Fannie Mae. The lead partner was Bob Maxant, who had previously handled the Enron board's in-house investigation.

OFHEO is not like most regulatory agencies; it is much weaker. Established in 1992, it is actually an illustration of Fannie's political power. When the legislation creating the agency was being debated, Fannie's allies in Congress made sure OFHEO was placed in the Department of Housing and Urban Development, which had no experience regulating financial markets. In the years prior to Falcon's appointment it was notoriously understaffed. Although its budget comes from fees paid by the GSEs, a Fannie-inspired amendment called for OFHEO to go through the appropriations process every year. Since Fannie and Freddie had numerous allies in Congress, this meant that the GSEs would effectively control their regulator. OFHEO, says one person who was there, had two choices: "Appease Fannie and Freddie or risk getting reamed in the budget." Former Treasury official Carnell once described OFHEO as a watchdog that was "hobbled, muzzled, and underfed."

It's fair to say that Fannie underestimated Falcon. The OFHEO chief, who is 44, seems shy and hesitates when he speaks. He's the middle of six children, raised outside San Antonio; his father was an aircraft mechanic. After attending St. Mary's, a Catholic college in San Antonio, he went to the University of Texas Law School and the Kennedy School of Government. He came to Washington in 1989 to work on the House Banking Committee under its populist chairman, Henry Gonzales, for eight years. After a failed political run in Texas, Falcon returned to D.C. and was appointed by Clinton to his current job. He didn't initially distrust Fannie or Freddie. But after wrangling with the GSEs, he became convinced that the last thing Fannie wanted was a capable regulator.

At first, it didn't look as if Falcon would last. (He is, after all, a Texas Democrat.) In February 2003 the White House announced that it planned to nominate a former J.P. Morgan executive named Mark Brickell to replace him. But Brickell's nomination was killed by foes who believed he was too close to the derivatives industry, and in the meantime the White House was warming up to Falcon. Later in 2003 the administration signaled its support for the agency by pointedly adding it to the President's corporate fraud task force. And it was the White House that got OFHEO the funds to hire Deloitte & Touche to investigate Fannie.

It would be wrong to say that OFHEO and the White House became allies. It was more like a wary marriage of convenience. What happened was that the White House's attitude toward the GSEs had changed—and it saw that OFHEO could help its cause.

There are people in Washington who will tell you that the White House turned on Fannie Mae because it's seen as a Democratic Party stronghold. There are others who will say it happened because of the Bush administration's pro-market ideology. There's probably some truth to both of those explanations. But the most important reason was self-preservation. The White House didn't want to be dragged into another business scandal—not after Enron. And when it looked to see where it might be vulnerable, well, considering what was going on with Freddie, it could hardly miss the GSEs.

First, there was the issue of Freddie's and Fannie's boards. Under their charters, five of the 18 directors on each board are appointed by the President. If something went wrong, wouldn't the President inevitably be blamed? In 2003 chief of staff Andrew Card was put in charge of a group to study the matter. The White House decided that it would not reappoint any presidential directors to either GSE board. (The posts are now vacant.) It also decided that their books needed to be cleaned up and they needed stronger oversight.

At the same time Alan Greenspan's public remarks about the GSEs were becoming increasingly pointed. His sharpest comments came in early 2004, when he told Congress that "to fend off future systemic difficulties, which we assess as likely if GSE expansion continues unabated, preventative actions are required sooner rather than later." In Greenspan-speak, those were strong words indeed.

The White House became part of a loose alliance that took on the Fannie Mae machine in a way no one had before. A short list of examples:

• In late 2003, Federal Reserve economist Wayne Passmore released a paper that put the value of the government's implied guarantee of the GSEs at as much as $164 billion. This subsidy "accounts for much of the GSEs market value," wrote Passmore, who added that "the GSEs' implicit subsidy does not appear to have substantially increased home-ownership or homebuilding." He also argued that the GSEs did very little to lower mortgage costs.

• HUD toughened its low-income housing goals for Fannie and Freddie—and then insisted the GSEs meet the new requirements. HUD had long felt that Fannie and Freddie were not doing enough to promote affordable housing. "HUD had permitted Fannie and Freddie to consistently dispute our findings and challenge us publicly," says Alphonso Jackson, the current head of HUD. "Not on my watch and not under this President." ("You just cannot appreciate how truly bad this is," a Fannie employee complained in an e-mail to a Republican staffer, referring to the prospect of HUD having more clout.)

• In the summer of 2004 the Justice Department rendered an opinion—which Fannie and Freddie had viewed as bad news—that Treasury could actually limit future debt issuance by the GSEs.

• Administration operatives began making anti-Fannie arguments to key opinion makers, such as the editorial boards of major newspapers. They seem to have had an impact. Over the past year anti-GSE editorials have appeared in key papers—not just *The Wall Street Journal*, but also *The Washington Post*, the *Los Angeles Times*, and the *Christian Science Monitor*.

Aides battling the GSEs came up with a half-joking code name for their assault: "Noriega"—as in Manuel Noriega, the former Panamanian dictator who was blasted with nonstop rock music from loudspeakers while holed up in the Vatican's diplomatic mission in Panama City, trying to avoid surrendering to the U.S. Attack mode, of course, has always been Fannie's way, but now the situation was reversed. As one former lobbyist for the GSEs put it: "Payback is hell."

On September. 10, 2003, then-Treasury Secretary John Snow and then-HUD head Mel Martinez outlined the administration's thinking on reforming Fannie and Freddie. Testifying before the House Financial Services Committee, Snow called for a new regulatory regime, one key element of which would be a receivership provision. Amazingly, there is no real procedure in place for reorganizing Fannie or Freddie in the event of a bankruptcy. By setting up a receivership mechanism, the government would be sending an unmistakable message: It would not stand behind Fannie and Freddie's debt.

It wasn't long before Fannie and the administration were effectively at war. Two bills to reform the GSEs were introduced—a Fannie-friendly bill in the House and a White House-friendly bill in the Senate sponsored by Republican Senator Richard Shelby of Alabama. The administration squashed the House bill; Wayne Abernathy, a Treasury official, said, "We must not settle for a crippled regulator." The Senate bill was moving along—until Republican Senator Bob Bennett of Utah (who had the backing of other Senators) added an amendment giving Congress a 45-day window to veto the receivership. That, of course, completely undercut the notion that the government would no longer back the GSEs. (Bennett's son was the deputy director of Fannie's Partnership Office in Utah.)

At every turn, Fannie declared publicly its desire for a strong new regulator. And at every turn, it stonewalled behind the scenes. "No, no, hell no," is how one person who watched the process describes Fannie's attitude. Some administration officials began to refer to Fannie's efforts to undermine the receivership provision as "deceivership."

On October 22, 2003, for instance, Raines sent Snow a letter. "Dear John," it began. "From the beginning of our discussions, you and I have agreed to avoid disrupting the capital markets by indicating a wish to change Fannie Mae's charter, status, or mission." After complaining about a comment that Raines said a high Treasury official had made about Fannie's line of credit, he wrote, "The result of his comment was that trading in our debt came to a halt for an extended period of time. I am disappointed and hope we can change course. Very truly yours, Frank."

In political terms the letter was an astonishment—what other CEO would dare dress down the Treasury Secretary, much less address him as "Dear John"?

Then, in 2004, Raines wrote another stern letter, this one to White House chief of staff Card, accusing him of misrepresenting Fannie's position on a regulation issue to the National Association of Home Builders. Card first learned of the letter from the NAHB because it got a copy before he did. After that, Card stopped returning Raines's phone calls. "It's hard to depersonalize these things," says NAHB CEO Jerry Howard. "It's hard to step back."

And then there was the TV ad Fannie ran on March 31, 2004—the day before the Senate Banking Committee was scheduled to work on its bill. The ad featured a worried-looking Hispanic couple.

MAN: "Uh-oh."

WOMAN: "What?"

MAN: "It looks like Congress is talking about new regulations for Fannie Mae."

WOMAN: "Will that keep us from getting that lower mortgage rate?"

MAN: "Some economists say rates may go up."

WOMAN: "But that could mean we won't be able to afford the new house.

MAN: "I know."

Even longtime Fannie watchers were stunned. "Here is an organization that was created by the Congress ... spending money questioning the Congress's right to take a serious look at oversight ..." sputtered Senator Hagel during the hearing that day. "I find it astounding. Astounding!"

By late spring 2004 it was clear that Fannie had fought the White House to a draw—there would be no bill, and hence no new regulator. But it's all too clear now that Fannie Mae had won a Pyrrhic victory. Raines would have been far better served by compromising. Thanks to the accounting scandal, the GSEs now face regulations that are likely to be far tougher than those in the bill Fannie helped kill.

FIGHTING FALCON

On September 22, 2004, OFHEO released results of its continuing investigation. The "Special Examination of Fannie Mae" was a dense 211 pages packed with technical accounting details. But the message was clear: OFHEO accused Fannie Mae of both willfully breaking accounting rules and fostering an environment of "weak or nonexistent" internal controls. OFHEO focused on exactly the issue that the skeptics had earlier noticed, which was Fannie's use of accounting rules to defer derivative losses onto its balance sheet. Except OFHEO said that Fannie hadn't just bent the rules, it had broken them.

What got the most attention, though, was OFHEO's charge that in 1998, when an internal model said Fannie would need to recognize a roughly $400 million expense, Fannie only recognized $200 million.

That, OFHEO charged, allowed the company to report earnings of $3.23 per share, which meant that Fannie paid out a total of about $27 million in bonuses. Both the SEC and Justice quickly announced their own investigations.

Two weeks later Falcon and Raines faced off against each other in a hearing before the House subcommittee on capital markets. Consider the circumstances. Falcon was Fannie's regulator and had leveled serious charges, amounting to fraud, against Fannie Mae. Most CEOs would have seen the wisdom of humility at this point, but Raines showed little. "These accounting standards are highly complex and require determinations on which experts often disagree," he said, adding that "there were no facts" that supported OFHEO's charge that Fannie executives had deferred an expense in 1998 to earn bonuses.

And most of the Democrats present agreed with him. "This hearing is about the political lynching of Franklin Raines," said Democratic Congressman William Lacy Clay of Missouri. Democratic Congressman Barney Frank of Massachusetts said, "I see nothing in here that suggests that safety and soundness are an issue." Other Democrats complained that the mere fact of releasing the report could increase the cost of home-ownership.

"Is it possible that by casting all of these aspersions ... you potentially are weakening this institution in the market, that you are potentially weakening the housing market in this country?" Congressman Artur Davis of Alabama demanded. When Falcon tried to answer, Davis acted like a prosecutor grilling a hostile witness. He wanted a one-word answer: yes or no. "Is that possible?" he asked again.

One of the few bad moments for Fannie came when Baker released information showing that over five years, Fannie had paid its 20 top executives a combined $245 million in bonuses. In 2002 its 21 top executives each earned more than $1 million in total compensation. Even the Democrats winced.

Fannie had one last card to play. Back in April, Republican Senator Kit Bond of Missouri, a member of the Senate Appropriations

Committee, had spurred the HUD inspector general to investigate OFHEO. (One of Bond's staffers, John Kamark, is a Fannie supporter who plays poker with Bill Maloni, Fannie's former chief lobbyist and current consultant.) Although the report had only been finished the previous day, and wasn't public, it was clear at the hearing that some members of Congress had already been briefed on it.

The report does not put Falcon or OFHEO in a flattering light. It quotes a "confidential source" inside OFHEO saying that Falcon's top deputy would become "almost gleeful" whenever Fannie's stock declined. This same source said that "OFHEO was trying to embarrass Fannie Mae." In other words, OFHEO wasn't just regulating Fannie Mae, it was out to get Fannie Mae. "This makes it difficult to assess the reliability of recent allegations by OFHEO against Fannie Mae," declared Congressman Frank.

It is true that the SEC would never have done some of the things OFHEO did. But OFHEO supporters say the agency had to play hardball. It was an outgunned regulator trying to investigate one of the nation's most politically powerful companies. And Fannie was being Fannie. For instance, one of the complaints Fannie's allies leveled at OFHEO was that it released the results of an ongoing investigation to the public, something no real regulator would do. But there is an explanation. One source close to the events says OFHEO had told Fannie's board that it wouldn't release the report. But the OFHEO people learned that Fannie lobbyists were telling members of Congress that the report was inconsequential and Falcon wouldn't release it because he didn't want to exonerate Fannie. And so OFHEO released the report.

For his part, Falcon refused to be moved by the barrage of criticism from his fellow Democrats. To him the problems at Fannie were reminiscent of the S&L crisis. He told a friend that the Democrats were "so blinded by their loyalty to Fannie that they can't see what's really happening. If they want to repeat history, I won't be part of it."

Wall Street, of course, was every bit as blind. After the hearing, analyst Bob Napoli at Piper Jaffray wrote: "We thought Frank Raines in particular made excellent points countering OFHEO accusations, in some cases directly contradicting OFHEO assertions." Jonathan Gray of Sanford Bernstein wrote that the "allegations lack cogency," and said, "Plausible charges against FNM are immaterial, while material charges are implausible."

And then Frank Raines overplayed his hand one last time. In a highly unusual move, Fannie insisted that the SEC review OFHEO's accounting allegations. Fannie hired the powerful law firm of Wilmer Cutler to help it make its case; Bill McLucas, the lead partner on the Fannie team, was formerly the SEC's chief enforcement officer. The potential danger of this request was obvious: In a worst-case scenario, if the SEC completely sided with OFHEO, Fannie would have to restate earnings going back to 2001. And the restatement would be massive—an estimated $9 billion in losses. Some Fannie people referred to the restatement possibility as the "ultimate penalty." But, in truth, they really did not seem to think that the SEC would rule against them.

FRANK'S FINALE

At a little after 6 p.m. on December 15, about 30 people piled into a conference room at the SEC's headquarters in Washington, D.C., and seated themselves around a large rectangular table. SEC officials first made it clear that they had not addressed any issues of individual culpability. Then, chief accountant Donald Nicolaisen announced that the SEC had decided that Fannie did not comply "in material respects" with accounting rules. Fannie would have to restate its results.

Raines looked stricken. One person who was there says it was the first time he'd ever heard Raines's voice waver. "What did we get wrong?" he asked. Nicolaisen held up a piece of paper. If the four corners of the sheet represented what was possible under GAAP, and the center was perfect compliance, he told Raines, "you weren't even on the page." Fannie representatives tried to argue that if they couldn't get it right, no one could. Nicolaisen wasn't having any of it. "Many companies out there get it right," he said.

It was over for Frank Raines. Falcon told the Fannie board that Raines and CFO Howard had to go. Raines resisted, but could not hang on; on December 21, he announced his resignation. "Although to my knowledge, the company has always made good faith efforts to get its accounting right, the SEC has determined that mistakes were made. By my early retirement, I have held myself accountable," he said.

Even in the wake of the Fannie Mae scandal, Raines still had legions of supporters. There are plenty of people who still believe that what's good for Fannie is good for home-ownership—and that the whole thing was little more than a political dirty trick. "They're just not dishonest in any way," says Martin Eakes, who runs the Self-Help Credit Bureau in North Carolina. "It's a little hard for me to swallow that what appears to me to be a hatchet job by OFHEO has basically been validated by the SEC.... You mark my words, you will not find scandal there or fraud."

As for Wall Street, it has its own reasons for defending Fannie, which is one of the Street's top fee-payers. "The overwhelming majority of FNM's accounting is correct," wrote a Lehman Brothers analyst. "We view this infraction as a speeding ticket, not a capital offense." Bear Stearns analysts concluded that Raines and Howard had been ousted because of OFHEO's "personal animosity."

A key tenet of the Street's defense of Fannie is that the $9 billion restatement doesn't really constitute an economic loss. It's just an accounting issue. The other view, of course, is that the $9 billion represents losses that Fannie should have taken—but didn't—since 2001. And that in avoiding those losses, Fannie's top executives collected millions in bonuses they didn't earn.

The restatement will put Fannie well below its regulatory capital requirements, which is why the company quickly sold $5 billion of preferred stock. Nothing says more about the Street's continued belief in Fannie than the ease with which it was able to raise that money.

Yet the notion that the worst is over may well turn out to be misguided. "Dig deep into what's there and you find more and more," says a person close to the investigation. One possible example: Critics note that Fannie has $9.1 billion of deferred tax assets included in its regulatory capital measure. Most of these assets were generated because Fannie suffered massive losses on its derivatives; they are an offset to future taxes Fannie might owe. But Lawrence Kam of hedge fund Sonic Capital says the inclusion of these assets in regulatory capital is unhealthy—he notes that bank regulators severely restrict the amount of such assets that can be included in a bank's regulatory capital. (Fannie has previously argued that the number is less than $9 billion, and that its regulatory statutes do not limit the inclusion of deferred tax assets in regulatory capital.)

Another question that has been lost in the political wrangling is whether Fannie's business has changed permanently for the worse. Over the past 18 months the growth in Fannie Mae's portfolio has slowed sharply because of competition from banks and hedge funds, which are financing their mortgage purchases with cheap, short-term debt (a technique known as the carry trade). Back in 2002 the spread between the yield of Fannie's mortgage portfolio and its long-term liabilities was 63 basis points. In the second quarter of 2004 it had fallen to two basis points. To keep profits up, it looks like Fannie, which has disparaged the carry trade as too risky, may now be using the strategy itself, which would make it more vulnerable to rising interest rates. The company disputes this analysis, pointing to its one-month duration gap as a sign that it is not taking interest rate risk. Still, Josh Rosner, an analyst at Medley Global Advisors, who has made a string of accurate calls on GSEs, says a diminished spread is "absolutely permanent."

And then there's the question of whether there will finally be new legislation. Senator Richard Shelby vows to try again. "They [Fannie] didn't listen because they thought they could thwart the whole deal, but time is on our side. We're coming back," he says. But the administration may no longer need legislation to force change at the GSEs. If other bad news emerges, if the spreads continue to shrink—there are a lot of things that could happen in the coming months that will force their own kind of reform.

What Fannie and Freddie may not be able to do any longer is to have it both ways. They can't profess to be devoted to the mission of providing affordable housing while generating turbocharged earnings growth. Freddie's new CEO, Dick Syron, concedes that the company won't grow at anywhere near the rates of the 1990s. He also concedes that the company has not done as much as it should have for affordable housing. "If we're going to have special privileges, then we have to do something special," he says. One of Syron's first moves was to redo management compensation to be weighted toward the achievement of affordable housing goals. "No one chartered us to be Goldman Sachs on the Potomac."

Fannie's new CEO, Dan Mudd, also insists that the mission has to come first. "To the extent that this company strays from its mission of financing affordable housing, we start to lose our compass." He also says that the company will begin to listen to its critics, and admits that "there are areas we have gotten arrogant."

But if Washington has learned anything about Fannie Mae, it's to watch what it does, not what it says.

◆

AFTERMATH

After the accounting fraud surfaced, many called for legislation that would dramatically reform Fannie Mae. Even Fannie was publicly supportive. "We are hopeful that legislation can be passed this year, and we will be doing everything we can to help support that goal," said a spokesman in early 2005. That summer, Senate Banking Committee Chairman Richard Shelby introduced a bill that would have forced Fannie to sell off a large part of its investment holdings. It passed the Senate, but the House then introduced another version calling for a new regulator. Critics said the House bill didn't give that regulator enough power. The legislation stalled.

In December 2006, Fannie Mae announced that the final reckoning of its earnings misstatements was $6.3 billion, and vowed to scrub its books. For its part, OFHEO vowed to pursue more than $100 million in fines from Fannie Mae's senior executives whose massive compensation was tied to the wrong numbers. No criminal charges were ever filed against Fannie Mae executives, but in April 2008, they were fined $31.4 million—a figure that was less dramatic than it sounded because much of it, as McLean later noted in Vanity Fair *"was an illusion," taking the form of foregone stock options that were under water anyway. In a statement, Raines said, "While I long ago accepted managerial accountability for any errors committed by subordinates while I was CEO, it is a very different matter to suggest that I was legally culpable in any way." Raines now sits on the board of Steve Case's company, Revolution Health.*

After Raines left, his successor, Daniel H. Mudd, faced a new set of pressures. The subprime mortgage business was booming, and Fannie was missing out on the profits. Unlike Fannie, Wall Street firms like Bear Stearns and Lehman Brothers weren't hesitating to pick up the riskier loans and then resell them to investors. On top of this, Washington regulators and lawmakers were raising Fannie's affordable-housing goals. Fannie Mae took on more risk. Though there were warnings against this trend, including from within Fannie Mae, efforts to modify the way Fannie did business failed repeatedly. Between 2005 and 2007, the number of mortgages it acquired with down payments of less than 10% tripled; the company specifically stated its intention to increase its exposure to the sub-prime market and also targeted Alt-A loans, in which income often went unverified.

The timing could not have been worse. By mid-2007, when it became clear that many high-risk borrowers were struggling to make their loan payments, Fannie began to wobble. In August 2008, according to the Washington Post, *loans from 2006 and 2007 accounted for almost 60% of its credit losses that quarter—a sign of just how risky Fannie's lending had become. From mid-October 2007 through mid-October 2008, the stock price crashed from $63 to less than $1.*

In mid-2008, legislation finally passed that would give regulators more power over Fannie's portfolio. But it was too late. In September 2008, Treasury Secretary Hank Paulson took control of Fannie Mae and Freddie Mac. The government acquired $1 billion of preferred shares in each company, pledged up to $200 billion to cover losses, and placed new executives in charge. The former head of TIAA-CREF, Herbert Allison, was called out of retirement and named Fannie's new CEO.

19

CRASH AND BURN

---

by ANN M. MORRISON

November 15, 1982

Dashing and handsome, with a former model for a wife and a glint in his eye, John De Lorean had a plan. He would make super-cool cars, while helping economically depressed, war-torn Belfast. That's not what happened.

John Z. De Lorean, 57, the founder, chairman, and chief executive of the auto company that bears his name, was discussing final details for the purchase of $24 million worth of cocaine with three undercover federal agents and an informant in a room at the Sheraton Plaza Hotel in Los Angeles in October 1982. As the five men talked, De Lorean cradled a kilo of what is known in the drug trade as China White. "This is better than gold," he said. "It came just in time."

In fact, time was running out for John De Lorean. Only six hours earlier the British government, which had invested $140 million in the De Lorean Motor Company, had announced that it was closing the Belfast, Northern Ireland, plant that built the stainless-steel, gull-winged "personal luxury" car. Then, as soon as De Lorean took possession of the cocaine, one agent identified himself and arrested him on charges of drug trafficking.

Following De Lorean's arraignment the next day, Bernard Minsky, one of his lawyers, said that the automaker was attempting save the company "for all of his shareholders." In fact, John De Lorean is the shareholder, controlling about 82% of De Lorean Motor Company. Other investors had given up hope of recovering their losses long ago.

While friends and business associates were shocked by the narcotics allegation, many of them were not surprised that De Lorean had run into trouble with the law. During recent year,s the onetime superstar at General Motors had become involved in a series of shady financial dealings involving both the De Lorean Motor Company and his personal financial holdings. Moreover, only one of seven former company executives interviewed for this article believes the explanation that De Lorean became involved in the alleged drug deal to raise money to save his firm. The associates argue that De Lorean was out to save himself, his reputation, his ego, and perhaps most of all, his glamorous style of living.

De Lorean's net worth—estimated at $28 million—includes a partnership in an offshore oil company, a ranch in Idaho, a Utah-based company that makes equipment for grooming ski slopes, an apartment on New York's Fifth Avenue, and the San Diego house that was put up last week as collateral for a $5 million bail. But none of those investments provided the ready cash needed for De Lorean's stylish living or to pay the two dozen or so employees still on his payroll.

De Lorean stumbled into an investigation actually aimed at catching a suspected major narcotics dealer. For five months the Drug Enforcement Administration, the Federal Bureau of Investigation, the Customs Service, and the Internal Revenue Service had been trailing William Morgan Hetrick, the owner of a small aircraft company, Morgan Aviation, in Mojave, Calif. As the trap was being laid for Hetrick, in walked De Lorean, who took part in five separate planning meetings with undercover agents, each one carefully videotaped for use later as evidence. Hetrick's associate, Stephen Arrington, was charged last week with possession of 25 kilos of cocaine, which were neatly packed behind the back seat of a specially outfitted Chevrolet Caprice.

The drug arrest was a radical turn for a man who sold his holdings in the San Diego Chargers at a loss in 1977 because the team psychiatrist gave drugs to football players. "I didn't want to have anything to do with those guys in relationship to their drug problem," De Lorean said at the time.

People close to De Lorean say the change reflected his relentless drive to maintain his youth, social connections, and wealth while his ambitious goal of building his own auto company was crumbling. A damaging pattern developed in De Lorean's business dealings over the past five years. He hired investigators to trace the home telephone calls of William Haddad, his vice president for planning, whom he suspected of being disloyal. After C. Richard Brown, the president of the firm's American operations, tried to prevent the forcible seizure of bank-owned cars, a company representative called and threatened Brown's wife and children. In addition came periodic accusations of misuse of funds: gold faucets for the company's Belfast guesthouse, two persons on the payroll who were De Lorean family servants, and company money spent on private De Lorean business schemes like a plan for a government-sponsored mass-transit vehicle called Transbus.

ONCE A SQUARE FELLOW

John Zachary De Lorean's rise in the auto industry was nearly as dramatic as his fall. He grew up in Detroit, the oldest of four sons of a Ford foundry worker. He worshipped the men who made the cars and made the car companies run. His mother, who separated from his father when John was 13, kept him in Los Angeles with her during the school year. He returned to Detroit in the summers to work at a Chrysler assembly plant.

After attending the Lawrence Institute of Technology in Detroit, De Lorean went to work at Chrysler in 1948. He switched to Packard in 1952, and then to General Motors in 1956, after Bunkie Knudsen, the general manager of the Pontiac division, offered him a job as his head of research and development. "He was a pretty square fellow when I hired him," Knudsen told FORTUNE in 1973.

That squareness and hard work helped De Lorean move quickly up the GM organizational chart. In 1965, at 40, he became the youngest general manager in Pontiac's history. De Lorean sponsored two hot-sellers, the Firebird and the Grand Prix, and then, in 1969, he was given the tough task of turning around the faltering Chevrolet division. De Lorean succeeded spectacularly by introducing new models like the Monte Carlo and winning back the loyalty of disgruntled dealers. In 1972 De Lorean was named president of the entire General Motors North American car and truck group, which was only one rung away from the company presidency.

The next year, De Lorean left GM.

By that time De Lorean's square edges had disappeared. His clothes ran more to turtlenecks and Nehru suits than button-downs and pin-stripes. He dyed his hair jet black and wore it long. He had a face-lift and started pumping iron to bring down his weight and preserve his physique. He was also now moving in broader circles than the General Motors management clique, counting among his friends film stars and sports celebrities. In 1969 De Lorean jettisoned his secretary-wife of 14 years and married Kelly Harmon, the 20-year-old daughter of former football star Tom Harmon. That ended in February 1973, and in May 48-year-old John De Lorean married Cristina Ferrare, 23, an actress-model.

By walking out on a $650,000-per-year job with one of the bastions of the American business establishment, De Lorean became a minor cultural hero in the Age of Aquarius. He spent one year as president of the National Alliance of Businessmen, a group of executives promoting the hiring of minorities. Then in 1974 he went to work creating a company to produce a visionary vehicle that would be safe, fuel efficient, affordable, and long lasting. He called it the "ethical car." Given his fast-track success record at GM and easygoing charm, De Lorean quickly raised $8.6 million from 345 automobile dealers and another $18 million from 134 limited partners to set up a company. By one estimate, he put up only $20,000 of his own money.

De Lorean ran into a small pothole in 1978 when he had to decide where to locate the assembly plant. Puerto Rican officials thought that De Lorean was committed to them, but when the British government offered him almost unlimited amounts of money if he built the plant in the civil-war-torn city of Belfast, De Lorean abruptly switched partners.

The day he was due to sign the deed with Puerto Rico, he simply failed to show up. Almost immediately the new company started getting into some questionable financial dealings. In November 1978 the firm authorized the payment of $18.8 million to GPD, a Swiss-based independent contractor that was supposed to be representing Lotus Cars of Norwich, England, whose famous designer, Colin Chapman, was doing development work on the De Lorean car. It turned out that GPD was no more than a one-room office in Geneva, was not a Swiss-registered company, and had nothing to do with making cars.

Richard Brown recalls another scheme to transfer all De Lorean Motor's $10 million in assets to De Lorean's personal corporation for only $600,000. Two outside directors had already approved the transfer before Brown became aware of it. At Brown's suggestion, they withdrew their signatures, and the proposal was dropped.

When the De Lorean cars finally reached dealers in June 1981, the $26,000 models were snatched up by an initially enthusiastic public. De Lorean also had other new grand plans. He was dreaming about a public stock offering, which would bring in more working capital and also give his shares a paper value of $120 million. When some executives, who had been hired on the promise of stock options as part of their compensation packages, learned their options would not be applied to the new public stock, at least one of them sued. The offering was postponed.

By early 1982, sales were slowing because of the recession, and owners were complaining the gull-winged doors did not close and the car was underpowered. Nonetheless, De Lorean continued to increase production, a strategy that led to bankruptcy in February. The company has not sold a single car at full price since March, but last week, after the cocaine bust, De Lorean sales suddenly became brisk as speculators bought on the expectation that they might become collectors' items.

In addition to troubles at the auto company, De Lorean was having problems with several private business deals around the country. These included a disputed sale of acreage in Idaho, a suit over patents in Phoenix, and a troubled Cadillac dealership in Wichita. Court battles followed in each case.

While his dealings have long raised questions, De Lorean had never previously been connected with hard drugs. His former associates said last week that they had never seen him using cocaine. Only one old partner reported seeing him smoking marijuana, and that was on a social occasion at his apartment. "Some of always figured that they would get him for something," says an insider, "but we never conceived of anything like this."

◆

AFTERMATH

De Lorean was acquitted in 1984, when the judge ruled that the government had entrapped him. Still, neither his career nor his reputation ever recovered, and his legal problems just kept coming.

The death of the De Lorean car also spelled the end of a certain kind of pseudo-industrial policy, in which governments would spend millions to attract dubious or poorly run businesses, and millions more to keep them going. Britain in the 1970's was particularly prone to this sort of thing. When Margaret Thatcher was elected in 1979, she brought in a very different kind of economic thinking, and it didn't take her long to shut down a clear loser. Although states and countries continue to offer incentives for new investment, the kind of expensive madness that the De Lorean factory represented now looks as dated as shag carpeting.

Fewer than 10,000 De Lorean cars were built, but they have gained an immortality of sorts, because of their starring role in Back to the Future *films. De Lorean himself managed to maintain a certain faded glamor almost to the end. He died from a stroke in 2005.*

20

MADOFF DOES MINNEAPOLIS

by DAVE KANSAS
January 16, 2009

The Bernard Madoff scandal emerged in late 2008 amidst a sharp selloff in the stock market and a wide-ranging financial crisis. Madoff, after a long and respected career on Wall Street, turned himself into authorities and allegedly stated that his investment business had been nothing more than an elaborate hoax.

Using an "affinity strategy," Madoff targeted primarily fellow Jewish investors, attracting clients from elite circles in New York City; Palm Beach, Fla.; Hollywood; Europe; and Latin America. He also successfully wooed large amounts of philanthropic foundation cash, and many of these non-profits suffered grievous losses. Some of them had to shut down.

While Madoff worked well-known centers of wealth, he also preyed on people in less-tony locales like Minneapolis and St. Paul. Investors in the region lost hundreds of millions of dollars and some charitable foundations were eviscerated. What follows is a story about how an alleged international charlatan found his way into a humble heartland community with devastating results.

T ucked into the rolling hills of Hopkins, a suburb west of Minne-apolis, the recently refurbished Oak Ridge Country Club looks much like a middle school: beige paneling, a limestone base, and—energy—efficient windows. Along the main road to the club is a mod-est apartment complex with four signs advertising units for rent. Be-yond Oak Ridge's modest doors, however, is a well-appointed interior that provides a gathering place for some of the wealthier families in the Twin Cities. In Minnesota's warm summers the club's golf course, tennis courts, and playground bustle with prosperity, but this winter, with the grounds buried in snow, the conversation at Oak Ridge has turned as grim as the weather. Typically at such clubs, members swap tips and ideas. People you golf with, after all, are usually people you trust. And for more than 20 years some of the members have enthusi-astically shared one notable financial strategy: investing with Bernard L. Madoff.

The predominantly Jewish country club, which dates back to 1921, is the hub of the Madoff scandal in the Twin Cities. While fraud vic-tims in Manhattan, Palm Beach, Hollywood, and European cities have grabbed the headlines, Madoff's alleged $50 billion Ponzi scheme reached other towns as well. He had a particularly painful impact on the Twin Cities, where his method of preying on Jewish families and foundations was highly effective in this close-knit and long-established community. While some regional reports put the losses at $300 mil-lion, a local attorney working with victims believes $600 million is a more accurate number. He knows of two families who lost a total of more than $130 million. Dozens of other families lost smaller amounts, representing everything from children's college savings to retirement accounts, while local Jewish-funded philanthropies find themselves scrambling to pay for basic core missions for the poor.

As a native of St. Paul, I returned to find my hometown stunned to be a victim of this kind of crime. I know it as a place of quiet money and conservative investors, where the banks rarely need bailouts and the great fortunes created by the likes of Pillsbury, General Mills, and

Cargill keep a low profile. But financial scandal has rocked the Twin Cities twice in one season. By a strange coincidence, just two months before the Madoff case broke open, the celebrated local tycoon Tom Petters was arrested and charged with 20 felony counts for his own alleged Ponzi scheme in which he took $3.5 billion from investors (at the end of the chapter). His tactics, in part, were similar to Madoff's, prosecutors allege: He preyed on a religious community, in this case members of his own evangelical Christian faith.

Madoff, operating remotely from Manhattan, developed a network of local feeders to steer business his way, and in the Twin Cities he had a good one: Mike Engler, an unassuming stockbroker. Engler, as part of Engler & Budd Securities, backed small, local stocks that traded on the more obscure edges of the financial markets, making him as different from the posh and powerful Madoff as Minneapolis is from Manhattan. Engler began his work in the 1980s, steering families into the Madoff machine with promises of sterling but not spectacular investment performance—usually returns of around 12% per year. The Oak Ridge Country Club, whose online history says it was founded for everyone in town "who knew the difference between a golf ball and a matzo ball," was fertile ground for Engler. The Madoff investors became like a club within a club. "The illusion was created that Bernard Madoff had to pick you to be in there," Minneapolis asset manager John Pohlad told the *St. Paul Pioneer Press*. "Madoff was one of the most difficult to compete against because he had so much momentum and mystique about him." Even after Engler's death in 1994, the money kept flowing to Madoff as estate lawyers and financial advisors kept up the tradition and families extended their participation, adding new generations to the Madoff mill. Besides soaking members of the Oak Ridge Country Club, Madoff worked the other side of the Mississippi River too, attracting a smaller following at Hillcrest Country Club, a predominantly Jewish golf course in St. Paul.

Bruce Graybow, president of Graybow Communications in the Minneapolis suburb of Golden Valley, became familiar with Madoff through Graybow's late father, Marvin, who had regarded Engler as an "honorable" and "trusted" family friend, Graybow told FORTUNE. After his father sold the family's plumbing and heating business, the family poured that money into Madoff's firm. Bruce built his own business, which provides corporate audio-visual systems, and eventually sold a chunk of it in 2007. As his father and friends had done, he placed most of the proceeds with Madoff. "I saw this as a safe and conservative investment, a good place to put my discretionary savings," says Graybow. "When I found out what happened, I was shocked and in absolute disbelief." He also felt physically ill and went into a cold sweat. "I put on my coat, and I walked to my friend's house down the street to gather my thoughts and sort things out."

The losses have affected people of much smaller means. One woman had kept her ties to Madoff secret for more than a decade. She was a mistress of a rich and powerful man in the Twin Cities. After a chance meeting in a park, they began a relationship that lasted nearly 20 years and included a promise that he would always take care of her. Once every quarter, a check from a Swiss bank account that included the name of Madoff's securities firm arrived in her mailbox. She moved into a new apartment, got a nice car, and like many associated with Madoff, gave away some of the money to charities and favored causes. She had a habit of reading *The New York Times* to keep track of the world she had intersected with in secret. Even after the man's death a few years ago, the checks continued to arrive on schedule. "Then one morning I pick up the *Times*, and there's Bernie," she recalls. "What's he doing in the paper? I read the article and realized that my life was over." Now she is struggling to find a way to survive, relying heavily on the generosity of friends. The check scheduled for the first week of January didn't arrive, as she expected, and her car has been repossessed.

Just as the Madoff scandal devastated charities on the coasts, including foundations associated with Elie Wiesel and Steven Spielberg, it hit hard in the Twin Cities, which are notably proud of their philanthropy.

The impact of Madoff's machinations can be seen down to the street level. "As difficult as this tragedy is for some families, it's the loss to the poor and to the charitable programs in the Twin Cities that is even worse," said Andy Parker, an attorney who represents some Madoff victims. Human-rights activism, a Minnesota passion that ranges from voting-rights efforts to campaigns aimed at shutting down the military prison at Guantánamo Bay, has been set back by the scandal.

"A lot of money has just disappeared. It's beyond shocking, the wide-spread damage that has resulted from this behavior," said Barbara Frey, director of the Human Rights Program at the University of Minnesota. "Local charities played a strong role in funding this work, and a lot of them are all of a sudden out of cash." Many of their sup-porters find themselves in the position of Violet Werner, a member of the Oak Ridge Country Club whose late husband owned a truck-ing company and set up a small foundation to support local arts and cultural groups. The foundation had $1.6 million in assets, much of it invested with Madoff. "The whole thing is just the most horrible scam I've ever heard of," she told the *Minneapolis Star Tribune.* "This money went to help people in need, and to people who do wonderful work. I'm so sad I can hardly speak."

Among the Minnesotans absorbing the news were workaday people who most likely had never heard of Madoff. One company, -Upsher-Smith Laboratories in suburban Maple Grove, a generic-drug com-pany with 650 employees, placed some of its profit-sharing programs for its employees with Madoff. These Upsher-Smith accounts, which reportedly had built up to more than $100,000 for some workers, were frozen when the Madoff scandal came to light. A representative of Upsher-Smith declined to comment.

Even the state government is concerned about Madoff's impact. Because of the allegedly fraudulent nature of returns associated with Madoff, many investors will have the right to reclaim taxes paid on phantom gains at the state and federal level. Given the parlous state of the economy, governments are already scrambling for tax revenue.

For a state like Minnesota, the highly localized impact of the losses and the potential for refunds on taxes paid by investors in both the Madoff and Petters cases could have significant consequences.

How is it that the Twin Cities found themselves sharing headline space with Palm Beach and Hollywood? While one seldom sees a Rolls-Royce or other public displays of wealth, the Twin Cities have no small number of rich families. Older money associated with James J. Hill's Great Northern Railroad and the Weyerhaeuser timber fortune clustered around St. Paul. In Minneapolis descendants of the early grain millers and grain traders held sway. This money moved quietly in the shadows, seldom drawing much attention to itself. The wealthy who came later, including the Jewish community, also embraced the understated approach to money. Since the Twin Cities aren't particularly large, some families preferred to invest with money managers in New York City or Chicago. "That made it less likely that you'd run into someone at a dinner party or other social function who knew exactly how rich you might be," said an attorney representing local victims.

FOR JEWISH MINNESOTANS, conforming to the quiet-money standards of the Twin Cities had another benefit: It kept latent anti-Semitism at bay. The Jewish population, despite its relatively small size of about 50,000, or 1% of the total, has had a large impact on philanthropy and politics in Minnesota. Al Franken and Norm Coleman, the two candidates in November's Senate race, are both Jewish. But despite this public-sector success, fear of a backlash has always lingered, especially since the Twin Cities were not a welcoming place for Jews as recently as the postwar era. In 1946 progressive author Carey McWilliams called Minneapolis the "capital of anti-Semitism in the United States." Indeed, many Jewish families have expressed alarm that the Madoff scandal will evoke darker thoughts. "There's always some anti-Semitism, and [the Madoff scandal] becomes fodder for those gristmills," says Harlan Jacobs, who runs a small-company investment incubator in the Twin Cities and is past president of the local

Jewish Community Relations Council. "People who hate will hate, and this unfortunately will give them more excuses to do so."

Members of Oak Ridge, meanwhile, have worried that the scandal might threaten the future of their 88-year-old club. Speculation reached such a pitch that club president Rom Zamansky, a Minneapolis attorney, sent a note to members saying that the club would pull through fine. In that letter he extolled the charitable work of Oak Ridge members and admonished members not to talk to the media about Madoff.

Most Jewish houses of worship are already struggling financially amid the economic downturn, and the Madoff situation could make things tougher in the near term. But some rabbis have sought to turn the Madoff scandal into a teaching moment. Not far from Oak Ridge, at the Beth El Synagogue in the Minneapolis suburb of St. Louis Park, Rabbi Alexander Davis maintains an optimistic mien. He acknowledges that people are shocked and that some feel the Madoff scandal has brought shame to the Jewish community. At the same time, he feels this is a chance to get a spiritual message across. "It's definitely an opportunity, whether we wanted it or not, to rethink our values," says Davis. "We need to examine the cultural norms that allowed us to get into this situation. There's an opportunity to reorganize our thinking so that it better reflects our priorities." In a letter to his members during Hanukkah in December, he decried Madoff as one who would steal from his own people. "This year the lights of Hanukkah may seem dimmer, the gifts may be fewer," he wrote. "But the message of Hanukkah continues to shine forth brightly. We will not allow Madoff—the Grinch who stole Hanukkah—to dampen the message of Hanukkah. For the light of Hanukkah is not the sparkle of gelt but the spirit of God."

What about the laws of men: Can they provide for any recourse to the alleged Madoff sins? Alas, attorneys representing victims are finding it hard to unlock the Madoff puzzle. Some prominent class-action attorneys see no real path to recover lost investments. "He cut a fairly large swath through here, and it's a terrible, awful tragedy," said Karl Cambronne, an attorney in Minneapolis at Chestnut & Brooks. "But as we look at the details, we just can't see anything we can do to help."

One reason that locals are so reticent is that not a small number, like the mistress who spoke to FORTUNE, received funds throughout the alleged scam. Foundations regularly drew down from their endowments invested with Madoff. The potential for "clawbacks," or litigation to wrest money from those who got cash out of Madoff before the scandal surfaced, remains high. Local attorneys are still scrambling to find some angle to recoup losses. The hunt includes a search for potential fiduciaries, those who might have offered enough advice to bear some responsibility for the failed investments. But many lawyers are skeptical about finding a successful legal strategy beyond the standard bankruptcy path and possible recovery of some assets via the Securities Investor Protection Corp.

Graybow, the communications entrepreneur and Madoff victim, is particularly incensed that the government failed to spot Madoff's mischief despite repeated warnings and several investigations into the firm. "It is shameful that after numerous inquiries from the investment community," Graybow says, "the regulators didn't thoroughly research and investigate the truth and uncover the underlying mechanics of the Madoff operations." He believes a government fund for victims is an appropriate solution, citing the failure of regulators to catch Madoff. At a time when everyone from auto companies to investment banks to state governments is holding a hand out to the government, Graybow's notion might have a chance, at least in theory. But in reality, the line at the government till is already very long and is likely to grow longer. For some members of the Oak Ridge club, the only solace may be springtime, which will come not a moment too soon.

THE HOMEGROWN MINNESOTA SCAM

Tom Petters looked like a pillar of the community. Now he's accused of building a giant Ponzi scheme.

Bernard Madoff targeted a community that had reason to trust him: his fellow Jews. In Minnesota, businessman Tom Petters is alleged to have played a similar game with his fellow Christians, setting himself up as a generous, high-profile philanthropist to help burnish his reputation as a can't-lose investor. Before his downfall, Petters had assembled a dog's breakfast of about 20 companies that included Sun Country Airlines, the Polaroid brand name, and Enable Holdings, an online marketplace for overstock merchandise. But according to federal investigators, the entire operation was a multibillion-dollar Ponzi scheme. It fell apart this past fall after Deanna Coleman, a Petters vice president, came forward as a whistleblower and investigators raided Petters Worldwide headquarters in the Minneapolis suburb of Minnetonka, where they allegedly found a massive paper trail of deceit. Petters, who has pleaded not guilty, has been held in jail awaiting trial.

Like Madoff, Petters secured most of his money from hedge funds and the very wealthy. But he also targeted smaller fish, especially from within his own religious community. Among those suing Petters and his businesses are a group of pastors, many of whom lost retirement savings by investing in the Petters scheme. He would often seek funding from church groups and nonprofits to support his business initiatives, especially when acquiring overstock items with plans to resell them to others at a higher price.

While Madoff promised merely above-average returns, Petters promised outsized returns to his investors. But he nonetheless had local credibility. "The Petters situation went on over a 12-year period of time," says Allan Caplan, a Minneapolis lawyer representing whistleblower Coleman. "So [what] appeared to people to be bona fide, valid, good investment opportunities suddenly come crashing down," he told CNNMoney.com's Poppy Harlow.

Unlike in the Madoff case, local attorneys are optimistic about recovering some of the losses for their clients. Madoff's billions seem to have gone to money heaven, but Petters owned some actual businesses, making a recovery of lost funds more feasible. Or maybe there's a good deal on some overstock merchandise.

◆

AFTERMATH: Madoff was charged with securities fraud; the case is so big, though, that it will likely be years before the legalities are sorted out. Said Andrew Calamari, an SEC enforcement officer in New York, "Our complaint alleges a stunning fraud that appears to be of epic proportions." In December Bernard L. Madoff Investment Securities officially entered bankruptcy. The bankruptcy trustee will determine the settlements; more than 8,000 forms were sent to possible claimants